Mexican Americans

& the Law

THE MEXICAN AMERICAN EXPERIENCE

Adela de la Torre,

EDITOR

Other books in the series:

Mexican Americans and Health: Sana! Sana!
  Adela de la Torre & Antonio L. Estrada

Chicano Popular Culture: Que Hable el Pueblo
  Charles M. Tatum

Mexican Americans and the U.S. Economy: Quest for Buenos Días
  Arturo González

Mexican Americans & the Law

¡El Pueblo Unido Jamás Será Vencido!

Reynaldo Anaya Valencia
Sonia R. García
Henry Flores
José Roberto Juárez Jr.

The University of Arizona Press   Tucson

The University of Arizona Press
© 2004 The Arizona Board of Regents
All rights reserved

www.uapress.arizona.edu

Library of Congress Cataloging-in-Publication Data
Mexican Americans and the law : ¡el pueblo unido jamás será vencido! /
Reynaldo Anaya Valencia . . . [et al.].
p. cm. —(The Mexican American experience)
Includes bibliographical references and index.
ISBN 978-0-8165-2279-8 (pbk. : acid-free paper)
1. Mexican Americans—Legal status, laws, etc. I. Title: ¡El pueblo unido
jamás será vencido!. II. Anaya Valencia, Reynaldo. III. Series.
KF4757.5.M4 M49 2004
342.73'0873—DC22   2003015701

Publication of this book is made possible in part by the proceeds of a
permanent endowment created with the assistance of a Challenge Grant
from the National Endowment for the Humanities, a federal agency.

Manufactured in the United States of America on acid-free, archival-
quality paper.

This book is dedicated to the memory of Carlos C. Cadena and Gus C. García, the first Mexican American lawyers ever to argue before the U.S. Supreme Court. The case, *Hernández v. Texas* (1954), was also the first time the Court applied the constitutional protections against discrimination to Mexican Americans. Cadena and García's unparalleled courage, conviction, and strength in preparing and arguing this case unquestionably opened many, many doors for all Mexican Americans. It is our sincere hope that this work will inspire others to ensure that these doors remain open.

■ Gus C. García.   ■ The Honorable Carlos C. Cadena.

■ CONTENTS

List of Illustrations xi
Acknowledgments xiii
Introduction xv
    Overview of the U.S. Court System xvi
    Structure of this Book xx
List of Acronyms xxiii

1. Mexican Americans and the Law 3

    Brief History of Mexican Americans and the Law 4
    People v. Zammora (Sleepy Lagoon, 1944) 7
    Securing the Rights of Mexican Americans 10
    The Legal Construction of Mexican American Identity 10
    Hernández v. Texas (1954) 11
    Other Legal Protections 13
    Theme of the Book 14
        Discussion Questions 17
        Suggested Readings 17
        Notes 18

2. Educational Equality 20

    Segregation 20
    Méndez v. Westminister School District of Orange County (1946) 23
    Unequal Funding 29
    San Antonio Independent School District v. Rodríguez (1973) 30
    Other Educational Challenges 35
    Concluding Thoughts 37
        Discussion Questions 37
        Suggested Readings 38
        Notes 39

3. Gender and the Law 41

    Reproductive Rights 42
    Madrigal v. Quilligan (1981) 44
    Sexual Harassment and Other Workplace Discrimination 47
    EEOC v. Hacienda Hotel (1989) 50
    Violence, Gender, and Sexual Identity 54
    Aguirre-Cervantes v. INS (2001) 55

Concluding Thoughts 61
  Discussion Questions 62
  Suggested Readings 63
  Notes 63

4. Law and Language 65

Early History of Language in the United States 67
Language as a Civil Rights Issue 69
Ýñiguez v. Arizonans for Official English (1995) 70
Language in the Workplace 77
García v. Gloor (1980) 78
Bilingual Education 81
Serna v. Portales Municipal Schools (1974) 83
Recent Challenges 85
Concluding Thoughts 86
  Discussion Questions 86
  Suggested Readings 88
  Notes 88

5. Immigration 89

Securing the U.S.–Mexico Border 90
U.S. v. Brignoni-Ponce (1975) 91
U.S. v. Martínez-Fuerte (1976) 94
The Challenge of Public Benefits 98
Plyler v. Doe (1982) 99
League of United Latin American Citizens v. Wilson (1997) 107
Other Important Developments 110
Concluding Thoughts 112
  Discussion Questions 112
  Suggested Readings 113
  Notes 113

6. Voting Rights 115

Voting Rights Litigation 115
Reapportionment and Redistricting 117
White v. Regester (1973) 119
Redistricting after *White* 121
Bush v. Vera (1996) 123
Combining Forces with African Americans 127

The Unrealized Hope of Statistical Sampling 129
Concluding Thoughts 131
    Discussion Questions 132
    Suggested Readings 133
    Notes 133

7.   Affirmative Action 134

Brief History of Affirmative Action 135
Legal Standards for Reviewing Affirmative Action Programs 137
Affirmative Action in Institutions of Higher Learning 139
Hopwood v. State of Texas (1996) 143
State Initiatives 152
Coalition for Economic Equity v. Wilson (1997) 153
Concluding Thoughts 155
    Discussion Questions 155
    Suggested Readings 156
    Notes 156

8.   The Criminal Justice System 157

Fourteenth Amendment Equal Protection and Jury Exclusion 159
Hernández v. Texas (1954) 160
Hernández v. New York (1991) 162
Voluntary Confessions and the Fifth Amendment Right against
Self-Incrimination 163
Miranda v. Arizona (1966) 164
Sixth Amendment Right to Legal Counsel 168
Escobedo v. Illinois (1964) 169
Concluding Thoughts 173
    Discussion Questions 174
    Suggested Readings 175
    Notes 176

Glossary 177
List of Websites 189
Figure Credits 191
Index 193

LIST OF ILLUSTRATIONS

Gus C. García v

The Honorable Carlos C. Cadena v

1. The thirteen federal judicial circuits xviii
2. Sleepy Lagoon defendants 6
3. A segregated school in Austin, Texas 22
4. Lemon Grove school children 22
5. Mexican American women railroad workers during World War II 42
6. Satirical map in response to the California English-Only referendum 66
7. Cartoon responding to denial of public education benefits to undocumented immigrants 99
8. Protesters marching against California's Proposition 187 106
9. Su Voto Es Su Voz 116
10. Society of American Law Teachers marching in Washington, D.C. 141
11. Cartoon satirizing the U.S. criminal justice system 158

ACKNOWLEDGMENTS

This book would not have been possible without the help of several individuals. First, we would like to thank María Vega, whose skills in typing, editing, and organizing the materials proved unparalleled. Law students Jenee Margo Gonzáles' and David Trevino's excellent research and general support throughout the process helped bring this work to its conclusion. Similarly, the exceptional assistance of Robert Leibold with photographs and art work is also greatly appreciated. We would also like to thank Dr. Marisela Márquez, Professor Lee Terán, and Professor John Schmolesky for reading versions of this work and making many helpful comments and insightful suggestions. Finally, we would like to thank the University of Arizona Press for its willingness to undertake publication of the visionary Mexican American Experience series, and Adela de la Torre, professor and director of the Chicana/o Studies program at University of California, Davis, for her suggestion to include our book in this groundbreaking and much-needed series.

■ INTRODUCTION

Mexican Americans and the Law is a volume in the Mexican American Experience series. It follows the same basic conventions as the others and is intended primarily as an undergraduate textbook. Accordingly, at the end of each chapter, you will find a set of discussion questions that serve as a review of, and springboard for further conversation about, key content in the chapter. Source notes and a list of suggested readings are also provided within each chapter. For anyone wishing to study a topic in more depth, a list of Internet sources appears at the end of the book. Technical and legal terms are in boldface on first reference in every chapter and are defined in the glossary at the end of the book.

We, the four authors of this book, are Mexican American scholars and activists who have a deep commitment to and interest in exploring issues relating to the experience of Mexican Americans and the law in the United States. In the book we cover a critical selection of issues and topics that affect Mexican Americans, and by implication and extension all Latinos, in the United States. We define *Mexican American* to refer to an individual of Mexican origin who was born in the United States, or who has become a naturalized citizen. Thus, the focus of the material in this book is on issues affecting Mexican-origin U.S. citizens, but many of the principles also apply to **legal residents,** undocumented immigrants, and other Latino groups, such as Cuban Americans and Puerto Ricans. Mexican American is often used interchangeably with *Chicano/a, Latino/a, Mexican, Mejicano,* and *Hispanic.* Although we have chosen to use *Mexican American* in this book, individuals may make a personal choice to identify themselves differently. Some of the preceding terms carry ideological underpinnings best understood and felt by the individual making the choice.

Through landmark court cases, federal and state laws, historical contextualizations, and policy discussions, we address the many and complex ways in which Mexican Americans affect and have been affected by the U.S. legal system. In addition to initiating a number of landmark cases, Mexican Americans have played crucial roles in significant cases that directly affect the educational, socioeconomic, and political status of Mexican Americans and all Latinos in the United States. Mexican Americans also worked in coalition with other individuals and organizations in several significant cases. Each chapter in this book contains abridged versions of significant state and federal cases involving Mexican Americans or issues of particular importance to Mexican Americans. Abridging cases for this book often involved dramatically shortening extremely lengthy court **opinions** to only a few pages. We have in all instances preserved the original language from the actual cases, unless otherwise indicated through the use of bracketed text—[text]—to denote a wording substitution. To render the cases as readable as possible, we have omitted most internal case citations and footnotes. In some instances, we found it necessary to omit or rearrange text within the case in order to make the abridged material flow more smoothly and be coherent and comprehensible. In short, all of the abridged text is actual language from reported court opinions, but we have used various mechanisms to promote the readability of the dramatically reduced text.

Because of the particular focus and structure of this book, some of the academic areas of Mexican American historical and cultural inquiry traditionally documented in other works are addressed only in passing, or sometimes not at all. We have not been able to deal at length with issues such as Chicanas' effective activism in labor, the United Farmworkers Movement, the general laws of immigration, efforts to reclaim lands in the Southwest, the **Chicano Movement** of the 1960s, and the emerging Mexican American voices within the lesbian and gay community. In not covering these important contributions, we do not mean to suggest that they are not worthy of academic inquiry and pursuit, or that the individuals not mentioned did not make significant contributions to the Mexican American cause. Indeed, we emphatically believe such areas and individuals should continue to be researched, documented, and discussed. However, this book is structured around litigated controversies that resulted in reported significant or landmark cases important to Mexican Americans. As such, both the focus and format of this book unfortunately dictate the exclusion of other significant and important contributions to Mexican American success.

■ Overview of the U.S. Court System

Like the casebooks used in law school classes, this textbook reprints language contained in court **decisions**. The information in this section is intended to help you understand the importance of these court decisions in the context of the U.S. legal system.

The legal system of the United States is based largely on the **common law** system developed in England and transported to the thirteen English colonies. The Spanish and Mexican legal systems heavily influenced particular areas of law, such as family law and water law, in the southwestern states. A thorough discussion of this influence is beyond the scope of this book, however. After securing its independence from Great Britain, the newly formed United States continued to use the common law system. As the territory of the United States expanded westward, the common law system was adopted or imposed in the new territories, including the southwestern states, that had previously operated under the Spanish and Mexican legal systems.

The common law system is based on the use of **precedents.** Like other courts around the world, common law courts will apply laws codified in **constitutions, statutes, ordinances,** and **regulations** to resolve a lawsuit. In the common law system, however, when a lawsuit is filed in a court, that court also looks at similar cases previously decided by other courts and tries to apply the rules of law announced in those previous cases. Under the doctrine of *stare decisis,* a court is required to apply the same rules applied by other courts in previous cases. In the abridged judicial opinions you will read in this book, you will therefore often see references to other court decisions. These previous decisions will always appear in italics and be followed by the year the case was decided; for example, *Regents of the University of California v. Bakke* (1978).

Federal courts exist throughout the United States. Federal courts have the power to decide lawsuits that raise claims based on the U.S. Constitution or federal law. Because many of the cases in this book raised such claims, they were brought in federal court. In the federal court system, a lawsuit is initiated in the U.S. District Court. Each state has at least one district court and some states have more than one. Following a trial in district court, the federal district court judge issues a written opinion or decision setting out an explanation of why she or he has ruled in favor of a particular party to the lawsuit.

Either party to the lawsuit has the right to file an appeal of the district court's decision to the U.S. Court of Appeals, which must hear the appeal. There are thirteen federal courts of appeals, each with jurisdiction over a particular group of states. Most of the cases in this book arose in the southwestern United States, where the majority of Mexican Americans have traditionally resided. Federal court cases from Texas are appealed to the U.S. Court of Appeals for the Fifth Circuit, often referred to as the "Fifth

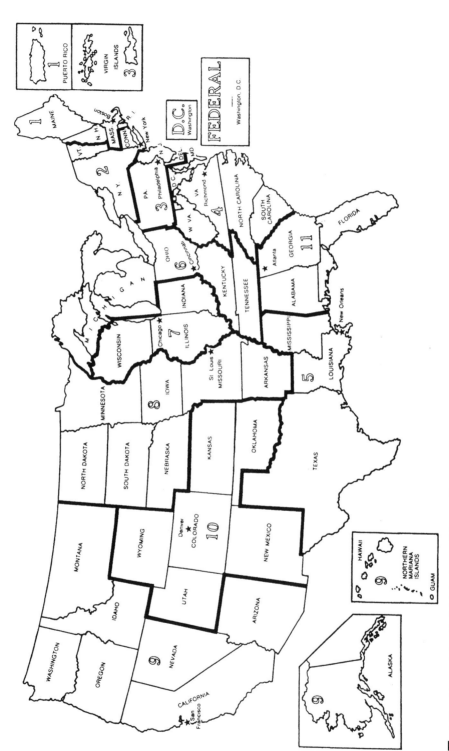

1. The thirteen federal judicial circuits; see 28 USCA 41.

Circuit." Cases from Arizona and California are appealed to the Ninth Circuit. Those from Colorado and New Mexico are appealed to the Tenth Circuit. Figure 1 illustrates the distribution of the federal courts of appeals.

Once the U.S. Court of Appeals has issued its decision, an appeal may be filed with the U.S. Supreme Court. Unlike the U.S. Courts of Appeals, the U.S. Supreme Court is not required to accept all appeals, and indeed has almost complete discretion in choosing which cases to review. In fact, the U.S. Supreme Court usually accepts fewer than one hundred appeals each year.

The opinions issued by the various courts have different weights, depending on the jurisdiction of the court. Once the Supreme Court issues a decision interpreting a federal law, that decision is binding on every other court in the United States. The decision of a U.S. Court of Appeals, on the other hand, is binding only on the federal courts in the circuit in which that court of appeals sits. Other courts outside that circuit may look to the decision, however, and may apply the same rule if they consider the case to provide persuasive authority. The decision of a U.S. District Court is not binding on any other court but may still be cited by other courts as persuasive authority.

The nine men and women who sit on the U.S. Supreme Court are referred to not as judges, but as *justices*. If five or more justices vote in the same manner on a case, the result is a majority opinion. Any justice who agrees or disagrees with the majority opinion or the reasoning that led to it may write a separate concurring or dissenting opinion explaining the grounds for agreement or disagreement. Although only majority opinions are binding and have value as precedents, law students, lawyers, legal scholars, and judges carefully review the arguments in dissenting opinions because these arguments may evolve into majority opinions in the future. At the court of appeals level, a similar process is followed. The various courts of appeal have a number of judges who are divided into three-judge panels for purposes of hearing and deciding appeals from the lower federal district courts. Two votes are necessary for a majority opinion from a court of appeals panel, and a judge who disagrees with the result or reasoning may file a dissenting opinion. A party who is not satisfied with a panel's decision may request that the matter be considered by all the judges of the court of appeals, a process known as an **en banc** hearing or review. A majority opinion from a panel and an en banc majority opinion are both binding precedents.

Each state also has its own state court system. The names of the courts differ from state to state, but each state has a structure similar to that of the federal court system: trial courts, intermediate appellate courts, and a final appellate court. The state courts hear many more cases than do the federal courts. The vast majority of criminal cases are heard in the state courts. If state court litigation raises an issue of federal law, and typically after the state supreme court has considered the matter, the U.S. Supreme Court has the power to hear an appeal of the federal law issue. Several of the cases in the chapter on criminal law were eventually decided by the U.S. Supreme Court but were filed originally in the state court system.

■ Structure of this Book

Legal appeals are the focus of this book, specifically with regard to discriminatory treatment of Mexican Americans in the following areas: education (at all levels from elementary to higher education); gender discrimination (reproductive rights, sexual harassment, and sexual violence); language (English-Only rules in government, the workplace, and schools); immigration (ranging from anti-immigrant sentiment to racial profiling along the U.S.–Mexico border and denial of benefits to undocumented persons); voting (in the voting booth and with respect to elected office); **affirmative action** (in education, the workplace, and government contracting); and the criminal justice system (not only as lawyers and judges, but also as defendants, witnesses, and jurors).

We begin chapter 1 with an overview of Mexican Americans' attempts to secure justice from the U.S. legal system, beginning with their incorporation in the United States under the **Treaty of Guadalupe Hidalgo.** We also lay out recurring themes that reappear throughout later chapters. Two cases are included: *People v. Zammora* "Sleepy Lagoon" (1944) and *Hernández v. Texas* (1954).

Educational equality is the focus of chapter 2. In the chapter we review some of the most important cases surrounding education, beginning with a background discussion of the landmark *Brown v. Board of Education* (1954), which abolished the doctrine of "separate but equal" in the realm of U.S. public education. We explore not only educational segregation but also the issue of equality of educational resources through two cases: *Méndez v. Westminster School District of Orange County* (1946) and *San Antonio Independent School District v. Rodríguez* (1973).

In chapter 3 we explore gender issues and consider the complex issue of being both Mexican American *and* female. We illustrate how the contributions of Mexican American women have played an integral role in the development of their own rights, as well as the rights of all Mexican Americans and all women in the United States. Three cases are included: *Madrigal v. Quilligan* (1978), EEOC *v. Hacienda Hotel* (1989), and *Aguirre-Cervantes v. INS* (2001).

In chapter 4 we focus on law and language, beginning with a brief history of language issues in the early United States. We then address the English-Only movement in the 1980s, as well as recent challenges to state statutes and proposed amendments to state constitutions, such as California's Proposition 227 eliminating bilingual education. Three cases are included: *Yñiguez v. Arizonans for Official English* (1995), *García v. Gloor* (1980), and *Serna v. Portales Municipal Schools* (1974).

Immigration law is highlighted in chapter 5, where we illustrate the complex and varied manner in which U.S. immigration policy has affected Mexican Americans through a focus on issues ranging from racial profiling along the U.S.–Mexico border to denial of benefits for undocumented immigrants and their children. Four cases are included: *U.S. v. Brignoni-Ponce* (1975), *U.S. v. Martínez-Fuerte* (1976), *Plyler v. Doe* (1982), and *League of United Latin American Citizens v. Wilson* (1997).

Chapter 6 is devoted to voting rights. We begin with a historical overview of voting rights generally and of those specific to Mexican Americans. We then address political representation and reapportionment issues affecting Mexican Americans, and conclude by addressing recent issues regarding coalitions with African Americans as well as the controversy surrounding the undercount in the U.S. Census. Two cases are included: *White v. Regester* (1973) and *Bush v. Vera* (1996).

Affirmative action is the focus of chapter 7. The chapter begins with a brief coverage of the landmark cases in this area, and ultimately focuses on admissions policies in higher education. Two cases are included: *Hopwood v. State of Texas* (1996), and *Coalition for Economic Equity v. Wilson* (1997).

The complexities of the criminal justice system are the focus of chapter 8. We discuss how landmark criminal justice decisions involving persons of Mexican descent established that criminal suspects cannot be denied their **Fifth Amendment** right against self-incrimination, Sixth Amendment right to counsel, and **Fourteenth Amendment** right to **equal protection** under the law. We emphasize how Mexican Americans, through their participation in the U.S. criminal justice system, have often been at the forefront of securing important constitutional rights for all citizens. Four cases are included: *Hernández v. Texas* (1954), *Hernández v. New York* (1991), *Miranda v. Arizona* (1966), and *Escobedo v. Illinois* (1964).

■ LIST OF ACRONYMS

BIA	Board of Immigration Appeals
EEOA	Equal Educational Opportunity Act
EEOC	Equal Employment Opportunity Commission
FBI	Federal Bureau of Investigation
INS	Immigration and Naturalization Service
IRA	Illegal Immigration Reform and Immigrant Responsibility Act
LULAC	League of United Latin American Citizens
MALDEF	Mexican American Legal Defense and Educational Fund
MAYO	Mexican American Youth Organization
MASO	Mexican American Student Organization
MEChA	Movimiento Estudiantil Chicano de Aztlán
NAACP	National Association for the Advancement of Colored People
SBA	Small Business Administration
VAWA	Violence Against Women Act

Mexican Americans

& the Law

Mexican Americans and the Law

The State of Texas would have us hold that there are only two classes—white and Negro—within the contemplation of the Fourteenth Amendment. . . . The Fourteenth Amendment is not directed solely against discrimination due to a "two-class" theory—that is, based upon differences between "white" and Negro.—*Hernández v. Texas* (1954)

The first Mexican Americans became U.S. citizens by virtue of a treaty signed between Mexico and the United States following the U.S.–Mexican War, which lasted from 1846 to 1848. With the **Treaty of Guadalupe Hidalgo** of 1848, Mexico accepted the Rio Grande as the Texas border, and ceded to the United States more than half its territory: what is presently Texas, California, New Mexico, Nevada, and parts of Colorado, Arizona, and Utah. Many Mexican Americans, therefore, are of the mindset that "we didn't cross the border, the border crossed us." Throughout negotiation of the treaty, Mexican negotiators were especially concerned for the Mexicans who chose to remain in the newly formed territories of the United States. Accordingly, the treaty specifically guaranteed these first Mexican Americans "the enjoyment of all rights of citizens of the U.S. and according to the principles of the **Constitution**; and in the meantime [they] shall be maintained and protected in the free enjoyment of their liberty and property, and secured in the free exercise of their religion without restriction." Many Mexican American activists also construe the treaty's provisions to protect pre-existing customs in language and culture.[1] The Treaty of Guadalupe Hidalgo thus defined and established the relationship between Mexican Americans and their new U.S. legal system.

Despite the treaty's language preserving the rights of Mexican Americans, the relationship between Mexican Americans and the U.S. legal system has been mixed. One of the main themes of this book will be to illustrate how the Mexican American experience has been marked by oppression from both the legal system and legal authorities in the United

States, while at the same time Mexican Americans have benefited from successful appeals to the same system. Another overriding theme will be an exploration of the ways in which Mexican Americans' legal identity has been constructed and developed throughout history, oftentimes without Mexican Americans' participation, and how this construction of identity was often informed and driven by racist and anti-immigrant sentiments.

■ Brief History of Mexican Americans and the Law

The early history of the relationship between Mexican Americans and the legal system chronicles abuse and violence at the hands of law enforcement agencies and the courts. Historian Manuel Gonzáles, in *Mexicanos: A History of Mexicans in the United States* (2000), presents anecdotal evidence highlighting the early violence Mexican Americans endured at the hands of the primitive legal system in the early history of the southwestern United States. Gonzáles discusses two incidents involving Mexican American women, one in the California gold-mining fields in 1851, and the other in South Texas in 1863. Both these women shot and killed Anglo males who were attempting to sexually assault them. The women were "arrested" by vigilante committees, tried by a vigilante court, and lynched for "killing white men." Gonzáles points out that if the racial orientations of the actors had been reversed, the white women would have been vindicated for attempting "to preserve their virtue" at the hands of purportedly dark, swarthy, and lascivious Mexicans.

Although these are only two examples, Mexican American history is replete with incidents of brutality perpetrated against Mexican American communities across the United States, from the copper and gold mines of Arizona and California in the nineteenth century to the streets of Houston, Los Angeles, Tucson, Chicago, Miami, and New York City today. As Professor Nicolás Kanellos notes,

> In the 1800s, brutality against Mexican Americans in the Southwest territories was commonplace. In fact, lynchings and murders of Mexican Americans became so common in California and Texas that, in 1912, the Mexican ambassador formally protested the mistreatment of Mexicans and cited several brutal incidents that had recently taken place.
>
> The prevailing conditions in the 1920s along the Texas-Mexico border

were intolerable. . . . No jury along the border would ever convict a white man for shooting a Mexican. Abuse of Mexican Americans by rangers and police continued unchecked in the 1930s. . . . Courts of law were rarely a source of justice for Mexican American victims of such abuse.

In 1943 *Time* magazine reported that two hundred navy men, angered by scuffles with Hispanic youth, commandeered taxicabs and began attacking Mexican Americans in East Los Angeles. The Los Angeles police followed the caravan of navy men and watched them beat the Hispanics and did nothing to stop them. Mexican-American boys were dragged, beaten, and left naked in the streets. Police did nothing to stop the attacks.[2]

The 1943 beatings Professor Kanellos refers to are better known as the Zoot Suit Riots. The Zoot Suit Riots are among the most notorious documented instances of violence by military servicemen and civilians against Mexican Americans, specifically zoot-suiters, young men and women so identified because of their distinctive clothing, language, and mannerisms. At this time—during World War II and after the Pearl Harbor attacks—racial tension in the Los Angeles area was high. In this highly charged context, a rumor spread that some sailors had been attacked by Mexican American youths for insulting a Mexican American woman. Various servicemen stationed at nearby bases, accompanied by several civilians, attacked first zoot-suiters then other Mexican Americans indiscriminately in retaliation, thus starting the ten-day Zoot Suit Riots. The riots did not subside until the navy declared the downtown Los Angeles area off-limits.[3] The city council then banned the wearing of zoot suits on the streets of Los Angeles.

A precursor to the riots was a murder case, *People v. Zammora* (1944), which also served as the basis for the popular play and film dramatization, *Zoot Suit,* by director Luis Valdez.[4] This case is more commonly referred to as the Sleepy Lagoon trial, after the Sleepy Lagoon reservoir where the body of a young Mexican American boy, José Díaz, was discovered. In this, the largest mass trial in California history, close to six hundred young Mexican American men and women (mostly zoot-suiters) were arrested, 24 young men were indicted, 22 were tried, and 12 were ultimately convicted of murder (figure 2). Importantly, the Sleepy Lagoon case occurred in a context in which newspapers in Los Angeles were creating, exacerbating, and capitalizing on anti-Mexican sentiment, including inventing terms such as "zoot-suit gangsters" and "pachuco killers." As a result,

2. The Sleepy Lagoon defendants: (kneeling left to right) Gus Zamora, Manuel Reyes, Bobby Telles, Manny Delgado, Jose "Chepe" Ruiz, Hank Ynostroza; (standing left to right) Jack Melendez, Victor Thompson, Angel Padilla, John Y. Matuz, Ysmael "Smiles" Parra, Henry Leyvas. Inscribed "To Alice with love from her boys."

the Sleepy Lagoon defendants were associated with other so-called undesirables such as the Japanese, communists, and other perceived subversives. Professors Wright and Graham have written about the background of this case:

> After an attempt to crash a party, a brawl broke out among groups of mostly Mexican-American youths in which one man was stabbed to death. An "expert" from the Los Angeles Sheriff's office told the grand jury that because of their descent from Mayans, who practiced ritual murder, Mexicans were "biologically" predisposed to violence. The grand jury indicted 22 young men for conspiracy. The trial was held in the midst of the sort of racial hysteria that Los Angeles newspapers were getting good at; "zoot-suit gangsters" and "pachuco killers" were the terms routinely used to describe the defendants. They were convicted despite evidence so weak that the Court of Appeals found it insufficient to support a verdict.[5]

Ultimately the murder convictions of the Sleepy Lagoon defendants were reversed by the California Court of Appeals. Despite its decision to overturn these convictions, the California Court of Appeals refused to give credence to the defendants' allegations that the charges and the trial were racially tinged and motivated.

People v. Zammora (Sleepy Lagoon)

California Court of Appeals, Second District
152 P.2d 180 (1944)

White, Justice.

In appellants' briefs filed herein, we note the charge that the prosecution of these defendants is the result of racial prejudice. This claim is without foundation and finds no support in the record. While it is true that practically all of the defendants are of Mexican birth or ancestry, it should be remembered that the victims named in the indictment are also of Mexican lineage. José Díaz, with whose murder the defendants were charged, had the right to live. The two victims named in counts II and III of the indictment possessed a natural right to freedom from illegal and unlawful attack and injury. The picture presented by the record in the case is one wherein the Delgadillo family, also of Mexican extraction, were holding a social gathering in honor of the birthday of the mother of that family. In so doing they were entitled, as is every other family under our form of government, to be protected against the invasion of their home and homelike activities by a band of hoodlums. It would be a sad commentary upon our vaunted protection of the right to "life, liberty and the pursuit of happiness" if law enforcement agencies did nothing to vindicate the right of this family to be free from such an attack as was allegedly made upon them and their guests. However, there is no ground revealed by the record upon which it can be said that this prosecution was conceived in, born, or nurtured by the seeds of racial prejudice. It was instituted to protect Mexican people in the enjoyment of rights and privileges which are inherent in every one, whatever may be their race or creed, and regardless of whether their status in life be that of the rich and influential or the more lowly and poor.

The judgments and orders denying motions for a new trial, from which this appeal was taken, are, and each of them is, reversed, and the cause remanded. ■

Historians also describe how the Texas Rangers brutalized Mexican American communities in Texas. The *rinches,* as many Mexican Americans called them, were originally a group of deputized gunmen hired to protect the land of Anglo ranchers and farmers from perceived predators. The reality was that in most instances, Mexican Americans were trying to retrieve land stolen from them by Anglos. Although the Texas Rangers are now a law enforcement agency of the state of Texas, when established in the nineteenth century, they were loosely organized and quickly gained a reputation among Mexican Americans as lawless and violent enforcers of the wishes of the large Anglo ranchers.[6] The Texas Rangers' early attitude and actions toward the Mexican American community may partially explain why many Mexican Americans hold law enforcement agencies suspect to this day.

In addition, Mexican Americans have faced other forms of discrimination. For instance, until 1966, many Mexican Americans, like African Americans, were segregated in elementary and secondary educational systems in the Southwest. In Texas and California, for instance, many school districts maintained Mexican schools where Mexican American children were taught, often by unqualified, inexperienced teachers. As late as the 1960s, restaurants in many southwestern towns and cities continued to post signs that prohibited serving "Mexicans and Dogs." Even today, restaurants that cater primarily either to Mexicans or to Anglos persist in rural areas of the Southwest. In many cities, public swimming pools and private pools franchised by local governments were closed to Mexicans. Even in funeral ceremonies, Mexican Americans were discriminated against in many communities in the Southwest. Many local cemeteries were either closed to Mexican Americans or segregated, with Mexican Americans buried on one side and Anglos buried on the other. Indeed, one of the first significant incidents that mobilized Mexican American efforts for civil rights occurred in 1949 and dealt with this type of discrimination. This incident involved the city of Three Rivers, Texas, where the only mortuary in town refused to bury Lt. Félix Longoria, a highly decorated war veteran, in a cemetery for whites only, despite Lt. Longoria's honorable and distinguished military career and service to his country. This refusal ultimately led to protests and the intervention of then–U.S. Senator Lyndon Baines Johnson, who secured Lt. Longoria's burial in Arlington Cemetery with full military honors. The incident outraged many Mexican Americans and ultimately gave rise to the founding of the **American GI Forum,** one of the most influential civil rights organizations for Mexican Americans.

In addition to the types of discrimination outlined so far, Mexican Americans have also been subjected to discrimination in the workplace, especially in hiring, promotion, evaluation, and termination. They have often been the "last hired and the first fired." Mexican Americans have even been terminated from places of employment for speaking Spanish to their co-workers, even when they were hired precisely for the purpose of communicating with and meeting the needs of the Spanish-speaking clientele.

Furthermore, as late as the 1960s, Mexican Americans were often excluded from serving on juries. With respect to voting, they were under-registered on the voting rolls, threatened and intimidated at the voting booths, and economically and in some cases physically intimidated to prevent their participation in the political process. On the west side of San Antonio, Texas, during the 1988 presidential election, individuals dressed in clothing similar to that of agents of the Immigration and Naturalization Service (INS) were even stationed at election precincts to ensure "ballot security" for one of the major political parties—a thinly veiled attempt to intimidate Mexican American voters in that neighborhood. Similar incidents took place in Southern California during the 1990s.

Sadly, violence and discrimination have all too often marked the relationship between Mexican Americans and the law since the Treaty of Guadalupe Hidalgo in 1848. The oppression experienced by Mexican Americans and synopsized here has been documented not only by historians (see Suggested Readings), but also chronicled through numerous appeals to legal authorities. At first many of these appeals were made by the Mexican national government, which felt a certain degree of responsibility for the welfare of Mexican American citizens and early immigrants from Mexico. As the Mexican American community matured and slowly experienced upward social mobility, however, it began using the legal system to seek redress for the discriminatory treatment it was experiencing throughout various aspects of American society.

Securing the Rights of Mexican Americans

As described throughout this book, in many instances of discriminatory treatment, Mexican Americans either filed suit or threatened to file suit in state and federal courts for redress of their grievances. Mexican American civil rights organizations, such as the **League of United Latin American Citizens** (LULAC), established in the 1920s, and the **Mexican American Legal Defense and Educational Fund** (MALDEF), established in the 1960s, usually spearheaded these court challenges. Although they took the lead in these litigation efforts, MALDEF and LULAC often worked closely with and relied on the efforts of other Mexican American and Latino civil rights organizations, including the National Council of La Raza, the National Association of Latino Elected and Appointed Officials, the Southwest Voter Registration Institute, the William C. Velásquez Institute, and the Tomás Rivera Center.[7] Significantly, although discrimination against Mexican Americans was prevalent throughout the Southwest, it was by most accounts worst in Texas. For this unenviable reason, therefore, much of the litigation regarding discriminatory practices against Mexican Americans was brought in and against the state of Texas.

Securing the legal rights of Mexican Americans has been a long, difficult, and often arduous process. As the cases in this book illustrate, the legal and constitutional history of Mexican Americans in the United States is disturbingly rich with examples of efforts by individuals and institutions to prevent Mexican Americans from gaining civil rights and participating fully in every aspect of American society. Thus, without doubt the myriad of legal, political, and socioeconomic rights currently enjoyed by Mexican Americans are the direct result of a very challenging history as well as hard-fought legal victories—many times by Mexican American lawyers.

 The Legal Construction of Mexican American Identity

Obviously, the relationship between Mexican Americans and the law is intertwined with the issue of racial identity. *Terrell Wells Swimming Pool Company v. Rodríguez* (1944)[8] was one of the first cases to demonstrate that the racial identity of Mexican Americans was still unclear under the law. This case involved a Mexican American male in San Antonio, Texas, who sued Terrell Wells Swimming Pool Company, Inc., because the company denied him and "all other persons of Hispanic or Mexican descent [from] equal accommodations, facilities and privileges at corporate defendant's swimming pool." The state trial court ruled that in "the absence of Civil Rights Legislation . . . the proprietor of a place of amusement which is privately owned can refuse to sell and exclude any person from the use of their facilities." Essentially, the court concluded that it could not extend the protection of anti-discrimination law to Mexican Americans because there was no law that specifically protected them. Ten years later, *Hernández v. Texas* (1954) resolved this dilemma for all federal and state courts. In *Hernández,* the U.S. Supreme Court, in a unanimous **decision,** held that Mexican Americans had historically been discriminated against, and accordingly constituted an identifiable class under the **Fourteenth Amendment** of the U.S. Constitution, thus requiring the protection of the law and the courts.

Hernández v. Texas

United States Supreme Court
347 U.S. 475 (1954)

Chief Justice Warren delivering the **opinion** of the Court.

This case featured a petition by Mr. Pete Hernández who was indicted for the murder of Joe Espinosa by a grand jury in Jackson County, Texas. He was convicted and sentenced to life imprisonment.

Prior to the trial, the petitioner, by his counsel, offered timely motions to quash the indictment and the jury panel. He alleged that persons of Mexican descent were systematically excluded from service as jury commissioners, grand jurors, and petit jurors, although there were such persons fully qualified to serve residing in Jackson County. The petitioner asserted that exclusion of this class deprived him, as a member of the class, of the **equal protection** of the laws guaranteed by the Fourteenth Amendment of the Constitution. After a hearing, the trial court denied the motions. At the trial, the motions were renewed, further evidence taken, and the motions again denied.

[This] Court has held that it is a denial of the equal protection of the laws to try a defendant of a particular race or color under an indictment issued by a grand jury, or before a petit jury, from which all persons of his race or color have, solely because of that race or color, been excluded by the State. The State of Texas would have us hold that there are only two classes—white and Negro—within the contemplation of the Fourteenth Amendment.

Throughout our history differences in race and color have defined easily identifiable groups which have at times required the aid of the courts in securing equal treatment under the laws. But community prejudices are not static, and from time to time other differences from the community norm may define other groups which need the same protection. Whether such a group exists within a community is a question of fact. When the existence of a distinct class is demonstrated, and it is further shown that the laws, as written or as applied, single out that class for different treatment not based on some reasonable classification, the guarantees of the Constitution have been violated. The Fourteenth Amendment is not directed solely against discrimination due to a "two-class" theory—that is, based upon differences between "white" and Negro.

The petitioner's initial burden in substantiating his charge of group discrimination was to prove that persons of Mexican descent constitute a separate class in Jackson County, distinct from "whites." One method by which this may be demonstrated is by showing the attitude of the community. Here the testimony of responsible officials and citizens contained the admission that residents of the community distinguished between "white" and "Mexican." The participation of persons of Mexican descent in business and community groups was shown as slight. Until very recent times, children of Mexican descent were required to attend a segregated school for the first four grades. At least one restaurant in town prominently displayed a sign announcing "No Mexicans Served." On the courthouse grounds at the time of the hearing, there were two men's toilets, one unmarked, and the other marked "Colored Men" and "Hombres Aquí" ("Men Here").

Having the existence of a class, petitioner was then charged with the burden of proving discrimination. [Note: The Court held that the petitioner met the burden of proof, as more fully explained in the discussion of this case in chapter 8.]

Reversed. ■

Hernández is important because the U.S. Supreme Court for the first time extended the protections of the **Due Process Clause** of the Fourteenth Amendment to Mexican Americans. Equally important, this case was the first time Mexican American attorneys argued before the U.S. Supreme Court. Carlos Cadena and Gus García[9] presented the argument on behalf of the petitioner in favor of including Mexican Americans under the protective veil of the Fourteenth Amendment. Essentially, they argued that since Anglos always identified Mexican Americans as separate, traditionally insisted that Mexicans Americans have separate accommodations, and easily singled out Mexican Americans for discriminatory treatment, Mexican Americans constituted a distinct class for Fourteenth Amendment purposes. That is to say, Mexican Americans were a class of people protected from discrimination under the Fourteenth Amendment. The irony of this brilliant and ultimately successful argument is that it was premised on the very racist beliefs and practices of many Anglos. Personal accounts reveal that both Cadena and García possessed wry senses of humor, and that the strategy and planning sessions for this landmark case were often marked by ample amounts of *Mexicano* humor. Ultimately, the U.S. Supreme Court found their argument had merit and ruled in their favor, holding that Mexican Americans constituted an identifiable class of individuals who deserved protection under the Fourteenth Amendment

■ Other Legal Protections

The Fourteenth Amendment protections at the core of the *Hernández* case were eventually extended to all Mexican Americans and other Latinos in all areas of public access and accommodations. Other important legal protections for Mexican Americans were obtained and secured through a variety of mechanisms, including litigation and legislation in state and federal forums. Access to public education, for instance, was achieved through an array of court cases brought in various courts beginning with *Méndez v. Westminster School District* (1946), a pre-*Hernández* case discussed in chapter 2. In addition to these state court cases, Title VI of the **Civil Rights Act of 1964,** passed subsequent to both the *Méndez* and *Hernández* cases, provided a powerful federal **statute** and yet another avenue for litigation challenging discriminatory treatment of Mexican Americans in the realm of public education. Similarly, Title VII of the Civil Rights Act of 1964 prohibits employment discrimination against Mexican Americans and women in the workplace. Equally important, rules, **regulations,** and guidelines promulgated by the **Equal Employment Opportunity Commission** (EEOC), which was created pursuant to the Civil Rights Act of 1964, provide a further basis of protection for Mexican American men and women in the workforce. Protection for participation in the economic marketplace has also been secured under various state and federal statutes, as well as various rules and regulations formulated by the **Small Business Administration** (SBA). Protection of voting rights for Mexican Americans was strengthened in 1972, when legislative changes to the **Voting Rights Act of 1965** finally made clear that Mexican Americans were a protected class under the statute.

In many of the cases included herein, Mexican Americans, individually or through Mexican American civil rights organizations, spearheaded efforts to secure justice. Equally important, however, in some cases Mexican Americans collaborated or formed coalitions with African Americans, other Latinos, other racial minorities, and women to fight for equality before the law. One of the best examples of Mexican Americans forming coalitions with other Latino groups is *Pérez v. Federal Bureau of Investigation* (1988).[10] Bernardo "Matt" Pérez, a Mexican American and the highest ranking Latino FBI special agent, was able to bring together 310 Mexican American, Cuban, Puerto Rican, and South and Central American FBI special agents in a **class action**. They successfully sued the FBI for workplace discrimination against all Latinos. The court in *Pérez* found "a pattern and practice of discrimination in conditions of employment and promotional opportunities as to the [Latino] Plaintiff Class."

■ Theme of the Book

The relationship between Mexican Americans and the U.S. legal system raises several very important questions concerning racial identity, notions of equality and justice, and the persistence of prejudice. Each of these issues occurs and reoccurs throughout our country's troubled history, having persisted since persons of Mexican ancestry first became part of American society and culture. This historical reality is particularly pertinent in a contemporary American culture that appears to be celebrating its recent "Latinoization." Yet, as *Hernández* and the other court cases throughout this book reveal, until somewhat recently, the U.S. government was often not willing even to recognize the existence and legal status of Mexican Americans.

Mexican Americans were "intentionally invisible" only half a century ago. Indeed, until *Hernández,* growing up Mexican American in the United States presented a perplexing legal status because the only two racial categories that existed were *colored* and *white.* Indeed, a common practice throughout the Southwest during the first half of the twentieth century was to identify Mexican Americans as white or Caucasian on their birth certificates. Under this strict racial delineation, Mexican Americans were deemed white or colored at the convenience of government or private actors seeking to deny Mexican Americans access to public places and accommodations. As long as Mexican American identity was defined and shaped by others, Mexican Americans had little control over their status within the legal system. And, as the court stipulated in *Terrell Wells,* Mexican Americans found themselves in a legal netherworld bereft of protection or rights simply because none had been specifically stipulated by the courts or legislative bodies. The *Hernández* case was the first to begin to remedy this problem. Influenced by academic research as well as activism by Mexican Americans and others, the U.S. government and society as a whole have only recently begun to move beyond this traditional black-white paradigm.

Among a host of other events, the **Chicano Movement** of the 1960s fueled further and extensive consciousness raising with regard to the racial and ethnic identity of Mexican Americans.[11] The outcomes of this new self-awareness and struggle for identity, in turn, informed the civil rights "litigation wars" with a more systematic and complete understanding of the identity, history, and struggles of Mexican Americans. Although already complex, Mexican American racial and ethnic identity was compounded in the 1980s when the federal government began to use a new official classification—*Hispanic.* This new Hispanic label included all Mexican Americans, Cuban Americans, Puerto Ricans, and Central and South Americans, despite the distinctive histories of these ethnic communities, and had a meaningful impact on the ability of members of this group to bring litigation.[12]

The relationship between Mexican Americans and the U.S. legal system also raises questions with regard to notions of equality and justice. Classic principles of democratic theory hold that in order for all citizens to have full incorporation into U.S. society, all discriminatory barriers, whether intentionally or unintentionally constructed, must be demolished. When applying these principles to the struggle for Mexican American equality under the law, it becomes clear that Mexican Americans cannot fully realize the fruits of citizenship or the protection of the laws of the United States until these barriers are destroyed and never reconstructed. The portrait painted in this book highlights and celebrates Mexican Americans' persistence in trying to achieve the inherent promise of democracy: that all residents of the United States shall be treated equally and justly in every avenue of life. This guarantee does not necessarily mean that all residents shall be socially or economically equal, only that they shall be equal in the eyes of the law.

Justice, according to the noted legal theorist John Rawls, is a mechanistic artifact of the workings of any system of government. Rawls defines justice as being based on two principles: "First: each person is to have an equal right to the most extensive scheme of equal basic liberties compatible with a similar scheme of liberties for others. Second: social and economic inequalities are to be arranged so that they are both (a) reasonably expected to be to everyone's advantage, and (b) attached to positions and offices open to all."[13] If we accept Rawls' definition of justice, then certain corollary principles become directly applicable in the effort to achieve equality for Mexican Americans within the legal system. The first is that justice can be obtained only if equality of access and treatment are guaranteed to all individuals within society. Second, the only inequalities that can be tolerated are those that "will work to everyone's advantage" and that are the result of equal participation and treatment.

Placing the Mexican American quest for justice within Rawls' conception of justice, it becomes clear why Mexican Americans continue to, and indeed *must* continue to, persist in this struggle. Both justice and equality under the law have been missing or terribly lacking for Mexican Americans in the broader U.S. society. The landmark *Hernández* decision was the first, most crucial step in the right direction, in that by achieving legal recognition of racial identity, Mexican Americans were able to lay the foundation for their demands for equal treatment under the law. Once identified as a separate and racially identifiable legal group, Mexican Americans began to demonstrate and prove that they had been treated unevenly and unequally in almost every social and political institution in U.S. society. As Rawls explains, the essential ingredient in having a just society is to allow each group and individual equal access to an institution or process. Without equal access, Mexican Americans would have remained forever at or near the bottom of the U.S. social and legal structure. Legal visibility, therefore, guarantees the ability of Mexican Americans to press and advocate for equal treatment and thus justice. After legal access has been granted and protected by the law, then it is in the best interests of the Mexican American community to take the necessary steps to close all remaining gaps between itself and all U.S. society.

◼ Discussion Questions

1. As mentioned in the chapter, Mexican American activists interpret the Treaty of Guadalupe Hidalgo as protecting their preexisting customs in language and culture. Do you think this argument is persuasive? Why or why not?

2. Do you agree that race or ethnicity did not play a role in the defendants' convictions in the Sleepy Lagoon case? Given the racial tension in Los Angeles, instigated largely by the local newspapers, do you believe the defendants received a fair trial? Can you draw any parallels to contemporary or recent trials?

3. Mexican Americans have endured a long history of discrimination by the dominant society. Do you believe Mexican Americans still experience discrimination today? If so, in what form or forms? Is the discrimination today different than it was in the past?

4. In *Hernández,* the attorneys for the petitioner argued that Anglos in Jackson County had always distinguished between "whites" and "Mexicans," and had treated Mexican Americans differently. Do you believe communities still exist in the United States where Mexican Americans are viewed in this fashion? If so, what is the nature of the discriminatory treatment?

5. As Rawls points out, justice cannot be achieved unless equality of access and treatment are guaranteed to all individuals. Do you believe equality has been achieved for Mexican Americans? Why or why not?

◼ Suggested Readings

Acuña, R. *Occupied America: A History of Chicanos.* 4th ed. Boston: Addison-Wesley Publishing Co., 1999.

Barrera, M. *Race and Class in the Southwest: A Theory of Racial Inequality.* Notre Dame: University of Notre Dame Press, 1980.

Bender, S. *Greasers and Gringos,* New York: New York University Press, 2003.

Delgado, R., and J. Stefancic. *The Latino Condition: A Critical Reader*. New York: New York University Press, 1998.

Gonzáles, M. *Mexicanos: A History of Mexicans in the United States*. Bloomington: Indiana University Press, 1999.

Griswold del Castillo, R. *The Treaty of Guadalupe Hidalgo: A Legacy of Conflict*. Norman: University of Oklahoma Press, 1992.

Haney-Lopez, I. F. *Racism on Trial: The Chicano Fight for Justice*. Cambridge, Mass.: Belknap Press, 2003.

McWilliams, C. *North from Mexico: The Spanish-Speaking People of the United States*, ed. M. S. Meier. Contributions in American History no. 140. Westport, Conn.: Praeger Press, 1990.

Montejano, D. *Anglos and Mexicans in the Making of Texas, 1836–1986*. Austin: University of Texas Press, 1987.

■ Notes

1. An unsuccessful attempt to make a legal claim on the basis of the Treaty of Guadalupe Hidalgo was *Tijerina v. Henry*, wherein the federal court refuted the plaintiff's rights to equal educational privileges, specifically with regard to the preservation and continuation of the Spanish language in the public schools. 48 F.R.D. 274 (D.N.M. 1969).

2. N. Kanellos, ed., *The Hispanic American Almanac: A Reference Work on Hispanics in the United States* (Gale Research Inc., 1993), 235.

3. For more information regarding the Sleepy Lagoon trial and the subsequent Zoot Suit Riots, see M. Mazón, *The Zoot-Suit Riots: The Psychology of Symbolic Annihilation*, Mexican American Monographs no. 8 (Austin: University of Texas Press, 1984); C. McWilliams, *North from Mexico: The Spanish-Speaking People of the United States*, ed. M. S. Meier, Contributions in American History no. 140 (Westport, Conn.: Praeger Press, 1990). Other sources of information about the case and the riots are R. S. Chang, "Los Angeles as a Single-Celled Organism," *Loyola of Los Angeles Law Review* 34 (2001): 843–862; E. J. Escobar, *Race, Police, and the Making of Political Identity: Mexican Americans and the Los Angeles Police Department, 1900–1945* (Berkeley and Los Angeles: University of California Press, 1999); and the Public Broadcasting Service website, The American Experience series, "Zoot Suit Riots": www.pbs.org/wgbh/amex/zoot.

4. Universal Pictures, 1981.

5. C. A. Wright and K. W. Graham Jr., "Hearsay," vol. 30A, chap. 9, sec. B; "Confrontation and Hearsay," 6360 "The Rights Revolution," in *Federal Practice and Procedure: Federal Rules of Evidence* (St Paul, Minn.: West Group, 2002).

6. For a detailed account of the Texas Rangers, see D. Montejano, *Anglos and Mexicans in the Making of Texas, 1836–1986* (Austin: University of Texas Press, 1987);

and J. Samora, J. Bernal, and A. Peña, eds., *Gunpowder Justice: A Reassessment of the Texas Rangers* (Notre Dame: University of Notre Dame Press, 1979).

7. For further information about these organizations and their efforts, please see the list of websites.

8. 182 S.W.2d 824. *Note:* Legal references follow the format of giving the volume number of the federal, regional, or state reporter in which the case appears, followed by an abbreviation for the title of the reporter (in this case *Southwestern Reporter,* second edition), and finally the starting page number of the case.

9. When he was hired to teach at St. Mary's University School of Law in San Antonio, Texas, Carlos Cadena became the first Mexican American ever hired as a law professor at a U.S. law school. He eventually rose to become the chief justice of the Fourth Court of Appeals in Texas. By the time he retired he was considered one of the most intellectual and brilliant jurists ever to have served on a Texas court. Equally impressive, Gus García was one of the earliest Mexican Americans to graduate from the University of Texas School of Law and was also considered one of the most brilliant attorneys ever to practice in Texas. Both of these exceptional and pioneering Mexican American attorneys are now deceased.

10. 707 F. Supp. 891.

11. For an elaborate discussion of the Chicano Movement, see A. Navarro, *Mexican American Youth Organization: Avant-Garde of the Chicano Movement in Texas* (Austin: University of Texas Press, 1995); J. Gómez Quiñones, *Chicano Politics: Reality and Promise 1940–1990* (Albuquerque: University of New Mexico Press, 1990); C. Muñoz, *Youth, Identity, and Power: The Chicano Movement* (New York: Verso Press, 1989); R. Acuña, *Occupied America* (New York: HarperCollins Publishers, 1988).

12. The challenge of this new category is best exemplified in *Pérez v. Federal Bureau of Investigation,* wherein the court addressed the ambiguity of this umbrella category in connection with certifying the class of Hispanic plaintiffs:

> Throughout the litigation, there seemed to be some question as to what is an "Hispanic." Some witnesses seemed to consider it a racial distinction. One witness for the Defense, not a member of the class and carrying a surname of Northern European origin, stated that because of a Latin maternal ancestor he "liked to think that he was Hispanic." The implication of his testimony is that he had not felt discrimination and bore Hispanic class members no ill will. No class members were in doubt that their ethnic heritage was from Spain or of Spanish origin and the Defendant does not dispute whether any individual member possesses this quality. . . . For the purposes of this class, the appellation "Hispanic" will signify ethnic and national origin categories.

13. J. Rawls, *A Theory of Justice,* rev. ed. (Cambridge, Mass.: Belknap Press, 1999), 53.

2

Educational Equality

The common segregation attitudes and practices of the school authorities
. . . pertain solely to children of Mexican ancestry and parentage. They
are singled out as a class for segregation.—*Méndez v. Westminister School
District of Orange County* (1946)

N
o U.S. Supreme Court case has received such widespread attention in
the twentieth century as the landmark *Brown v. Board of Education*
(1954).[1] In this case, the Supreme Court concluded that "separate-
but-equal" public schools for white and African American schoolchildren
were inherently unequal, thereby overruling *Plessy v. Ferguson* (1896).[2] In
Brown, the U.S. Supreme Court held that segregating children in public
schools on the basis of race placed "a badge of inferiority" on black children
in violation of the **Equal Protection Clause** of the **Fourteenth Amendment**
of the U.S. **Constitution.** Anticipating resistance from school boards, particularly in the South, the Supreme Court required public schools to deseg-
regate "with all deliberate speed." As some scholars have argued, however,
the Court in effect allowed school systems to integrate at their own pace, so
that true integration still has not been achieved. Following the *Brown*
decision, federal courts tackled the arduous task of supervising the **desegregation** plans of school boards, as well as busing to address the continual
problem of **de facto segregation,** particularly in the North. A reconstituted
and more conservative Supreme Court in the 1990s ultimately held that so
long as schools were making "a good faith" effort toward integration,
federal judicial supervision of school systems was no longer necessary.

■ Segregation

During the 1920s and 1930s, as the number of Mexican immigrants increased due to the **Mexican Revolution,** several school districts created
"Americanization" schools for children of Mexican ancestry. Both recent
immigrants and Mexican American U.S. citizens were placed in these

separate schools, primarily to learn the English language and be inculcated in American culture and customs (see figures 3 and 4). The main argument school boards gave to justify this practice was that Mexican American children would better integrate in American society if they learned to assimilate into the dominant culture. In most cases, however, stereotypical assumptions and racism toward Mexican Americans motivated school boards to treat Mexican American students differently and provide them with an inferior education. Much like African American schoolchildren, children of Mexican ancestry were segregated because of deep-seated prejudice. It was common, for instance, for Mexican Americans to be viewed as inferior and dirty.

How does school segregation, and specifically the *Brown* decision, apply to Mexican Americans? Few students of civil rights know that before the U.S. Supreme Court's decision in *Brown,* state and federal courts were already struggling with the issue of Mexican American segregation in the public educational system.[3] In the early 1930s, organizations such as LULAC led the drive in the courts for educational rights. Of these early cases, the one that received the most attention was *Méndez v. Westminister School District of Orange County* (1946), a precursor to the *Brown* decision. In *Méndez,* legal services were obtained through and largely funded by LULAC. Additionally, the **National Association for the Advancement of Colored People** (NAACP) closely watched *Méndez* as a potential **test case.** The case was brought by the parents of Mexican American schoolchildren in southern California who had been segregated on the basis of Mexican ancestry. The federal trial court held that the Fourteenth Amendment Equal Protection Clause was not met by furnishing a separate school for children of Mexican ancestry. The U.S. Court of Appeals for the Ninth Circuit affirmed the decision a year later. In addition to *Méndez,* a federal court in Texas in 1948 also held that segregation of Mexican Americans violated the Fourteenth Amendment.[4]

■ 3. A segregated school in Austin, Texas.

■ 4. Mexican American students targeted for segregation in Lemon Grove, California, during the 1930s.

Méndez v. Westminister School District of Orange County

United States District Court for the
Southern District of California
64 F. Supp 544 (1946)

McCormick, District Judge.

Gonzalo Méndez . . . , as [a] citizen[ ] of the United States, and on behalf of [his] minor children . . . [and] on behalf of 'some 5000' persons similarly affected, all of Mexican or Latin descent, filed a class suit . . . against the Westminister (Garden Grove and El Modeno) School Districts, and the Santa Ana City Schools, all of Orange County, California. The complaint, grounded upon the Fourteenth Amendment to the Constitution of the United States, alleges a concerted policy and design of class discrimination against 'persons of Mexican or Latin descent or extraction' of elementary school age by the defendant school agencies in the conduct and operation of public schools of said districts, resulting in the denial of the equal protection of the laws to such class of persons among which are the petitioning school children.

Specifically, plaintiffs allege: 'That for several years respondents have and do now in furtherance and in execution of their common plan, design and purpose within their respective Systems and Districts, have by their **regulation,** custom and usage and in execution thereof adopted and declared: That all children or persons of Mexican or Latin descent or extraction, though Citizens of the United States of America, shall be, have been and are now excluded from attending, using, enjoying and receiving the benefits of the education, health and recreation facilities of certain schools within their respective Districts and Systems but that [the] children are now and have been segregated and required to and must attend and use certain schools in [these] Districts and Systems reserved for and attended solely and exclusively by children and persons of Mexican and Latin descent, while other schools are maintained, attended, and used exclusively by and for persons and children purportedly known as White or Anglo-Saxon children. That in execution of [these] rules and regulations, each, every and all the foregoing children are compelled and required to and must attend and use the schools in [these] respective Districts reserved for and attended solely and exclusively by children of Mexican and Latin descent and are forbidden, barred and excluded from attending any other school in [the] District or System solely for the reason that [these] children or child are of Mexican or Latin descent.

The petitioners demand that the alleged rules, regulations, customs and usages be adjudged void and unconstitutional and that an **injunction** issue restraining further application by defendant school authorities of such rules, regulations, customs, and usages. It is conceded by all parties that there is no question of race discrimination in this action. It is, however, admitted that segregation is practiced in the school districts as the Spanish-speaking children enter school life and as they advance through the grades in [these] school districts. It is also admitted by the defendants that the petitioning children are qualified to attend the public schools in the respective districts of their residences. In the Westminister, Garden Grove and El Modeno school districts the respective boards of trustees had taken official action, declaring that there be no segregation of pupils on a racial basis but that non-English-speaking children (which group, excepting as to a small number of pupils, was made up entirely of children of Mexican ancestry or descent), be required to attend schools designated by the boards separate and apart from English-speaking pupils; [and] that such group should attend such schools until they had acquired some proficiency in the English language.

The petitioners contend that [this] official action evinces a covert attempt by the school authorities in [these] school districts to produce an arbitrary discrimination against school children of Mexican extraction or descent and that such illegal result has been established in [these] school districts respectively. The school authorities of the City of Santa Ana have not memorialized any such official action, but petitioners assert that the same custom and usage exists in the schools of the City of Santa Ana under the authority of appropriate school agencies of such city. The concrete acts complained of are those of the various school district officials in directing which schools the petitioning children and others of the same class or group must attend. The segregation exists in the elementary schools to and including the sixth grade in two of the defendant districts, and in the two other defendant districts through the eighth grade. The record before us shows without conflict that the technical facilities and physical conveniences offered in the schools housing entirely the segregated pupils, the efficiency of the teachers therein and the curricula are identical and in some respects superior to those in the other schools in the respective districts.

The ultimate question for decision may be thus stated: Does such official action of defendant district school agencies and the usages and practices pursued by the school authorities operate to deny or deprive the so-called non-English-speaking school children of Mexican ancestry or descent within such school districts of the equal protection of the laws? We therefore turn to consider whether under the record before us the school boards and administrative authorities in the respective defendant districts have by their segregation policies and practices transgressed applicable law and Constitutional safeguards and limitations and thus have invaded the personal right which every public school pupil has to the equal protection provision of the Fourteenth Amendment to obtain the means of education.

We think the pattern of public education promulgated in the Constitution of California and effectuated by provisions of the Education Code of the State prohibits segregation of the pupils of Mexican ancestry in the elementary schools from the rest of the school children. Section I of Article IX of the Constitution of California directs the legislature to 'encourage by all suitable means the promotion of intellectual, scientific, moral, and agricultural improvement' of the people. The common segregation attitudes and practices of the school authorities in the defendant school districts in Orange County pertain solely to children of Mexican ancestry and parentage. They are singled out as a class for segregation.

Obviously, the children referred to in these laws are those of Mexican ancestry. And it is noteworthy that the educational advantages of their commingling with other pupils is regarded as being so important to the school system of the State that it is provided for even regardless of the citizenship of the parents. We perceive in the laws relating to the public educational system in the State of California a clear purpose to avoid and forbid distinctions among pupils based upon race or ancestry except in specific situations not pertinent to this action. Distinctions of that kind have recently been declared by the highest judicial authority of the

United States 'by their very nature odious to a free people whose institutions are founded upon the doctrine of equality.' Our conclusions in this action, however, do not rest solely upon what we conceive to be the utter irreconcilability of the segregation practices in the defendant school districts with the public educational system authorized and sanctioned by the laws of the State of California. We think such practices clearly and unmistakably disregard rights secured by the supreme law of the land.

'The equal protection of the laws' pertaining to the public school system in California is not provided by furnishing in separate schools the same technical facilities, text books and courses of instruction to children of Mexican ancestry that are available to the other public school children regardless of their ancestry. We think that under the record before us the only tenable ground upon which segregation practices in the defendant school districts can be defended lies in the English language deficiencies of some of the children of Mexican ancestry as they enter elementary public school life as beginners. But even such situations do not justify the general and continuous segregation in separate schools of the children of Mexican ancestry from the rest of the elementary school population as has been shown to be the practice in the defendant school districts—in all of them to the sixth grade, and in two of them through the eighth grade.

The evidence clearly shows that Spanish-speaking children are retarded in learning English by lack of exposure to its use because of segregation, and that commingling of the entire student body instills and develops a common cultural attitude among the school children which is imperative for the perpetuation of American institutions and ideals. It is also established by the record that the methods of segregation prevalent in the defendant school districts foster antagonisms in the children and suggest inferiority among them where none exists. One of the flagrant examples of the discriminatory results of segregation in two of the schools involved in this case is shown by the record. In the district under consideration there are two schools, the Lincoln and the Roosevelt, located approximately 120 yards apart on the same school grounds, hours of opening and closing, as well as recess periods, are not uniform. No credible language test is given to the children of Mexican ancestry upon entering the first grade in Lincoln School. This school has an enrollment of 249 so-called Spanish-speaking pupils, and no so-called English-speaking pupils; while the Roosevelt (the other) school has 83 so-called English-speaking pupils and 25 so-called Spanish-speaking pupils. Standardized tests as to mental ability are given to the respective classes in the two schools and the same curricula are pursued in both schools and, of course, in the English language as required by State law. In the last school year the students in the seventh grade of the Lincoln School were superior scholarly to the same grade in the Roosevelt School and to any group in the seventh grade in either of the schools in the past. It further appears that not only did the class as a group have such mental superiority but that certain pupils in the group were also outstanding in the class itself. Notwithstanding this showing, the pupils of such excellence were kept in the Lincoln School.

The natural operation and effect of the Board's official action manifests a clear purpose to arbitrarily discriminate against the pupils of Mexican ancestry and to deny to them the equal protection of the laws. The court may not exercise legislative or administrative functions in this case to save such discriminatory act from inoperativeness. There are other discriminatory customs, shown by the evidence, existing in the defendant school districts as to pupils of Mexican descent and extraction, but we deem it unnecessary to discuss them in this memorandum. We conclude by holding that the allegations of the complaint (petition) have been established sufficiently to justify **injunctive relief** against all defendants, restraining further discriminatory practices against the pupils of Mexican descent in the public schools of defendant school districts. ■

It is important to note that both *Méndez* and *Brown* addressed what is known as **de jure segregation,** which was prevalent through the 1950s and 1960s. What these cases did not address, however, was the de facto discrimination that persisted as a result of segregated residential patterns. Most neighborhoods were already segregated on the basis of race as a result of laws or practices that discriminated against Mexican Americans or African Americans attempting to purchase homes in white neighborhoods. In addition, Mexican Americans were more likely to move into predominantly Mexican American neighborhoods, in many cases in order to be closer to friends and families. The result of these dynamics was that the student body of neighborhood schools in these areas was also predominantly Mexican American. Indeed, by the 1960s and early 1970s, most Mexican Americans lived in highly segregated areas of urban centers such as Los Angeles, Albuquerque, Dallas, and Phoenix, and as a result attended largely qualitatively inferior segregated schools.

In addition to its earlier decision in *Brown* striking down de jure segregation, and in response to de facto segregation, the U.S. Supreme Court through subsequent cases required that school boards take steps to integrate public schools—a decision that applied to Mexican Americans. Despite the clear mandate from the Supreme Court, school boards and school officials used various evasive tactics to delay integration. Often the problem was simply ignored or Mexican Americans were segregated in separate classrooms within the school. More often than not, however, school districts claimed to meet integration requirements by combining African Americans and Mexican Americans in a school rather than by integrating racial minorities with whites.

It was not until the late 1960s that the federal courts directly addressed the issue of desegregation for Mexican American schoolchildren.[5] In *Cisneros v. Corpus Christi School District* (1970),[6] a federal trial court held that Mexican Americans were an "identifiable ethnic group" and concluded that integrating Mexican Americans only with African Americans but not with whites was unconstitutional. In a separate case out of Denver, Colorado, the U.S. Supreme Court in *Keyes v. Denver School District* (1973)[7] reaffirmed that Mexican Americans were a "protected ethnic minority group" and called for integration. In short, the courts began to make clear that desegregation efforts had to include all racial minorities and whites.

During the same period, the growing dissatisfaction among an increasingly politicized youth in the public schools led to the first mass school blowouts and walkouts in Los Angeles in 1968. Other cities and towns in the Southwest, including Crystal City, Texas, and Denver, Colorado, also experienced these demonstrations in 1969. Influenced by the **Civil Rights Movement** and the **Anti–Vietnam War Movement,** student activists and student organizations such as the Mexican American Youth Organization (MAYO), the Mexican American Student Organization (MASO), and Movimiento Estudiantil Chicano de Aztlán (MEChA) protested against racist teachers and school policies.[8] These organizations demanded, in most cases successfully, the hiring of Mexican American teachers and administrators, and the creation of classes in Mexican American history and culture. In Texas, students especially fought for the elimination of the rule against speaking Spanish on school grounds. Until these challenges, it was not unusual for students to face discrimination because they spoke Spanish, and in some cases to be reprimanded, spanked, suspended, or expelled from school for doing so. As discussed in chapter 4, although bilingual education programs had existed in the past for other immigrant groups, these programs were not implemented for Mexican Americans until the late 1960s and the 1970s. These programs were a way to address the linguistic and cultural differences of these children, and as a means to rectify past systematic discrimination against Mexican American students.

■ Unequal Funding

Despite the elimination of de jure segregation, schools remained segregated even in integrated communities, usually because of neglect and unequal resources. Unlike in the *Méndez* decision, most of these purportedly "separate-but-equal" schools were typically not equal in resources, instructional facilities, or course instruction.

In the landmark *San Antonio Independent School District v. Rodríguez* (1973) case, the U.S. Supreme Court addressed whether a state system of financing public education through property taxes violated the Equal Protection Clause of the Fourteenth Amendment because it discriminated on the basis of wealth. Petitioners in the case also claimed that the U.S. Constitution provided a fundamental right to an education under the **Due Process Clause** of the Fourteenth Amendment. Brought by the parents of Mexican American children living in San Antonio, Texas, the case highlighted the blatant disparities in resources among San Antonio school districts. The federal trial court ruled in favor of Rodríguez, holding that the Texas system for funding public schools was in violation of the Equal Protection Clause of the Fourteenth Amendment. As the case extract illustrates, however, on appeal the U.S. Supreme Court disagreed, holding in a five-to-four decision that education is a responsibility of the states, not the federal government. The Court also noted that it had never held that disparities in resources based on wealth constituted a violation of the Constitution. The Court's decision had the effect of setting a less progressive tone for educational equality during the 1980s and 1990s.

San Antonio Independent School District v. Rodríguez

United States Supreme Court
411 U.S. 1 (1973)

Mr. Justice Powell delivered the **opinion** of the Court.

This suit attacking the Texas system of financing public education was initiated by Mexican-American parents whose children attend the elementary and secondary schools in the Edgewood Independent School District, an urban school district in San Antonio, Texas. They brought a **class action** on behalf of school children throughout the State who are members of minority groups or who are poor and reside in school districts having a low property tax base. The school district in which appellees reside, the Edgewood Independent School District, has been compared throughout this litigation with the Alamo Heights Independent School District. This comparison between the least and most affluent districts in the San Antonio area serves to illustrate the manner in which the dual system of finance operates and to indicate the extent to which substantial disparities exist despite the State's impressive progress in recent years. Edgewood is one of seven public school districts in the metropolitan area. The district has 25 elementary and secondary schools situated in the core-city sector of San Antonio in a residential neighborhood that has little commercial or industrial property. The residents are predominantly of Mexican-American descent: approximately 90 percent of the student population is Mexican-American and over 6 percent is Negro. The average assessed property value per pupil is $5,960—the lowest in the metropolitan area—and the median family income ($4,686) is also the lowest. At an equalized tax rate of $1.05 per $100 of assessed property—the highest in the metropolitan area—the district contributed $26 to the education of each child for the 1967–1968 school year above its Local Fund Assignment for the Minimum Foundation Program. The Foundation Program contributed $222 per pupil for a state-local total of $248. Federal funds added another $108 for a total of $356 per pupil.

Alamo Heights is the most affluent school district in San Antonio. Its six schools, housing approximately 5,000 students, are situated in a residential community quite unlike the Edgewood District. The school population is predominantly 'Anglo,' having only 18 percent Mexican-Americans and less than 1 percent Negroes. The assessed property value per pupil exceeds $49,000, and the median family income is $8,001. In 1967–1968 the local tax rate of $.85 per $100 of valuation yielded $333 per pupil over and above its contribution to the Foundation Program. Coupled with the $225 provided from that Program, the district was able to supply $558 per student. Supplemented by a $36 per-pupil grant from federal sources, Alamo Heights spent $594 per pupil.

We must decide, first, whether the Texas system of financing public education operates to the disadvantage of some **suspect class** or impinges upon a fundamental right explicitly or implicitly protected by the Constitution, thereby requiring [review under the **strict scrutiny standard**]. The Texas scheme must still be examined to determine whether it rationally furthers some legitimate, articulated state purpose and therefore does not constitute an **invidious discrimination** in violation of the Equal Protection Clause of the Fourteenth Amendment.

First, in support of their charge that the system discriminates against the 'poor,' appellees have made no effort to demonstrate that it operates to the peculiar disadvantage of any class fairly definable as indigent, or as composed of persons whose incomes are beneath any designated poverty level. Indeed, there is reason to believe that the poorest families are not necessarily clustered in the poorest property districts. Second, lack of personal resources has not occasioned an absolute deprivation of the desired benefit. The argument here is not that the children in districts having relatively low assessable property values are receiving no public education; rather, it is that they are receiving a poorer quality education than that available to children in districts having more assessable wealth. Apart from the unsettled and disputed question whether the quality of education may be determined by the amount of money expended for it, a sufficient answer to appellees' argument is that, at least where wealth is involved, the Equal Protection Clause does not require absolute equality or precisely equal advantages. For these two reasons—the absence of any evidence that the financing system discriminates against any definable category of 'poor' people or that it results in the absolute deprivation of education—the disadvantaged class is not susceptible of identification in traditional terms. We thus conclude that the Texas system does not operate to the peculiar disadvantage of any suspect class.

[Petitioners] also assert that the State's system impermissibly interferes with the exercise of a 'fundamental' right. It is this question—whether education is a **fundamental right,** in the sense that it is among the rights and liberties protected by the Constitution—which has so consumed the attention of courts and commentators in recent years. In *Brown v. Board of Education* (1954), a unanimous Court recognized that 'education is perhaps the most important function of state and local governments.' But the importance of a service performed by the State does not determine whether it must be regarded as fundamental for purposes of examination under the Equal Protection Clause. It is not the province of this Court to create substantive constitutional rights in the name of guaranteeing equal protection of the laws. Thus, the key to discovering whether education is 'fundamental' is not to be found in comparisons of the relative societal significance of education as opposed to subsistence or housing. Nor is it to be found by weighing whether education is as important as the right to travel. Rather, the answer lies in assessing whether there is a right to education explicitly or implicitly guaranteed by the Constitution.

Education, of course, is not among the rights afforded explicit protection under our Federal Constitution. Nor do we find any basis for saying it is implicitly so protected. As we have said, the undisputed importance of education will not alone cause this Court to depart from the usual standard for reviewing a State's social and economic legislation. It is appellees' contention, however, that education is distinguishable from other services and benefits provided by the State because it bears a peculiarly close relationship to other rights and liberties accorded protection under the Constitution. Specifically, they insist that education is itself a fundamental personal right because it is essential to the effective exercise of **First Amendment** freedoms and to intelligent utilization of the right to vote. In asserting a nexus between speech and education, appellees urge that the right to speak is meaningless unless the speaker is capable of articulating his thoughts intelligently and persuasively. The 'marketplace of ideas' is an empty forum for those lacking basic communicative tools. Likewise, they argue that the corollary right to receive information becomes little more than a hollow privilege when the recipient has not been taught to read, assimilate, and utilize available knowledge. A similar line of reasoning is pursued with respect to the right to vote.

We need not dispute any of these propositions. The Court has long afforded zealous protection against unjustifiable governmental interference with the individual's rights to speak and to vote. Yet we have never presumed to possess either the ability or the authority to guarantee to the citizenry the most effective speech or the most informed electoral choice. That these may be desirable goals of a system of freedom of expression and of a representative form of government is not to be doubted. These are indeed goals to be pursued by a people whose thoughts and beliefs are freed from governmental interference. But they are not values to be implemented by judicial intrusion into otherwise legitimate state activities. We have carefully considered each of the arguments that education is a fundamental right or liberty and have found those arguments unpersuasive.

Because of differences in expenditure levels occasioned by disparities in property tax income, appellees claim that children in less affluent districts have been made the subject of invidious discrimination. The [trial court] found that the State had failed even 'to establish a reasonable basis' for a system that results in different levels of per-pupil expenditure. We disagree. Appellees further urge that the Texas system is unconstitutionally arbitrary because it allows the availability of local taxable resources to turn on 'happenstance.' They see no justification for a system that allows, as they contend, the quality of education to fluctuate on the basis of the fortuitous positioning of the boundary lines of political subdivisions and the location of valuable commercial and industrial property. But any scheme of local taxation—indeed the very existence of identifiable local governmental units—requires the establishment of jurisdictional boundaries that are inevitably arbitrary. It is equally inevitable that some localities are going to be blessed with more taxable assets than others.

In sum, to the extent that the Texas system of school financing results in unequal expenditures between children who happen to reside in different districts, we cannot say that such disparities are the product of a system that is so irrational as to be invidiously discriminatory. Texas has acknowledged its shortcomings and has persistently endeavored—not without some success—to ameliorate the differences in levels of expenditures without sacrificing the benefits of local participation. The Texas plan is not the result of hurried, ill-conceived legislation. It certainly is not the product of purposeful discrimination against any group or class.

Reversed.

Mr. Justice Stewart, concurring.

The method of financing public schools in Texas, as in almost every other State, has resulted in a system of public education that can fairly be described as chaotic and unjust. It does not follow, however, and I cannot find, that this system violates the Constitution of the United States.

Mr. Justice Brennan, dissenting.

Although I agree with my Brother White that the Texas statutory scheme is devoid of any rational basis, and for that reason is violative of the Equal Protection Clause, I also record my disagreement with the Court's rather distressing assertion that a right may be deemed 'fundamental' for the purposes of equal protection analysis only if it is 'explicitly or implicitly guaranteed by the Constitution.'

Mr. Justice White, with whom Mr. Justice Douglas and Mr. Justice Brennan join, dissenting.

The majority and the State concede, as they must, the existence of major disparities in spendable funds. But the State contends that the disparities do not invidiously discriminate against children and families in districts such as Edgewood, because the Texas scheme is designed 'to provide an adequate education for all, with local autonomy to go beyond that as individual school districts desire and are able. . . . It leaves to the people of each district the choice whether to go beyond the minimum and, if so, by how much.' The majority advances this rationalization: 'While assuring a basic education for every child in the State, it permits and encourages a large measure of participation in and control of each district's schools at the local level.' I cannot disagree with the proposition that local control and local decisionmaking play an important part in our democratic system of government. Much may be left to local option, and this case would be quite different if it were true that the Texas system, while insuring minimum educational expenditures in every district through state funding, extended a meaningful option to all local districts to increase their per-pupil expenditures and so to improve their children's education to the extent that increased funding would achieve that goal. The system would then arguably provide a rational and sensible method of achieving the stated aim of preserving an area for local initiative and decision. The difficulty with the Texas system, however, is that it provides a meaningful option to Alamo Heights and like school districts but almost none to Edgewood and those other districts with a low per-pupil real estate tax base.

Mr. Justice Marshall, with whom Mr. Justice Douglas concurs, dissenting.

The Court today decides, in effect, that a State may constitutionally vary the quality of education which it offers its children in accordance with the amount of taxable wealth located in the school districts within which they reside. The majority's decision represents an abrupt departure from the mainstream of recent state and federal court decisions concerning the unconstitutionality of state educational financing schemes dependent upon taxable local wealth. More unfortunately, though, the majority's holding can only be seen as a retreat from our historic commitment to equality of educational opportunity and as unsupportable acquiescence in a system which deprives children in their earliest years of the chance to reach their full potential as citizens. The Court does this despite the absence of any substantial justification for a scheme which arbitrarily channels educational resources in accordance with the fortuity of the amount of taxable wealth within each district. ∎

▪ Other Educational Challenges

Concurrent with the *Rodríguez* case, many states and state courts began to address funding disparities in the public schools. In *Serrano v. Priest,*[9] for instance, the California Supreme Court in 1971 ruled that financing schools through local property taxes violated state and federal constitutional provisions guaranteeing equal protection under the law. In contrast, the Colorado Supreme Court in *Luján v. Colorado School Board of Education* (1982),[10] much like the result in the *Rodríguez* decision, held that the financing system was permissible even though extreme disparities existed among school districts within the state and that the state constitution did not forbid disparities in wealth.

Having lost in the federal courts, the Mexican American plaintiffs in *Rodríguez* turned their efforts to the Texas state courts, alleging that the Texas system of funding public schools violated the Texas state constitution. More than fifteen years after the *Rodríguez* decision, the Texas Supreme Court in *Edgewood Independent School District v. Kirby* (1989)[11] confirmed the existence of funding inequities in the Texas public school system and struck down the system. Relying on the Texas Constitution, the court held that the state legislature had an obligation to ensure that public schools are "efficient." By so holding, the Texas Supreme Court in effect interpreted the meaning of efficiency to relate to the use of resources and a right to equitable distribution of funds. The Texas Supreme Court required the state legislature within a year to create a method to begin reducing these inequities. After a series of court battles by both wealthy and poor school districts regarding school funding laws, as well as a failed effort to address this problem through a constitutional amendment, the Texas legislature ultimately approved a school funding law that passed constitutional muster in 1994. The law identifies roughly ninety wealthy districts in the state of Texas and gives them one of several options for sharing their resources with poorer school districts. Then in 1995, the Texas Supreme Court narrowed its decision in *Kirby* by concluding that efficiency does not require equality of resources at all levels, such as educational resources, instructional materials, and extracurricular activities.[12] By 2003, some wealthy districts had brought lawsuits challenging any requirement that they must share resources with poor districts. Initially, these lawsuits were summarily dismissed and had no success, but appeals and efforts to keep these lawsuits viable continue. In addition, the Texas legislature continues to struggle with legislative proposals to dismantle the current, more equitable funding scheme.

Tied to the issue of educational funding in the public schools is that of allocation of funding for colleges and universities. In a case originating in South Texas, where Mexican Americans constitute the overwhelming majority of the population, plaintiffs argued that the allocation of funds for colleges and universities discriminated against Mexican Americans living along the U.S. border with Mexico. In the history of South Texas, very few four-year public universities have existed throughout the border communities, and until recently there were no law schools, medical schools, or other professional schools in this region. Thus, a student from South Texas who wanted to attend college or pursue a post-baccalaureate degree had to travel a significant distance, effectively denying South Texas residents access to and benefits of quality higher education programs and resources. A state trial court agreed with the plaintiffs' claims. When *Richards v. LULAC*[13] reached the Texas Supreme Court in 1993, the Court rejected the plaintiffs' claims and found no direct evidence of discriminatory intent or **disparate impact,** since some Mexican American students have the advantage of higher educational resources in other parts of the state. Additionally, the Texas Supreme Court rejected the notion that higher education is a fundamental right protected under the Texas Constitution, a result that mirrors the *Rodríguez* holding at the federal level with regard to elementary and secondary education. During the same time period, however, the Texas legislature created the South Texas Border Initiative, allocating millions of dollars to existing South Texas colleges and universities and creating new institutions of higher learning.

■ Concluding Thoughts

Educational access and equality will no doubt continue to be pressing issues for Mexican Americans in the twenty-first century. Historical discrimination and segregation in the U.S. public school system has contributed to present-day inequalities in educational attainment. Although there have been some successes, such as the *Méndez* and *Kirby* decisions, these court cases have had little lasting impact overall. Moreover, some recent studies indicate that Mexican American segregation in public schools continues to occur in communities with large Spanish-speaking populations. In some cases, Mexican Americans are more likely to be segregated than African Americans, indicating that resegregation is taking place. Furthermore, recent census figures also demonstrate that Mexican Americans in some southwestern states rank highest in high school dropout (or pushout) rates, and Mexican Americans continue to be less likely than whites and other racial or ethnic groups to have a college degree.

■ Discussion Questions

1. What reasons do you suppose were given to justify the segregation of Mexican American children in *Méndez* and throughout the 1920s and 1930s?

Do stereotypical assumptions about Mexican Americans persist today, and if so, do these assumptions affect their educational attainment?

2. Mexican American student organizations on college campuses have always been involved with pursuing educational equality in the public schools. In what way, if any, do students on your campus address these issues today?

3. How might the K–12 school system work differently today if the U.S. Supreme Court had ruled in favor of Rodríguez? If you were a state legislator, how would you propose equalizing the disparities in funding within school districts and between school districts?

4. One of the more recent educational challenges facing the Mexican American community has been the new requirement in many states that students pass a standardized test before graduating from high school. In recent years, litigation has challenged this practice, alleging that since Mexican Americans often obtain low or failing test scores, requiring passage of the test for high school graduation has a disproportionate impact on these students. Given the discriminatory impact on Mexican American students, do you believe making passage of these tests a requirement for high school graduation is a good idea?

■ Suggested Readings

Contreras, R. *Emerging Politics of Hispanic Education: From Politics to the Courts and Back Again.* Available from the Arizona State University website at www.asu.edu/educ/hbli/pubs/policypapers/policypaper1.htm.

Donato, R. *The Other Struggle for Equal Schools: Mexican Americans during the Civil Rights Movement.* Albany: State University of New York Press, 1997.

González, G. G. *Chicano Education in the Era of Segregation.* Philadelphia: Balch Institute for Ethnic Studies Press, 1990.

Harders, R., and M. N. Gómez. *Separate and Unequal: "Méndez v. Westminster* and Desegregation in California Schools." In *A Family Changes History: Méndez v. Westminster,* ed. M. DeMartino. Irvine: University of California, 1998.

Loya, A. C. "Chicanos, Law, and Educational Reform." *La Raza Law Journal* 3 (1994): 28–50.

Martínez, G. A. "Legal Indeterminacy, Judicial Discretion, and the Mexican American Litigation Experience: 1930–1980." *University of California Davis Law Review* 27, no. 3 (1994): 555–618.

San Miguel, G. *"Let All of Them Take Heed:" Mexican Americans and the Campaign for Educational Equality in Texas, 1910–1981.* Austin: University of Texas Press, 1987.

■ Videos

The Lemon Grove Incident. Los Angeles: UCLA Powell Media Library.

Ruiz, L. (executive producer), and S. Racho (segment producer). *Taking Back the Schools. Chicano: A History of the Mexican American Civil Rights Movement.* Los Angeles: National Latino Communications Center and Galan Productions, 1996.

■ Notes

1. 347 U.S. 483.

2. 163 U.S. 537. Although the *Plessy* case dealt with state laws mandating separate accommodations in trains, segregation in public schools was subsequently upheld by the U.S. Supreme Court in *Cummings v. Richmond County Board of Education,* 175 U.S. 528 (1899).

3. In 1931, in *Del Rio Independent School District v. Salvatierra,* a Texas appellate court held that school authorities could not segregate students on account of Mexican ancestry. The school district later argued successfully that Mexican children's language deficiencies justified separate schooling. Also in 1931, in *Alvarez v. Owen,* a California county court reached the same decision. For a discussion of these early cases, see G. San Miguel, "Mexican American Organizations and the Changing Politics of School Segregation in Texas, 1945–1980," *Social Science Quarterly* 63, no. 4 (1982): 701–15. *See also The Lemon Grove Incident* video above.

4. *Delgado v. Bastrop Independent School District* (W.D. TX, June 15, 1948) (unreported decision). This case was argued in part by Gus García, to whom this book is dedicated.

5. The California courts also reviewed several cases, such as *Jackson v. Pasadena City School District,* 59 Cal.2d 876 (1963), where the California Supreme Court declared the segregation of schoolchildren unconstitutional. Several court cases relied on the 1968 hearings before the U.S. Commission on Civil Rights. The report produced as a result of these hearings was titled *Ethnic Isolation of Mexican Americans in Public Schools of the Southwest, Mexican American Education Study, 1970.*

6. 324 F.Supp. 499. In 1972, the U.S. Court of Appeals for the Fifth Circuit affirmed this decision, holding that segregation of Mexican American schoolchildren is constitutionally impermissible and that "contours of unlawful segregation extend beyond statutorily mandated segregation . . . to include actions and policies of school authorities . . . separating them ethnically and racially in public schools." 467 F.2d 142 (1972).

7. 413 U.S. 189. State supreme courts also reviewed school desegregation cases. In *Crawford v. Board of Education of the City of Los Angeles,* the California Supreme Court held that school boards had a constitutional obligation to undertake feasible steps to alleviate the racial segregation that persisted in Los Angeles. 17 Cal.3d 280 (1976).

8. For an elaboration of Chicano student organizations, see C. Muñoz, *Youth,*

Identity and Power: The Chicano Movement (New York: Verso Press, 1989); and A. Navarro, *Mexican American Youth Organization: Avant-Garde of the Chicano Movement in Texas* (Austin: University of Texas Press, 1995). Also see the websites list for URLs for these organizations.

9. 5 Cal.3d 584 (1971). The California Supreme Court reaffirmed the decision in 1976 (18 Cal.3d 728). But in a later case, the Court of Appeals in California set the standards for assessing school finance equity, concluding that the California system of school finance was not equitable, and that absolute equality is neither possible nor required. 226 Cal.Rptr. 584 (1986).

10. 649 P.2d 1005.

11. 777 S.W.2d 391.

12. *Edgewood I.S.D. v. Meno,* 829 S.W.2d 450 (1995). The court held that the legislature's latest efforts to reform the education finance system satisfied the Texas Constitution.

13. 868 S.W.2d 306.

3

Gender and the Law

[The doctor] told her the Mexican people were very poor and that she should not have any more children because she could not support them. She does not remember signing any consent form [for the sterilization] although there is one in the file.—*Madrigal v. Quilligan* (1981)

book on Mexican Americans and the law would be incomplete without consideration of the complex issue of being both Mexican American *and* female. While researchers in history and social science have documented and illustrated the oppression Mexican American women face, which is qualitatively different than the discrimination experienced by either Mexican American men or women of other races and ethnicities,[1] their distinct experience within the U.S. legal system has been largely ignored. Undoubtedly, Mexican American women have played an integral and crucial role in every struggle for equality and justice for the Mexican American community. Indeed, Mexican American women were either plaintiffs or lawyers representing parties in some of the most significant cases contained in this book. Equally important, Mexican American women's organizations—such as Comisión Femenil Mexicana Nacional (established in 1970), the MALDEF Chicana Rights Project (established in 1974), Equal Rights Advocates (established in 1974), and other women's legal organizations—played key roles in bringing some of the cases contained in this chapter to fruition. Although historically there has been a paucity of materials, an area of academic research has begun to surface addressing legal issues that specifically impact Mexican American women and Latinas.[2] These issues range from reproductive rights, pregnancy discrimination, workplace discrimination, equal pay, and **affirmative action** to sexual harassment, domestic violence, and sexual violence (particularly by law enforcement agents). Thus, throughout this chapter and this book, remember that the contributions of Mexican Americans include not only those of fathers, sons, brothers, nephews, and husbands, but equally those of mothers, daughters, sisters, nieces, and wives (see figure 5).

■ 5. Mexican American women railroad workers employed by Southern Pacific during World War II.

▓ Reproductive Rights

Reproductive rights advocates assert that women should have a constitutional right to "control their bodies," including the right to determine whether or not to procreate, to continue to bear children, and to carry a pregnancy to term. One of the best examples of Mexican American women playing an integral role in shaping the law has been precisely with respect to reproductive rights—an area that has historically been of interest to all women but of particular challenge to Mexican American women.

As is commonly known, *Roe v. Wade* (1973)[3] was the landmark case in which the U.S. Supreme Court declared that a women's choice regarding whether or not to have an abortion is a constitutionally protected right. Since *Roe,* however, Congress and the states have consistently imposed restrictions that make it increasingly difficult for women, and women of color in particular, to obtain abortions. Restrictions on women seeking abortions—such as a mandatory twenty-four-hour waiting period, written informed consent, parental consent for minors, and restrictions on public funding for abortions—have been upheld by the U.S. Supreme Court. One of the only requirements to be struck down has been the requirement that women notify their spouses in order to obtain abortions.

Advocates for Mexican American women's rights argue that while all restrictions on abortion are relevant to Mexican American women, public funding for abortions is among the most crucial. In this area of case law, the U.S. Supreme Court has rejected the argument that state and federal governments have a constitutional obligation to pay for abortions for indigent women, even in "medically necessary" situations. Simultaneously, the Court has upheld restricting publicly funded abortions to cases of rape, incest, or danger to the mother's life. Some state courts, including the Texas courts, have come to the same conclusion. Most women's rights advocates argue that these court **decisions** have limited the right to an abortion to only those women who can afford it and have access to such facilities.

In addition to abortion, the issue of voluntary consent for sterilization is an area of reproductive rights of particular relevance to Mexican American women. In *Madrigal v. Quilligan* (1981), a federal court in California heard a challenge by ten Mexican and Mexican American women who alleged that the University of Southern California–Los Angeles County Medical Center performed illegal and unwanted sterilizations upon them without their consent. The background of the case revealed that the hospital at issue was a training ground for medical students and residents, and that various kinds of procedures, including sterilizations, were practiced on patients. The plaintiffs presented evidence that hospital staff pressured or coerced most of the women into signing consent forms during labor, presented these forms when the women were under heavy sedation, or in some cases never presented consent forms at all.[4] Most of the women were presented with forms printed in English although their primary language was Spanish. Some of the plaintiffs did not even discover that they had been sterilized until after they had given birth or in some cases until years later. While language barriers and cultural differences were relevant factors, these forced sterilizations were arguably a function of overt discrimination and hostility based on ethnicity, gender, class, and immigrant status. In fact, many of the women encountered hospital staff who were "openly hostile to them because of their ethnicity or poverty status."[5]

The trial court in *Madrigal* denied the women's claims, reasoning that any unwanted sterilizations were the result of two factors: the women's limited English abilities and their "cultural background." In dismissing their complaints, the trial judge asserted that given these two factors, "misunderstandings are bound to occur." In effect, the judge placed the blame on the women, without considering how their reproductive rights were violated.

Madrigal v. Quilligan

**United States District Court for the
Central District of California
No. CV 75-2057-JWC (June 30, 1978),
affirmed, 639 F.2d 789 (9th Cir. 1981)**

Curtis, J.

The rather subtle but underlying thrust of plaintiffs' complaint appears to be that they were all victims of a concerted plan by hospital attendants and doctors to push them, as members of a low socio-economic group who tend toward large families, to consent to sterilization in order to accomplish some sinister, invidious social purpose. A careful search of the record fails to produce any evidence whatever to support this contention. It did appear that the hospital had received funds for the establishment of a family planning program, and that discussion and encouragement of alternative methods of birth control, including sterilization, were carried on in the outpatient prenatal care clinic. In the obstetrics ward, however, whenever a sterilization procedure was suggested or advised, it was done on the initiative of the individual employee. Consequently, this case in its present posture consists of ten separate and distinct claims against the individual doctors who actually performed the sterilizations.

This case is essentially the result of a breakdown in communications between the patients and the doctors. All plaintiffs are Spanish speaking women whose ability to understand and speak English is limited. [The staff] have acquired enough familiarity with the language to get by. There is also an interpreter available. . . . But, even with these precautions, misunderstandings are bound to occur. Furthermore, the cultural background of these particular women has contributed to the problem in a subtle but very significant way. According to plaintiffs' anthropological expert, they are members of a traditional Mexican rural subculture, a relatively narrow spectrum of Mexican people living in this country whose lifestyle and cultural background derive from the lifestyle and culture of small rural communities in Mexico. He further testified that a cultural trait which is very prominent with this group is an extreme dependence on family. Most come from large families and wish to have large families for their own comfort and support. Furthermore, the status of a woman and her husband within that group depends largely upon the woman's ability to produce children. If for any reason she cannot, she is considered an incomplete woman and is apt to suffer a disruption of her relationship with her family and husband. When faced with a decision of whether or not to be sterilized, the decision process is a much more traumatic event with her than it would be with a typical patient and, consequently, she would require greater explanation, more patient advice, and greater care in interpreting her consent than persons not members of such a subculture would require. But this need for such delicate treatment is not readily apparent. It is not surprising therefore that the staff of a busy metropolitan hospital . . . would be unaware of these atypical cultural traits.

The plaintiff [Dolores] Madrigal was born in a small town in Mexico and attended school there through the sixth grade. She does not read or speak English fluently. The medical file contains an early note that [she] wished a tubal ligation. [She] apparently changed her mind as she refused the suggestion several times prior to the operation. During labor, and having indicated that she did not wish a tubal ligation, her husband was called to the hospital. She overheard an interpreter telling him that because of the complications she might die in the event of a future pregnancy. She was then told that her husband had agreed to the operation and she was again presented with a consent form which she signed. . . . She complains that some pressure was put upon her to sign the consent. . . . [Under] the circumstances [the doctor] performed the operation in a bona fide belief that [she] had given her informed and voluntary consent.

Mrs. [María] Figueroa is a thirty-one year old Mexican woman, the mother of three, all of whom were delivered by cesarean section. At the time of the birth of [her] first child, [she] had executed a consent form for a possible emergency tubal ligation or hysterectomy prior to the delivery of the child by cesarean section. However, this was not necessary and no such operation was performed. At the time of her most recent previous cesarean section, [conditions arose] significantly increas[ing] the risk in the event of a subsequent pregnancy. [When] these conditions were revealed [during the surgery to her husband] . . . he consented to the tubal ligation for his wife and signed a consent. . . . [The doctor] performed the operation in a bona fide belief that Mrs. Figueroa would have consented had she been able to, since she had done so once before when a cesarean procedure seemed imminent. This belief was further supported by the written consent form signed by her husband after the risks had been explained to him.

Helena Orozco was born in Fort Worth, Texas, and speaks both English and Spanish. All of her six children were born by cesarean section. She received her prenatal care at the Medical Center and was on many occasions advised by personnel that she should have her tubes tied . . . because she had already had "too many cesarean sections." She at first indicated that she did not want a tubal ligation but did consent to the cesarean. At a later time, however, she did sign her written consent because, she says, of the insistence of some members of the staff. [The doctor] performed the cesarean section and tubal ligation in reliance upon the written consent found in the file. There is no evidence that [the doctor] was present or participated in obtaining the written consent. . . . [he] was acting in the bona fide belief that he had the plaintiff's consent.

Mrs. [Georgina] Hernández is a thirty-eight year old Mexican-American woman who understands some English and who had no prenatal care at the Medical Center. She first came to the hospital with complications as she was already bleeding and experiencing labor pains. As she progressed it became apparent that a cesarean section was necessary, at which time the doctor asked her about having her tubes tied. He told her the Mexican people were very poor and that she should not have any more children because she could not support them. She does not remember signing any consent form although there is one in the file. Plaintiff contends that her handwriting on this consent form shows indications of medication and traumatic shock. The handwriting expert believed this signature was written under abnormal conditions. One [possibility] was that she was in severe labor pains and another possibility, which seems to me to be more credible, was that the consent was signed while she was lying in her hospital bed. In any event, there was nothing about this signature which would suggest to the surgeon that her consent was equivocal. The doctor testified that [she] had been offered a sterilization at the time of her admission but had refused. As delivery arrived he again discussed sterilization but she was unwilling. As the time for delivery arrived and it became apparent that a cesarean section would be required, he again discussed the sterilization process with [her], at which time she signed the consent for [a] cesarean but was not yet willing to consent to the sterilization. Shortly before going into the operating room, she indicated the decision to have the [sterilization] and this was noted in the file. The doctor denied . . . that he made the statement that she should not have any more children because the Mexican people were too poor to support them. He further stated that the consent was obtained before any anesthetic was applied. . . . I find therefore that . . . [the doctor] was acting in the bona fide belief that he had the voluntary and knowing consent of the plaintiff, and that such belief was reasonable.

There is no doubt that these women have suffered severe emotional and physical stress because of these operations. One can sympathize with them for their inability to communicate clearly, but one can hardly blame the doctors for relying on these indicia of consent which appeared to be unequivocal on their face and which are in constant use in the Medical Center. ■

■ Sexual Harassment and Other Workplace Discrimination

Among the most important federal **statutes** affecting women are the **Civil Rights Act of 1964** and the Equal Pay Act of 1963. Title VII of the Civil Rights Act forbids discrimination on the basis of either gender or race in hiring, promoting, and firing in the workplace. The original bill did not include sex discrimination, and the inclusion of sex as a protected category was actually an attempt by several southern congressmen to defeat the entire bill and thereby deny civil rights to racial minorities. In short, this effort to defeat the bill resulted in the passage of civil rights protections not only for racial minorities, but also for women. The Equal Pay Act of 1963 requires employers to give men and women equal pay for equal work. Exactly what constitutes "equal work" is not defined in the act, however, which has given rise to considerable debate centered on the issue of "comparable worth."

In addition to legislative efforts, court decisions have secured women's rights. Not until 1971 did the U.S. Supreme Court hold that discrimination on the basis of sex was unconstitutional under the **Equal Protection Clause** of the **Fourteenth Amendment.**[6] The case heralded a long series of court rulings invalidating a variety of laws and practices that discriminated against women. Equally important, the U.S. Supreme Court, in other cases, has upheld the use of **affirmative action** that takes into account sex as a basis for remedying underrepresentation of women in "traditionally segregated" workplaces.[7] Social science research, in turn, has repeatedly demonstrated that white women are the greatest beneficiaries of affirmative action programs. Despite these gains and protections, however, women continue to be subjected to sex discrimination in hiring, promotion, training, pay, and compensation and continue to be segregated in so-called "pink-collar" jobs.

The challenges women face are compounded for Mexican American women, especially when one considers the intersection of various factors, including gender, race and ethnicity, class, language ability, and immigrant status. As a result of the cumulative effect of these factors, Mexican American women are more likely to work in traditionally segregated jobs, such as secretaries, custodians, maids, nannies, and garment workers. They are also more likely to be the lowest paid workers in comparison to men and other women.

Relatedly, the realities of Mexican American women's work lives, including the fact that they are overrepresented among garment and manufacturing workers, also means that they are more likely to be directly affected by plant closings and relocations to other countries. Latina organizations, such as Fuerza Unida in San Antonio and La Mujer Obrera in El Paso, have begun to seek legal remedies from employers in connection with plant closings, specifically regarding back pay and loss of pensions and benefits.[8]

Immigrant status is often an issue for Mexican American women in the workplace. And while it is true that Mexican American rights organizations such as MALDEF and LULAC have always fought for the rights of immigrants, both legal and illegal, only recently has the broader Mexican American community followed suit. Given the realities of the nation's segregated workforce, Latino/a undocumented immigrants, **legal residents,** and U.S. citizens often work side by side. Thus, for most proponents of Mexican Americans' civil rights, being undocumented is not a particularly relevant factor in the workplace, because unfair and unjust conditions exist and persist for Mexican Americans and other Latinos irrespective of legal status.

As in the arena of reproductive rights, Mexican American women and Latinas have been instrumental in securing important rights for all workers. For instance, in *EEOC v. Tortilleria La Mejor* (1991),[9] the **Equal Employment Opportunity Commission** and a Latina plaintiff successfully argued that the protections under Title VII of the Civil Rights Act were available to all workers irrespective of their legal status. The case was important because a significant percentage of the workers were Latinas and because the plaintiff secured important workplace protections for all workers. The federal court judge concluded,

> The question posed in the present case . . . is not whether aliens are protected from illegal discrimination under the Act, but what kinds of discrimination the Act makes illegal. Certainly it would be unlawful for an employer to discriminate against aliens because of race, color, religion, sex, or **national origin**—for example, by hiring aliens of Anglo-Saxon background but refusing to hire those of Mexican or Spanish ancestry. Aliens are protected from illegal discrimination under the Act, but nothing in the Act makes it illegal to discriminate on the basis of citizenship or alienage. Consequently, the court concludes, as a matter of law, that the protections of Title VII were intended by Congress to run to aliens, whether documented or not, who are employed within the United States.

Another reality for women in the workplace is sexual harassment. In recognizing this increasing widespread problem, the U.S. Supreme Court has held that two forms of workplace sexual harassment, "quid pro quo" and "a hostile work environment," constitute sex discrimination under Title VII of the Civil Rights Act of 1964.[10] Quid pro quo harassment occurs when an employer bases employment decisions (including hiring, firing, promotion, and salary) on sexual behavior or acts or both, whereas "hostile work environment" harassment occurs when an employer creates or allows an environment of unwelcome conduct based on sex that is severe or pervasive enough to alter a person's working conditions. Once again, despite the legal gains women have made, sexual harassment is a persistent problem. Like other women, Mexican American women and Latinas have challenged intolerable circumstances in which they were placed in the workplace. In the highlighted case, for example, Mexican and Mexican American women who worked as maids in a hotel challenged the discrimination and sexual harassment in their environment. The Ninth Circuit ultimately sided with them.

EEOC v. *Hacienda Hotel*

United States Court of Appeals for the Ninth Circuit
881 F.2d 1504 (1989)

Cynthia Holcomb Hall, Circuit Judge:

On May 30, 1986, the Equal Employment Opportunity Commission ("EEOC" or "the Commission") initiated this employment discrimination action against appellant Hacienda Hotel ("Hacienda" or "the Hotel"), an establishment operated by Las Freres Hacienda in El Segundo, California. The Commission alleged that the Hacienda, its General Manager (Frank Godoy), its Executive Housekeeper (Alicia Castro), and its Chief of Engineering (William Nusbaum) had engaged in unlawful employment practices against female employees in the Hacienda housekeeping department by sexually harassing them, terminating them when they became pregnant . . . and retaliating against them for opposing Hacienda's discriminatory practices. Relief was sought and obtained on behalf of five current and former Hacienda maids, all but one of whom were undocumented aliens, who were alleged to have been victims of appellant's discriminatory employment practices during 1982 and 1983. We affirm.

The Hotel hired Teodora Castro in June 1980. Teodora became pregnant in late 1981 and continued to work for defendant. During the course of her pregnancy, both Alicia Castro and Nusbaum made numerous crude and disparaging remarks regarding her pregnancy. Nusbaum, for example, told Teodora that "that's what you get for sleeping without your underwear"; he also asked why she was pregnant by another man and made comments about her "ass." Nusbaum often subjected her to sexually offensive remarks in the presence of Alicia Castro, who merely laughed. Alicia Castro herself told Teodora that she did not like "stupid women who have kids," and on many occasions called her a "dog" or a "whore" or a "slut." In late 1981 and early 1982, Teodora Castro complained to Frank Godoy and Jose Ortiz, the union representative, about Nusbaum's and Alicia Castro's comments, but the situation did not improve. On June 30, 1982, Teodora Castro was terminated, as Alicia Castro admitted in her deposition and at trial, because of her pregnancy. She was rehired in November 1982, following the birth of her child.

The Hotel hired Flora Villalobos in April of 1980. After she became pregnant in early 1982, she was regularly subjected to sexually offensive remarks from Alicia Castro and Nusbaum. Castro often called her a "dog" or a "whore," and Nusbaum told her that women "get pregnant because they like to suck men's dicks." On many occasions, Nusbaum threatened to have her fired if she did not submit to his sexual advances. Castro witnessed some of Nusbaum's behavior and laughed at his sexual remarks. On October 31, 1982, when Villalobos was approximately seven months pregnant and still able and willing to work, Castro terminated her employment because of her pregnancy. Villalobos had obtained a statement from her doctor indicating that she was able to continue working until two or three weeks before her estimated delivery date of December 28, 1982. On February 9, 1983, Villalobos provided Castro a written statement from her doctor indicating that she was able to return to work immediately. Villalobos was not rehired until April 8, 1983. The Hotel hired two maids, one rehire and one new employee, while Villalobos was awaiting rehire.

Leticia Cardona was employed by the Hotel from May 15, 1981, to September 28, 1982. After she became pregnant in early 1982, she was subjected to sexually offensive comments by Alicia Castro and Nusbaum.

In September 1982, when Cardona was six months pregnant, Castro told her that she was too fat to clean rooms and fired her on September 28, 1982. Although at trial Castro testified that Cardona was terminated for poor work performance, Castro had previously admitted in a deposition that she terminated Cardona pursuant to her practice of terminating pregnant employees. Cardona's notice of termination form, which was completed by Castro, states that she was terminated because of her pregnancy. In December 1982, after the birth of her baby, Cardona returned to the Hotel and requested her job back, but Castro refused. Castro testified that Cardona was not rehired because she was a poor worker.

Throughout her term of employment from October 8, 1978, to March 10, 1983, William Nusbaum made sexual advances and offensive sexual comments to Mercedes Flores. Nusbaum regularly offered, for example, to give her money from his paycheck and an apartment to live in if she would "give him [her] body." He also assured her that she would never be fired if she would have sex with him. Flores claimed to have heard Nusbaum make offensive sexual comments to other maids, including complainants Cardona, Castro, and Villalobos. On one occasion, for example, she heard him say to Villalobos: "You have such a fine ass. It's a nice ass to stick a nice dick into. How many dicks have you eaten?"

On February 17, 1987, the district court heard the EEOC's motion for partial summary judgment on the issue of appellant's liability for pregnancy discrimination. The district court concluded that the Hacienda's practice of terminating pregnant employees, while granting leaves of absence and reinstatement upon recovery to other "temporarily disabled" employees, violated [Section 703(a)] of Title VII. The court entered partial summary judgment in favor of the Commission with respect to Castro's, Cardona's, and Villalobos' pregnancy claims on March 2, 1987. The remaining issues were tried before the court from September 21 to 25, 1987. After trial, the district court entered judgment for the EEOC, based on the following findings and conclusions. The court . . . found the sexual harassment claims supported by the evidence and concluded that the Hacienda was liable for the conduct of Alicia Castro and William Nusbaum, and for the failure of Frank Godoy to take prompt remedial action upon learning of the employees' allegations.

The Supreme Court recently recognized the "hostile or offensive work environment" theory of liability for sexual harassment [in] *Meritor Savings Bank v. Vinson,* 477 U.S. 57 (1986). To establish a Title VII violation under this theory, a plaintiff must show that: (1) she was subjected to sexual advances, requests for sexual favors, or other verbal or physical conduct of a sexual nature; (2) that the conduct was unwelcome; and (3) that the conduct was sufficiently severe or pervasive to alter the conditions of her employment and create an abusive working environment.

Appellant raises three challenges to the district court's conclusion that it is liable for sexual harassment in which its employees Alicia Castro and William Nusbaum engaged. First, Hacienda argues that the sexually harassing conduct in which Castro and Nusbaum were proven to have engaged was not sufficiently severe or pervasive to be actionable under Title VII. Appellant also contends that it could not be held liable for the acts of Nusbaum and Castro of which it had no notice. We consider each of Hacienda's contentions in turn.

There is no dispute in this case that the acts of sexual harassment complained of occurred, and that they were unwelcome. The contested issue about a . . . cause of action here is whether the harassment was sufficiently "severe or pervasive" to alter the terms and conditions of the claimants' employment and to create a sexually hostile work environment. As the record reveals, and as the district court found, Nusbaum repeatedly engaged in vulgarities, made sexual remarks, and requested sexual favors from the complainants. The complainants' direct supervisor, Alicia Castro, also frequently witnessed, laughed at, and herself made these types of comments. As the district court also found, Castro had direct authority to hire, discharge, and discipline housekeeping employees, and Nusbaum threatened at least one of the claimants that he would have Castro fire her if she did not submit to his sexual advances. Upon . . . review of the evidence in this case, we agree with the district court's conclusion that the complainants were subjected to severe and pervasive sexual harassment that "seriously tainted" the working environment and altered the terms and conditions of their employment.

[The court also held that] Hacienda can be held liable for Castro's and Nusbaum's actions. As the district found, the general manager of the Hacienda, Frank Godoy, had actual knowledge of allegations of harassment, as did Alicia Castro, a supervisor with authority to hire, discharge, and discipline employees in the housekeeping department. The court also found, by implication, that appellant should have known (or constructively knew), of the harassment because it was severe and pervasive and "seriously tainted" the complainants' working environment. The district court did not err in concluding that appellant could be held liable for Castro's and Nusbaum's conduct.

For all of the foregoing reasons, the judgment of the district court is AFFIRMED.

Violence, Gender, and Sexual Identity

Sexual violence is another pressing issue facing Mexican American women. The issue is not exclusive to women in the United States but also implicates women immigrating from other countries. One of the more disturbing cases of immigrant women enduring sexual violence took place along the Texas-Mexico border, where border patrol officers were ultimately convicted in a federal district court for sexually abusing and coercing sexual favors from illegal immigrants who were being detained.[11]

Fortunately, among the more positive pieces of legislation for Mexican immigrants and Mexican Americans are the Violence Against Women Act of 1994 (VAWA I) and the Violence Against Women Act of 2000 (VAWA II), both of which contain provisions addressing the rights of battered immigrant women. Prior to the passage of these two statutes, Mexican and other immigrant women who were victims of domestic violence had a very difficult time obtaining legal residence status in the United States independent of their abusive husbands. As a result, many were forced to stay with their abusive spouses, who often used the threat of deportation as yet another form of abuse. As a result of these two statutes, immigrant women who are victims of domestic violence may now seek legal residency on their own.

Additionally, immigrant women who are victims of domestic violence in their home country are now beginning to have some success in qualifying as "refugees" under the relevant provisions of the **Immigration and Nationality Act** (INA). Under this law, individuals fleeing their home country may qualify as refugees if they are able to prove that they have been persecuted or fear that they will be persecuted "on account of" one of the following: (1) race, (2) religion, (3) nationality, (4) membership in a particular social group, or (5) political opinion. An individual who is able to prove that he or she is a refugee is granted "political asylum" and is entitled to remain in the United States.

Foreigners who have experienced domestic violence in other countries and are seeking political asylum in the United States have begun to argue that they have been persecuted or fear persecution on account of membership in a particular social group, namely that of domestic violence victims. This legal argument has had some success, and Mexican women have been at the forefront of some of these cutting-edge cases. In *Aguirre-Cervantes v. INS* (2001), for instance, the U.S. Court of Appeals for the Ninth Circuit granted a nineteen-year-old Mexican woman's petition for political asylum on the basis that she had suffered extreme and severe abuse by her father in Mexico, and suspended the government's efforts to remove her from the United States.

Aguirre-Cervantes v. INS

United States Court of Appeals for the Ninth Circuit
242 F.3d 1169 (2001)

David R. Thompson, Circuit Judge:

Rosalba Aguirre-Cervantes ("petitioner"), a 19-year-old native of Mexico, petitions for review of an order of the Board of Immigration Appeals ("BIA"), which **vacated** a decision by the Immigration Judge granting her request for asylum. Over many years, the petitioner was subjected to extreme abuse by her father. She contends this abuse constituted persecution, and that it occurred on account of her membership in a particular social group consisting of her immediate family, all of whose members were abused by her father. At the hearing before the Immigration Judge ("IJ"), the petitioner presented evidence that the country of Mexico was unable or unwilling to do anything about this abuse, and that if she returned to Mexico the abuse would likely continue.

The IJ concluded that the petitioner had satisfied the statutory requirements for asylum, but denied her request for withholding of removal. The INS appealed to the BIA, which agreed that the petitioner had suffered persecution but concluded that she was not eligible for asylum on the ground of persecution on account of membership in a particular social group.

The primary issue is whether the petitioner's immediate family, all of whose members lived together and were subjected to abuse by the petitioner's father, constitutes a protected particular social group under the asylum statute. We conclude that it does. We also conclude that the petitioner was persecuted by her father on account of her membership in that social group, that she has a well-founded fear of future persecution, and that Mexico is unable or unwilling to interfere with that persecution.

We grant the petitioner's petition for review and hold that she is eligible for asylum. We further hold that she is entitled to withholding of removal because she has established a clear probability of persecution if she returns to Mexico.

The petitioner lived in Michoacan, Mexico, with her parents and six of her nine siblings. Two of her brothers now live in the United States, and another sister lives with her grandfather in Michoacan.

In January 1998, at the age of 16, the petitioner left Mexico because of severe, repeated physical abuse by her father. She testified that from the time she was about three years old, her father beat her frequently and severely, sometimes daily and sometimes weekly. In administering these beatings, he employed a horse whip, tree branches, a hose and his fists. The petitioner suffered a dislocated elbow and lost consciousness as a result of some of this abuse, and bears various scars on her forehead, hand, arm and leg. Her father refused to allow her to seek medical treatment for any of the injuries he inflicted. Furthermore, she testified that her mother did not allow her to go to the police, telling her that her father had the right to do with her what he wanted. Several times, the petitioner went to live with her grandfather to escape her father's beatings, but each time her father came after her and forced her to return with him.

The petitioner testified that she was not aware of any shelters, agencies or children's services in Mexico that would help her. In addition, she testified that she believed the police would not have helped her even if she had been able to contact them.

Petitioner's father, Mr. Aguirre, abused not only the petitioner, but all of her siblings and her mother as well. He abused petitioner's mother (his wife) especially frequently during her pregnancies. The petitioner testified that whenever she tried to protect her mother by intervening, she was also beaten.

The petitioner presented evidence that in Mexico domestic violence is pervasive, officially tolerated, and in some areas legally approved. The State Department concluded that women who suffer domestic violence "are reluctant to report abuse or file charges, and even when notified, police are reluctant to intervene in what society considers to be a domestic matter." Evidence in the record further establishes that in Mexico there are very few shelters or social services available to domestic violence victims, and that few women avail themselves of these services.

The IJ found that the petitioner's testimony was "credible and consistent and detailed." The IJ ruled that she was a member of a social group of "victims of domestic violence," or of "the family which is a victim of domestic violence."

The BIA agreed with the IJ that the petitioner's severe abuse by her father constituted persecution. The BIA also credited "the [petitioner's] testimony in general" and stated that "[t]he determinative issue . . . is whether the harm experienced by the [petitioner] was, or in the future may be inflicted 'on account of' a statutorily protected ground." The BIA characterized the relevant social group as "Mexican children who are victims of domestic violence," and determined that such a group had not adequately been shown to be a particular social group for asylum purposes. The BIA reversed the decision of the IJ, and this petition for review followed.

To be eligible for asylum, an applicant must establish that she is a refugee. A refugee is a person "who is unable or unwilling to return to, and is unable or unwilling to avail himself or herself of the protection of," his or her country of nationality "because of persecution or a well-founded fear of persecution on account of race, religion, nationality, membership in a particular social group, or political opinion."

We have defined a "particular social group" as a collection of people closely affiliated with each other, who are actuated by some common impulse or interest. Of central concern is the existence of a voluntary associational relationship among the purported members, which imparts some common characteristic that is fundamental to their identity as a member of that discrete social group.

Consistent with decisions from our circuit, our sister circuits and the BIA, we hold that a family group may qualify as a particular social group within the meaning of [the law]. This is not to say, however, that every family group will qualify. Qualification will depend upon the circumstances of each case. In the domestic violence context, Mexican society . . . treats members of a family differently from nonmembers because it regards violence within a family as a "domestic matter," rather than a matter for government intervention.

The INS concedes that the petitioner was persecuted. It does not concede, however, that she was persecuted "on account of" her family membership. Establishing persecution on account of family membership is a burden the petitioner bears. She must present evidence, either direct or circumstantial, from which it is reasonable to conclude that her persecutor harmed her at least in part because of her membership in what we have held to be a particular social group, her immediate family. We conclude the petitioner carried this burden.

The petitioner presented extensive documentary evidence that domestic violence is practiced to control and dominate members of the abuser's family. The undisputed evidence demonstrates that Mr. Aguirre's goal was to dominate and persecute members of his immediate family. He abused his wife and all of his children to whom he had access. There is no evidence that he ever acted violently toward any non-family member. The petitioner's uncle also testified that two of the petitioner's brothers, who now live in the United States, fled Mexico because of frequent abuse by their father. It was the immediate family that was the target of Mr. Aguirre's assaults. It was established by abundant evidence— and undisputed—that it was the petitioner's status as a member of that family that prompted her beatings. The conclusion is inescapable that she suffered those beatings on account of her family membership.

We next consider whether the petitioner established that the Mexican government was unable or unwilling to control Mr. Aguirre's abusive behavior. When persecution is inflicted by a non-governmental entity, an applicant must be able to show that the persecutor was someone the government was "unable or unwilling to control." In commenting on the documentary evidence, the BIA stated that the evidence "appears to establish that [in Mexico] 'the most pervasive violations of women's rights involve domestic and sexual violence which is believed to be widespread and vastly under-reported.'"

In addition to the sources cited by the BIA, there was additional documentary evidence that domestic violence is widely condoned in Mexico and that law enforcement authorities are unwilling to intervene in such matters. As of 1997, in all but a few of Mexico's thirty-two states, it was "legal for husbands to use 'correction' discipline to handle wives and children.'" At that time, Mexico City, with a population of 23 million, had only one battered women's shelter, with only eight beds, and battered wives' shelters existed in only five Mexican states.

We conclude that any reasonable fact finder considering the evidence in this case would conclude that the Mexican government is unable or unwilling to control Mr. Aguirre's abusive behavior directed toward his immediate family.

[T]he record does not contain any evidence that the petitioner could reasonably relocate within Mexico. When she previously tried to live with her grandfather, her father came after her and forced her to return home. Moreover, Mr. Aguirre has personal information about the petitioner that would assist him in tracking her down if she were to return to Mexico. She is still quite young and most likely would have to turn to relatives or family friends for assistance. Finding her would not likely prove difficult.

Considering all of the relevant circumstances, we are convinced that any reasonable fact finder would conclude that the petitioner's relocation away from her former home in Mexico would not effectively negate the likelihood of her future persecution by her father.

For these reasons, we grant the petition for review and grant withholding of removal. We **remand** to the Attorney General to exercise his discretion and determine whether to grant asylum.

Petition for Review GRANTED.

Following this decision, the government appealed for rehearing of the case **en banc,** that is, by all of the judges of the Ninth Circuit, a request that was granted. The panel decision by the Ninth Circuit was subsequently vacated, leaving the panel's **opinion** with no binding effect. Then, in an unexpected turn of events, the father of Ms. Aguirre-Cervantes was killed in an unrelated incident, so the full circuit court never actually ruled on the case. Consequently, the Ninth Circuit ultimately remanded the case to the BIA by agreement of the parties. Irrespective of this outcome, what is most important about the case is that it provided another avenue for immigrants, specifically Mexican women immigrants who are victims of domestic violence, to seek justice.

In another groundbreaking case involving a Mexican national and the issue of political asylum, the U.S. Court of Appeals for the Ninth Circuit in *Hernández-Montiel v. INS* (2000)[12] overturned an immigration judge's and the BIA's denial of an asylum request for a gay male "with [a] female sexual identity." The petitioner was only fifteen years old upon his original illegal entry into the United States, and the evidence established that while in Mexico, the petitioner had been thrown out of his parents' home, expelled from school, raped by police and attacked by other men for his sexual identity. As a result, the petitioner claimed he met the requirements for political asylum because he had been persecuted and feared further persecution because of his membership in a particular social group. On appeal, much as in *Aguirre-Cervantes,* the primary issue was whether the petitioner was a member of a particular social group. The INS argued that petitioner had not established his membership in a particular social group, in part because of his own conduct and in part because his sexual identity was not immutable. More specifically, with respect to the petitioner's rape by police officers and experiences of gay bashing, the BIA "reasoned that 'the respondent's mistreatment arose from his [own] conduct . . . thus the rape by the policemen, and the attack by a mob of gay bashers are not necessarily persecution.'" As an initial matter, the Ninth Circuit ruled that the BIA had erred in defining the petitioner's social group as "homosexual males who dress as females" and held instead that the "primary issue" in the case was "whether gay men with female sexual identities in Mexico constitute a protected 'particular social group' under the asylum statute." In rejecting the BIA's problematic assertions that the petitioner's own conduct caused his persecution, the Ninth Circuit forcefully stated, "Perhaps, then, by 'conduct,' the BIA was referring to [petitioner's] effeminate dress or his sexual orientation as a gay man, as a justification for the police officer's raping him. The 'you asked for it' excuse for rape is offensive to this court and has been discounted by courts and commentators alike." Finally, the Ninth Circuit granted the petitioner's request, holding, "We conclude as a matter of law that gay men with female sexual identities in Mexico constitute a 'particular social group' and that [petitioner] is a member of that group. His female sexual identity is immutable because it is inherent in his identity; in any event, he should not be required to change it. Because the evidence compels the conclusion that [petitioner] suffered past persecution and has a well-founded fear of persecution if he were forced to return to Mexico, we conclude that the record compels a finding that he is entitled to asylum and withholding of deportation."

■ Concluding Thoughts

Mexican American women have been at the forefront of legal battles in the fight for equality and justice for not only Mexican American women but all women. As the cases in this chapter illustrate, Mexican American women have had to struggle with the dual challenge of being not only Mexican American but also female. The intersection of these two forces means that Mexican American women face unique issues, as in the realm of reproductive rights, sexual harassment, and other workplace discrimination.

Moreover, it is often the case that these struggles pertain to women who are Mexican nationals. Mexican American and Mexican women encounter nearly identical challenges of workplace segregation, educational inequities, and lack of access to political resources. Thus, whether the issue is reproductive rights, domestic violence, or workplace discrimination, the documented versus undocumented distinction is largely irrelevant for Mexican American women. In short, removing legal status from the equation would not eliminate or substantially reduce sex discrimination in the workplace.

Equally important, with the exception of the political asylum issues, all the challenges facing Mexican American and Mexican women explored in this chapter occurred not in Mexico but here in the United States. Significantly, the cases highlighted here are but a small sampling of the innumerable instances that are certain to have occurred but were never reported. It is also fair to say that certain topics, such as abortion, sexual harassment, and transgendered identities are still considered taboo within the Mexican American community and remain exceptionally difficult to address through traditional legal means. So Mexican American women's rights advocates must continue to confront these dilemmas.

Finally, few of the legal advances spearheaded by Mexican American women were obtained alone. Rather, as is true in the struggle for Mexican American rights generally, Mexican American women often collaborated with various community-based organizations, or relied on the EEOC and other law-enforcement agencies to help vindicate their rights. Until all barriers that prevent women from achieving true equality have been eliminated, Mexican American women, who face particular discrimination, will continue to play an integral role in the advancement of the legal system within the United States.

■ Discussion Questions

1. Do you agree with the district court's conclusion in *Madrigal v. Quilligan* that given the women's limited English abilities and cultural background, "misunderstandings are bound to occur"? Do doctors have a professional or moral responsibility to be culturally sensitive?

2. Social science research repeatedly demonstrates that populations with low educational and income levels and those with a young median age—all of which are true of the Mexican American population—consistently have higher reproduction rates than the general population. Is it ever appropriate for government to formulate a policy, either through sterilization efforts or otherwise, that seeks to reduce or limit a particular population's reproduction level?

3. In the case of *EEOC v. Hacienda Hotel* Ms. Castro, presumably a Mexican American or Latina herself, participated in the discrimination and exploitation of other Mexican American women. Without necessarily justifying her actions, how would you characterize the complex dynamics of which Ms. Castro was a part (for example, power, racism, anti-immigrant sentiment, cultural self-hatred, or something else)? Is it possible Ms. Castro was also being manipulated to acquiesce to Mr. Nusbaum's behavior?

4. Mexican American women, in particular, face a serious dilemma. They are more likely to be segregated in the workplace, be trapped in low-wage jobs,

drop out of high school, and get pregnant at a young age. Yet they are also more likely to be stereotyped as sultry and sexualized, an image reinforced by Latina celebrities such as Jennifer Lopez and Christina Aguilera. Should these competing forces be addressed by Mexican American women and the broader Mexican American community? Given the reality of Latinas' lives and work, do you believe these competing forces will continue to present barriers to Mexican American women's success?

5. Do you believe victims of domestic violence and "gay men with female sexual identities" from Mexico or other countries should qualify as members of a "particular social group" for asylum purposes and thereby be allowed to remain in the United States?

6. Given your knowledge of and experience in Mexico (if any), do you agree with the Ninth Circuit's grim characterization of women, domestic violence, and gender issues in general in Mexican culture? Does this characterization hold true for Mexican American culture in the United States?

■ Suggested Readings

Hernández, A. "Chicanas and the Issue of Involuntary Sterilization: Reforms Needed to Protect Informed Consent." *Chicano Law Review* 3 (1976): 3–37.

López, A. S. "Latina Issues: Fragments of Historia (ella) (Herstory)." In *Latinos in the United States: History, Law and Perspective,* vol. 2. New York: Garland Publishing, 1999.

López, G. "The Work We Know So Little About." *Stanford Law Review* 42 (1989): 1–13.

Ontiveros, M. "Three Perspectives on Workplace Harassment of Women of Color." *Golden Gate University Law Review* 23 (1993): 817–28.

Padilla, L. M. "Intersectionality and Positionality: Situating Women of Color in the Affirmative Action Dialogue." *Fordham Law Review* 66 (1997): 843–930.

Vellos, D. "Immigrant Latina Domestic Workers and Sexual Harassment." *American University Journal of Gender and the Law* 5 (1997): 407–32.

■ Notes

1. For some of the earliest works addressing this issue, see M. Vidal, *Chicanas Speak Out* (New York: Pathfinder Press, 1971); M. B. Melville, ed., *Twice a Minority: Mexican-American Women* (St. Louis: C. V. Mosby, 1980).

2. See the suggested readings for this chapter, as well as E. Arriola, "Voices from the Barbed Wires of Despair: Women in the Maquiladoras, Latina Critical Legal Theory

and Gender at the U.S.–Mexico Border," *DePaul Law Review* 49 (2000): 729–815; L. G. Espinoza, "Dissecting Women, Dissecting Law: The Court Ordering of Cesarean Section Operations and the Failure of Informed Consent to Protect Women of Color," *National Black Law Journal* 13 (1994): 211–37; L. Galindo and M. D. Gonzáles, eds., *Speaking Chicana: Voice, Power, and Identity* (Tucson: University of Arizona Press, 1999); L. M. Padilla, "Latinas and Religion: Subordination or State of Grace?," *University of California at Davis Law Review* 33 (2000): 973–1008; J. Rivera, "Domestic Violence against Latinas by Latino Males: An Analysis of Race, National Origin, and Gender Differentials," *Boston College Third World Law Journal* 14 (1994): 231–57.

3. 410 U.S. 113.

4. C. G. Velez-I., "The Nonconsenting Sterilization of Mexican American Women in Los Angeles," in Melville, *Twice a Minority.*

5. A. Hernandez, "Chicanas and the Issue of Involuntary Sterilization: Reforms Needed to Protect Informed Consent," *Chicano Law Review* 3 (1976): 3–37.

6. *Reed v. Reed,* 404 U.S. 71.

7. *Johnson v. Transportation Agency, Santa Clara County,* 480 U.S. 616 (1987).

8. For an overview of these organizations and their impact, see I. Minjarez, "Unraveling the Cloth That Binds Latina Workers in Texas: A Critical Analysis of the Texas Pay Day Act," *The Scholar: St. Mary's Law Review on Minority Issues* 1 (Spring 1999): 207–52.

9. 758 F.Supp 585.

10. *Meritor Savings Bank v. Vinson,* 477 U.S. 57 (1986).

11. *U.S. v. Davila,* 704 F.2d 749 (1983).

12. 225 F.3d 1084.

4

Law and Language

Since language is a close and meaningful proxy for national origin, restrictions on the use of languages may mask discrimination against specific national origin groups.—*Yñiguez v. Arizonans for Official English* (1995)

Although there is no official language of the United States, the abilities to speak, read, and write English are essential to economic success in this country. Nevertheless, almost forty-five million people—approximately 18 percent of the U.S. population—speak a language other than English at home, and more than 19 million people report to the U.S. Census Bureau that they speak English less than "very well."[1]

How should the U.S. legal system respond to the diversity of languages spoken within the borders of our country? This question is important for the Mexican American community since language is a fundamental part of its personal and cultural identity. It is especially important for those who are fluent in English and continue to speak Spanish, and it is of critical importance for the roughly twelve million Mexican Americans and other Latinos who do not speak English well or do not speak it at all. Proponents of Mexican American language rights have long cited the **Treaty of Guadalupe Hidalgo** as a basis for their position.

Language issues have historically generated a great deal of controversy in the United States. Since the 1980s, English-Only activists have been seeking to ban government use of any language other than English and to have English declared the nation's official language. The English-Only movement, fueled by racist and **nativist** sentiments, spread in direct response to the increase in undocumented immigration from Latin America and Asia in the 1980s.

The English-Only movement makes, and is based upon, a number of false and unsupportable assertions, namely that (1) the United States has always been an English-speaking country (see figure 6); (2) government officials in the United States used only English to communicate with citizens and residents prior to the mid-twentieth century; (3) European immi-

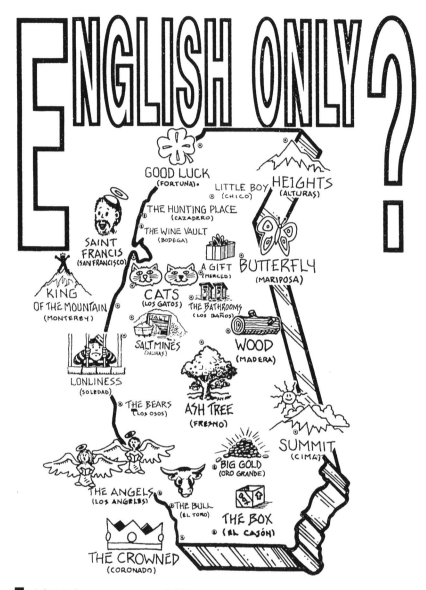

■ 6. Satirical map in response to California voters' passage of the English-Only referendum.

grants to the United States learned English on their own without receiving bilingual assistance from the government; and (4) bilingual services were an invention of the 1960s designed to aid Latinos who, unlike other immigrants, refused to learn English.

■ Early History of Language in the United States

The United States has always been a multilingual country. Prior to the arrival of Europeans in North America, Native Americans spoke approximately one thousand distinct languages. The arrival of Europeans had devastating effects on the indigenous population, but even today more than two hundred Native American languages are spoken in the United States. In addition, during the colonial era, large numbers of English-, German-, and French-speaking immigrants arrived in this country. Large groups speaking other European languages settled in territories that would later become part of the United States. For instance, French was spoken in Louisiana and Spanish was spoken in Arizona, California, Colorado, Florida, New Mexico, and Texas.

Equally important, the United States has a rich history of providing services in languages other than English. The Continental Congress, for instance, issued official publications during the Revolutionary War in German, French, and English. Furthermore, after the Louisiana Territory was purchased from France in 1803, the laws in Louisiana were published in French and English. Louisiana also authorized bilingual French-English public schools in the 1879 Louisiana **Constitution**.

The sympathetic views of English-speaking Americans toward language-appropriate government services were clearly evident in the early years of our nation in various southwestern states, such as California, New Mexico, and Texas. During the 1820s and 1830s, English-speaking immigrants settled in northern Mexico, in what would later become the state of Texas. Very few of these Anglo American immigrants spoke Spanish. Despite their status as immigrants, these Anglo Americans demanded that the Mexican government provide them services in English. In response, the Mexican government maintained bilingual (English-Spanish) records. Furthermore, elections were conducted, local **ordinances** were enacted, and official notices were published in English. The government also authorized bilingual schools. These widespread bilingual services did not however satisfy Anglo immigrants, who declared their independence from Mexico. These immigrants claimed a right to do so in part on the basis that the Mexican government was sacrificing their welfare "in an unknown tongue." After its independence from Mexico was secured, government proceedings in Texas were conducted in both Spanish and English. This tradition of multilingual government continued after Texas became part of the United States. Indeed, with the influx of large numbers of German immigrants, the state of Texas began publishing its laws in German as well as Spanish and English. Local governments operated in English and in the languages spoken by the local population. Public schools also operated in the languages spoken in each locality, including Spanish, German, Czech, Polish, Danish, Wendish, and English.

After the U.S.–Mexican War, Californios—those who were native to and had lived in Mexican California prior to 1848—in the newly annexed U.S. state of California also received bilingual government services. Translators were provided for the Spanish-speaking native Californio delegates to the first California Constitutional Convention. The first California Constitution was published in Spanish and English. The California Legislature in 1850 also authorized the dissemination of all laws, supreme court **decisions,** and other government documents in Spanish and English.

Similarly, laws in New Mexico were published in Spanish and English from 1846 until 1953. Bilingual schools were also established. In fact, New Mexico did not become a state until 1912 in large part because of concerns that a majority of its population did not speak English. After statehood, however, government services continued to be provided in Spanish.

Clearly, therefore, throughout the early history of the U.S. Southwest, state and local government services were provided in many languages other than English. Yet, most contemporary residents are unfamiliar with this history because multilingual government services were suppressed in the late nineteenth and early twentieth centuries, usually in response to nativist political pressure. These efforts occurred in California as early as 1879, as Spanish-speaking Californios became a minority population in their native land. Even after bilingualism was no longer officially permitted, bilingual government services continued to be offered informally in areas where a large percentage of the population spoke a language other than English.

■ Language as a Civil Rights Issue

In the 1950s and 1960s as African Americans succeeded in expanding their opportunities through the **Civil Rights Movement,** Mexican Americans joined in demanding legislative guarantees of their basic civil rights. A number of important legislative programs implemented in the 1960s and 1970s explicitly guaranteed language rights. The **Voting Rights Act of 1965** discussed in chapters 1 and 6, for example, was amended in 1972 to guarantee the voting rights of language minorities by requiring that bilingual ballots and voting information be provided whenever 5 percent of the relevant population belongs to a single language minority. Many civil rights **statutes,** however, do not explicitly protect against discrimination on the basis of language, even though they do prohibit discrimination on the basis of **national origin.** Thus, one of the more complex issues the courts have struggled with is whether a ban on national origin discrimination also prohibits language-based discrimination. As we will illustrate in the remainder of the chapter, the courts have addressed the extent to which language rights are guaranteed under U.S. law. As you read these materials, consider the extent to which they reflect the heritage and history of multilingualism in the United States.

As we have shown, the United States has always been a land in which many different languages have been and are spoken. Moreover, the use of these diverse languages has often been supported, encouraged, and facilitated by official government actions. To the surprise of many Americans, there is currently no national law that makes English the official language of the United States. A few states—such as Hawaii, Louisiana, and New Mexico—officially recognize their multilingual heritage. Hawaii's constitution declares Hawaiian and English official languages of the state. Louisiana's constitution recognizes the right of Louisianans to preserve and promote their linguistic origins. Likewise, New Mexico's constitution requires certain government functions to be carried out in Spanish and English.

Before the 1980s, only two states had declared English the sole official language of their state: Illinois (1923) and Nebraska (1920). Such declarations did not prevent these states from offering multilingual services.[2] But since the 1980s, in excess of twenty states in diverse areas of the nation have declared English their official language.[3] Many of these state constitutional amendments and statutes, unlike the Arizona one described below, simply declared English to be the official language for purposes of conducting government business but did not prohibit the use of any other languages in such contexts.

In November 1988, Article XXVIII of the Arizona Constitution was approved by 50.1 percent of the voters. The article declared English the official language of Arizona and provided that "[t]his State and all political subdivisions of this State shall act in English and in no other language." Two days after the amendment passed, María-Kelly F. Ýñiguez, a bilingual Latina state employee, filed suit in federal district court challenging the constitutionality of Article XXVIII. Ms. Ýñiguez' job involved handling medical malpractice claims. Prior to the passage of Article XXVIII, she communicated in Spanish with monolingual Spanish-speaking claimants, and in a combination of English and Spanish with bilingual claimants. The federal trial court agreed with her that Article XXVIII violated her free speech rights under the **First Amendment** to the U.S. Constitution. Arizonans for Official English, the organization supporting Article XXVIII, appealed the trial court's judgment to the U.S. Court of Appeals for the Ninth Circuit. The Ninth Circuit affirmed the trial court's holding.

Ýñiguez v. Arizonans for Official English

United States Court of Appeals for the Ninth Circuit
69 F.3d 920 (1995)

Reinhardt, Circuit Judge:

These consolidated appeals require us to consider an important area of constitutional law, rarely reexamined since a series of cases in the 1920s in which the Supreme Court struck down laws restricting the use of non-English languages. See *Meyer v. Nebraska,* 262 U.S. 390 (1923).

[T]here are valid concerns on both sides. In our diverse and pluralistic society, the importance of establishing common bonds and a common language between citizens is clear. Equally important, however, is the American tradition of tolerance, a tradition that recognizes a critical difference between encouraging the use of English and repressing the use of other languages. In deciding this case, therefore, we are guided by what the Supreme Court wrote in *Meyer:* "The protection of the Constitution extends to all, to those who speak other languages as well as those born with English on the tongue. Perhaps it would be highly advantageous if all had ready understanding of our ordinary speech, but this cannot be coerced by methods which conflict with the Constitution—a desirable end cannot be promoted by prohibited means."

We conclude that Article XXVIII constitutes a prohibited means of promoting the English language and affirm the district court's ruling that it violates the First Amendment.

Article XXVIII's ban on the use of languages other than English by persons in government service could hardly be more inclusive. The provision plainly states that it applies to "the legislative, executive, and judicial branches" of both state and local government, and to "all government officials and employees during the performance of government business." This broad language means that Article XXVIII on its face applies to speech in a seemingly limitless variety of governmental settings, from ministerial statements by civil servants at the office to teachers speaking in the classroom, from town-hall discussions between constituents and their representatives to the translation of judicial proceedings in the courtroom. Accordingly, it is self-evident that Article XXVIII's sweeping English-Only mandate limits the speech of governmental actors serving in a wide range of work-related contexts that differ significantly from that in which Yñiguez performed her daily tasks. The speech rights of all of Arizona's state and local employees, officials, and officers are thus adversely affected in a potentially unconstitutional manner by the breadth of Article XXVIII's ban on non-English governmental speech. Similarly, the interests of non-English-speaking Arizonans in receiving all kinds of essential information are severely burdened.

Arizonans for Official English argues vehemently that First Amendment scrutiny should be relaxed in this case because the decision to speak a non-English language does not implicate pure speech rights. Rather, the group suggests, "choice of language . . . is a mode of conduct"—a "*nonverbal* expressive activity."

A bilingual person does, of course, make an expressive choice by choosing to speak one language rather than another. As Yñiguez explained, her choice to speak Spanish with other bilingual people can signify "solidarity" or "comfortableness." Nonetheless, this expressive effect does not reduce choice of language to the level of "conduct," as posited by Arizonans for Official English.

Ýñiguez's comments regarding her use of Spanish [mirrored those made in a prior Supreme Court **opinion** wherein the Court] stated that "words are often chosen as much for their emotive as their cognitive force"—to such an extent, in fact, that this emotive aspect "may often be the more important element of the overall message sought to be communicated."

Under Article XXVIII, of course, the state is not singling out one word for repression, but rather entire vocabularies. Moreover, the languages of Cervantes, Proust, Tolstoy, and Lao-Tze, among others, can hardly be described as "scurrilous." In this case, therefore, the [Supreme] Court's admonishment that "in a society as diverse and populous as ours" the state has "no right to cleanse public debate" of unpopular words, rings even truer. While Arizonans for Official English complains of the "Babel" of many languages, the [Supreme Court has stated] that this "verbal cacophony is . . . not a sign of weakness but of strength."

As we have noted, it is frequently the need to convey information to members of the public that indicates the decision to speak in a different tongue. If all state and local officials and employees are prohibited from doing so, Arizonans who do not speak English will be unable to receive much essential information concerning their daily needs and lives. To call a prohibition that precludes the conveying of information to thousands of Arizonans in a language they can comprehend a mere regulation of "mode of expression" is to miss entirely the basic point of First Amendment protections. [S]peech in any language is still speech, and the decision to speak in another language is a decision involving speech alone.

Arizonans for Official English next contends, incorrectly, that Ýñiguez seeks an affirmative right to have government operations conducted in foreign tongues. In the case before us, there is no claim of an affirmative right to compel the state to provide multilingual information, but instead only a claim of a negative right: that the state cannot, consistent with the First Amendment, gag the employees currently providing members of the public with information and thereby effectively preclude large numbers of persons from receiving information that they have previously received. Such a claim falls squarely within the confines of traditional free speech doctrine, and is in no way dependent on a finding of an affirmative duty on the part of the state.

If this case involved a statewide ban on all uses of languages other than English within the geographical jurisdiction of the state of Arizona, the constitutional outcome would be clear. A state cannot simply prohibit all persons within its borders from speaking in the tongue of their choice. Such a restriction on private speech obviously could not stand. *Meyer v. Nebraska* (1923). However, Article XXVIII's restraint on speech is of more limited scope. Its ban is restricted to speech by persons performing services for the government. Thus, we must look beyond first principles of First Amendment doctrine and consider the question of what limitations may constitutionally be placed on the speech of government servants. For nearly half a century, it has been axiomatic in constitutional law that government employees do not simply forfeit their First Amendment rights upon entering the public workplace. In deciding whether to afford constitutional protection to prohibited employee speech, we must consider both the general interest of the public servant in speaking freely . . . and the importance to the public of the speech involved. The employee speech banned by Article XXVIII is unquestionably of public import.

The practical effects of Article XXVIII's *de facto* bar on communications by or with government employees are numerous and varied. For example, Spanish-speaking residents of Arizona cannot, consistent with the article, communicate effectively with employees of a state or local housing office about a landlord's wrongful retention of a rental deposit, nor can they learn from clerks of the state court about how and where to file small claims court complaints. They cannot obtain information regarding a variety of state and local social services, or adequately inform the service-givers that the governmental employees involved are not performing their duties properly or that the government itself is not operating effectively or honestly. Those with a limited command of English will face commensurate difficulties in obtaining or providing such information. Moreover, as we suggested earlier, the restrictions that

Article XXVIII imposes severely limit the ability of state legislators to communicate with their constituents concerning official matters. The legislative fact-finding function would, in short, be directly affected. Because Article XXVIII bars or significantly restricts communications by and with government officials and employees, it significantly interferes with the ability of the non-English-speaking populace of Arizona "to receive information and ideas."

Arizonans for Official English claims, as it and others did when the initiative was on the ballot, that Article XXVIII promotes significant state interests. The organization enumerates these interests as: protecting democracy by encouraging "unity and political stability"; encouraging a common language; and protecting public confidence. In plain fact, Arizonans for Official English offers us nothing more than "assertion and conjecture to support its claim" that Article XXVIII's restrictions on speech would serve the alleged state interests. We also reject the justifications for even more basic reasons. Our conclusions are influenced primarily by two Supreme Court cases from the 1920s in which nearly identical justifications were asserted in support of laws restricting language rights. See *Meyer v. Nebraska*, 262 U.S. 390 (1923); *Farrington v. Tokushige*, 273 U.S. 284 (1927). *Meyer* involved a Nebraska statute that prohibited the teaching of non-English languages to children under the eighth grade level; *Tokushige*, similarly, involved a Hawaii statute that singled out "foreign language schools," such as those in which Japanese was taught, for stringent government control. [T]he [Supreme] Court explicitly characterized the language restriction in *Meyer* as designed "to promote civic cohesiveness by encouraging the learning of English." Despite these worthy goals, the Court ruled [in *Meyer*] that the repressive means adopted to further them were "arbitrary" and invalid.

Meyer demonstrate[s] the weakness of the second justification for Article XXVIII proffered by Arizonans for Official English: that of encouraging a common language. In *Meyer*, the statute reflected the belief that "the English language should be and become the mother tongue of all children reared in this state." Although there is probably no more effective way of encouraging the uniform use of English than to ensure that children grow up speaking it, [the] statute [was] struck down on the ground that these interests were insufficient to warrant such restrictions on the use of foreign languages.

Like the Court in *Meyer*, we recognize the importance of (1) promoting democracy and national unity and (2) encouraging a common language as a means of encouraging such unity. We cannot agree, however, that Article XXVIII is in any way a fair, effective, or appropriate means of promoting those interests, or that even under a more deferential analysis its severely flawed effort to advance those goals outweighs its substantial adverse effect on first amendment rights. As we have learned time and again in our history, the state cannot achieve unity by prescribing orthodoxy. Notwithstanding this lesson, the provision at issue here "promotes" English only by means of proscribing other languages and is, thus, wholly coercive. Next, the measure inhibits rather than advances the state's interest in the efficient and effective performance of its duties. Finally, the direct effect of the provision is not only to restrict the rights of all state and local government servants in Arizona, but also to severely impair the free speech interests of a portion of the populace they serve.

We should add that we are entirely unmoved by the third justification—that allowing government employees to speak languages other than English when serving the public would undermine public confidence and lead to "disillusionment and concern." To begin with, it is clear that the non-English-speaking public of Arizona would feel even greater disillusionment and concern if their communications with public employees and, effectively, their access to many government services, were to be barred by Article XXVIII. Moreover, numerous cases support the notion that the interest in avoiding public hostility does not justify infringements upon constitutional rights. In short, the "concern" that some members of the Arizona public may feel over the use of non-English languages provides no basis for prohibiting their use no matter the degree of scrutiny we apply. [T]he range of potential injuries to the public is vast. By comparison, the benefits that the initiative purports to offer are minimal, especially in light of the state's concession that its interests in "efficiency" and "effectiveness" are not served by the Article. Thus, Article XXVIII must be held unconstitutional.

We note that the adverse impact of Article XXVIII's over-breadth is especially egregious because it is not uniformly spread over the population, but falls almost entirely upon Hispanics and other national origin minorities. *Spun Steak*, 998 F.2d at 1486 (English-Only rule in the workplace may disproportionately affect Hispanic employees). Since language is a close and meaningful proxy for national origin, restrictions on the use of languages may mask discrimination against specific national origin groups or, more generally, conceal nativist sentiment. *See Hernández v. Erlenbusch*, 368 F.Supp. 752 (1973) (tavern's English-Only rule constitutes illegal discrimination against Mexican-American patrons). In light of these considerations, the equal protection ramifications of Article XXVIII's restrictive impact strongly support our holding, as well.

[T]his country has historically prided itself on welcoming immigrants with a spirit of tolerance and freedom—and it is this spirit, embodied in the Constitution, which, when it flags on occasion, courts must be vigilant to protect. In closing, we note that tolerance of difference—whether difference in language, religion, or culture more generally—does not ultimately exact a cost. To the contrary, the diverse and multicultural character of our society is widely recognized as being among our greatest strengths. Recognizing this, we have not, except for rare repressive statutes such as those struck down in *Meyer* [and other cases], tried to compel immigrants to give up their native language; instead, we have encouraged them to learn English. The Arizona restriction on language provides no encouragement, however, only compulsion: as such, it is unconstitutional.

Fernandez, Circuit Judge, with whom Chief Judge Wallace and Judges Hall and Kleinfeld join, dissenting:

María-Kelley F. Ýñiguez does not like Article XXVIII as a matter of policy. I can understand and sympathize with that. It is when she goes beyond the realm of policy and seeks to show that the Article violates the First Amendment to the United States Constitution that she goes astray. It is there that we part company. Of course, I recognize that a State's restrictions upon its employees must not be so irrational that they may be branded arbitrary. Can this Article of the Arizona Constitution be so branded if we believe it to be ill-conceived?

Kozinski, Circuit Judge, with whom Judge Kleinfeld joins, dissenting:

A house divided against itself cannot stand. Abraham Lincoln.

María-Kelly Ýñiguez was hired by the State of Arizona to perform various functions connected with processing medical malpractice claims. The people of Arizona—Ýñiguez's ultimate superiors—then augmented her duties: They charged her with promoting English by using only that language for official business. The people of Arizona were warned that this might disrupt services and make government employees less efficient. Arizonans nevertheless chose to make this tradeoff. Since they were paying Ýñiguez's salary, I had assumed it was their call whether Ýñiguez spent her work-time processing claims, promoting English or twiddling her thumbs. While I understand my colleagues' eagerness to do away with a law they see as misguided and divisive, the price they pay is too high. No rational society can afford it. ■

Subsequently, the decision of the Ninth Circuit was appealed to the U.S. Supreme Court, which found that the federal courts did not have authority to decide this case because Ms. Ýñiguez had left her job with the state of Arizona in 1990, thus rendering the whole case legally **moot.** The Supreme Court **vacated** the Ninth Circuit's opinion, leaving the Ninth Circuit's opinion with no legally binding effect, and ordered the dismissal of the case in the federal courts. Although *Ýñiguez* was not successful in the *federal* courts, a challenge to Article XXVIII had also been filed in the Arizona *state* courts. In this state court proceeding, the Arizona Supreme Court held that Article XXVIII violated the First and **Fourteenth Amendments** to the U.S. Constitution. In doing so, the Arizona Supreme Court agreed "with the result and with much of the reasoning of the Ninth Circuit opinion." An Alaska state court also found that Alaska's English-Only law violated the First Amendment.[4]

■ Language in the Workplace

The Ninth Circuit decision in *Ýñiguez* holds that the U.S. Constitution bars the government from prohibiting the use of languages other than English. What *Ýñiguez* did not address, however, was whether private, nongovernmental actors may prohibit the use of other languages. In considering this issue, it is important to keep in mind that most of the rights set out in the U.S. Constitution protect individuals from discriminatory action by the government, not from discriminatory action by private, nongovernmental actors. Title VII of the **Civil Rights Act of 1964** makes it unlawful for any employer, public or private, to discriminate in employment on the basis of an individual's "race, color, religion, sex, or national origin." Discrimination in the workplace against individuals on the basis of national origin is explicitly prohibited, but Title VII is wholly silent with respect to language discrimination. Given the connection between language and national origin, courts have struggled with whether Title VII's prohibition of discrimination on the basis of national origin forbids language discrimination.

This was the very issue raised in *García v. Gloor* (1980). This lawsuit was filed by Hector García, a twenty-four-year-old bilingual Mexican American who spoke Spanish at home. Mr. García worked as a salesman at Gloor Lumber and Supply, Inc., in Brownsville, Texas, a city along the U.S.–Mexico border. Although the majority of the population in Brownsville was and still is Mexican American and many of Gloor Lumber Company's customers were Spanish speaking, Gloor prohibited employees from speaking Spanish on the job unless they were communicating directly with Spanish-speaking customers. On June 10, 1975, Mr. García was asked a question by another Mexican American employee and responded in Spanish, for which he was fired. He challenged his firing as a violation of Title VII of the Civil Rights Act.

García v. Gloor

United States Court of Appeals for the Fifth Circuit
618 F.2d 264 (1980)

Alvin B. Rubin, Circuit Judge:

[W]e conclude that the "speak-only-English" rule, as applied to Mr. García by his employer, does not discriminate on the basis of national origin. We therefore affirm the district court's judgment that Mr. García's discharge for violating the rule was not unlawful.

Mr. Gloor testified that there were business reasons for the language policy: English-speaking customers objected to communications between employees that they could not understand; pamphlets and trade literature were in English and were not available in Spanish, so it was important for employees to be fluent in English apart from conversations with English-speaking customers; if employees who normally spoke Spanish off the job were required to speak English on the job at all times and not only when waiting on English-speaking customers, they would improve their English; and the rule would permit supervisors, who did not speak Spanish, better to oversee the work of subordinates. The district court found that these were valid business reasons and that they, rather than discrimination, were the motive for the rule.

[Title VII of the Civil Rights Act of 1964] forbids discrimination in employment on the basis of national origin. Neither the statute nor common understanding equates national origin with the language that one chooses to speak. Language may be used as a covert basis for national origin discrimination, but the English-Only rule was not applied to García by Gloor either to this end or with this result.

Mr. García was fully bilingual. He chose deliberately to speak Spanish instead of English while actually at work. He was permitted to speak the language he preferred during work breaks.

The refusal to hire applicants who cannot speak English might be discriminatory if the jobs they seek can be performed without knowledge of that language, but the obverse is not correct: if the employer engages a bilingual person, that person is granted neither right nor privilege by the statute to use the language of his personal preference.

Let us assume that, as contended by Mr. García, there was no genuine business need for the rule and that its adoption by Gloor was arbitrary. [Title VII] does not prohibit all arbitrary employment practices. It does not forbid employers to hire only persons born under a certain sign of the zodiac or persons having long hair or short hair or no hair at all. It is directed only at specific impermissible bases of discrimination[:] race, color, religion, sex, or national origin. National origin must not be confused with ethnic or sociocultural traits or an unrelated status, such as citizenship or alienage, or poverty.

The argument is made that the rule is discriminatory in impact, even if that result was not intentional, because it was likely to be violated only by Hispanic-Americans and that, therefore, they have a higher risk of incurring penalties. The **disparate impact** test . . . forbids the use of any employment criterion, even one neutral on its face and not intended to be discriminatory, if, in fact, the criterion causes discrimination as measured by the impact on a person or group entitled to equal opportunity. However, there is no disparate impact if the rule is one that the affected employee can readily observe and nonobservance is a matter of individual preference. Mr. García could readily comply with the speak-English-Only rule; as to him nonobservance was a matter of choice.

[Title VII] does not support an interpretation that equates the language an employee prefers to use with his national origin. To a person who speaks only one tongue or to a person who has difficulty using another language than the one spoken in his home, language might well be an immutable characteristic like skin color, sex or place of birth. However, the language a person who is multi-lingual elects to speak at a particular time is by definition a matter of choice. No claim is made that García and the other employees engaged in sales were unable to speak English. Indeed, it is conceded that all could do so and that ability was an occupational qualification because of the requirement that they wait on customers who spoke only English or who used that language by choice. Nor are we confronted with a case where an employee inadvertently slipped into using a more familiar tongue.

The rule was confined to the work place and work hours. It did not apply to conversations during breaks or other employee free-time. In some circumstances, the ability to speak or the speaking of a language other than English might be equated with national origin, but this case concerns only a requirement that persons capable of speaking English do so while on duty.

Reduced to its simplest, the claim is "others like to speak English on the job and do so without penalty. Speaking Spanish is very important to me and is inherent in my ancestral national origin. Therefore, I should be permitted to speak it and the denial to me of that preference so important to my self-identity is statutorily forbidden." The argument thus reduces itself to a contention that the statute commands employers to permit employees to speak the tongue they prefer. We do not think the statute permits that interpretation, whether the preference be slight or strong or even one closely related to self-identity.

The judgment [in favor of Gloor Lumber Company] is AFFIRMED.

After the Fifth Circuit's decision in *García v. Gloor,* the EEOC, the federal agency charged with enforcing Title VII, enacted its "Guidelines on Discrimination Because of National Origin," which interpreted Title VII to prohibit English-Only rules, unless justified by **business necessity.** In a subsequent case, *García v. Spun Steak Co.* (1993),[5] the U.S. Court of Appeals for the Ninth Circuit cited *García v. Gloor* when it upheld another English-Only rule challenged by bilingual employees of a private company in California. The Ninth Circuit refused to defer to the interpretation of Title VII in the EEOC guidelines. The bilingual employees unsuccessfully asked the Ninth Circuit to reconsider its decision. On the other hand, several federal district courts have applied the EEOC guidelines in striking down English-Only rules in the workplace.

In 2001, the California Legislature enacted a statute that provides the protection sought by the plaintiffs in *Gloor* and *Spun Steak Co.* The California statute makes it an unlawful employment practice for an employer to limit or prohibit the use of any language in any workplace, unless the language restriction is justified by a "business necessity" and the employer has notified the employees of when the language restriction applies and of the consequences of violating it. The statute defines business necessity very narrowly as "an overriding legitimate business purpose such that the language restriction is necessary to the safe and efficient operation of the business, . . . the language restriction effectively fulfills the business purpose it is supposed to serve, and there is no alternative practice to the language restriction that would accomplish the business purpose equally well with a lesser discriminatory impact." Because few language restrictions are likely to meet this standard, the statute provides broad protection to California employees who speak languages other than English.

■ Bilingual Education

English-Only advocates have often portrayed bilingual education as a special benefit sought by Mexican Americans and other language minorities, and have argued that these communities should be provided the same English-language education purportedly provided to European immigrants in the past. In fact, education in languages other than English has existed in the United States since the earliest years of our nation. Bilingual education began to fall into disfavor only in the late nineteenth century. States that had previously provided bilingual education began to require that educational instruction be conducted only in English. In the late 1800s,

Texas made it a crime to teach in any public school using any language other than English. Anti-German hysteria during World War I led to the formal abolition of bilingual education in those areas that still maintained it. By the 1900s, some states had banned the use of languages other than English in private and parochial schools, some going so far as to make it a crime. Although the U.S. Supreme Court held that such restrictions were unconstitutional in *Meyer v. Nebraska*, the 1923 case cited and relied upon by the Ninth Circuit in *Yñiguez*, such statutes remained on the books for much of the twentieth century. As mentioned in chapter 2, Mexican Americans who attended school through the 1960s often recall teachers punishing them for speaking Spanish—even if Spanish was the only language they could speak. Many Mexican Americans found schools to be hostile places that were not conducive to their learning. Therefore, not surprisingly, dropout rates for Mexican Americans during this period were very high and remain so to this day.

During the 1960s, the government initiated efforts to improve Mexican American educational success. The U.S. Congress in 1968 enacted the first federal statute providing funds to local school districts for bilingual education programs. Congress had previously passed Title VI of the Civil Rights Act of 1964, which provides, "No person shall, on the basis of race, color, or national origin, be excluded from participation in, be denied the benefits of, or be subjected to discrimination under any program or activity receiving federal financial assistance." Note that, like Title VII which was applied in *Gloor,* Title VI does not explicitly prohibit discrimination on the basis of language, despite its express prohibition of discrimination based on national origin. As a result, courts have struggled with whether Title VI's prohibition against discrimination on the basis of national origin protects language-minority children. The U.S. Supreme Court addressed this issue in *Lau v. Nichols* (1974).[6] Although the case dealt with students of Chinese ancestry in California, it had significant implications for the educational language rights of Mexican Americans. The Court in *Lau* held that "there is no equality of treatment merely by providing students with the same facilities, textbooks, teachers, and curriculum; for students who do not understand English are effectively foreclosed from any meaningful education."

Six months after the Supreme Court decision in *Lau,* the U.S. Court of Appeals for the Tenth Circuit decided an appeal by the Portales, New Mexico, school district in an action brought by Mexican American students who alleged language discrimination.

Serna v. Portales Municipal Schools

United States Court of Appeals of the Tenth Circuit
499 F.2d 1147 (1974)

Hill, Circuit Judge:

The City of Portales, New Mexico, has a substantial number of Spanish surnamed residents. Accordingly, a sizable minority of students attending the Portales schools are Spanish surnamed. Evidence indicates that many of these students know very little English when they enter the school system. They speak Spanish at home and grow up in a Spanish culture totally alien to the environment thrust upon them in the Portales school system. The result is a lower achievement level than their Anglo-American counterparts, and a higher percentage of school dropouts.

For the 1971–72 school year approximately 34 percent of the children attending Portales' four elementary schools, Lindsey, James, Steiner and Brown, were Spanish surnamed. The junior high school and senior high school enrollments of Spanish surnamed students were 29 percent and 17 percent, respectively. Unquestionably as Spanish surnamed children advanced to the higher grades, a disproportionate number of them quit school.

Appellees in their complaint charge appellant with discriminating against Spanish surnamed students in numerous respects. Allegedly there is discrimination in appellant's failure to provide bilingual instruction which takes into account the special educational needs of the Mexican-American student.

[I]n 1969 the report by Portales Municipal Schools to [the] United States Commission on Civil Rights indicated that at Lindsey, the 86 percent Spanish surnamed school, only four students with Spanish surnames in the first grade spoke English as well as the average Anglo first grader. [A]ppellants neither applied for funds under the federal Bilingual Education Act, nor accepted funds for a similar purpose when they were offered by the State of New Mexico.

Undisputed evidence shows that Spanish surnamed students do not reach the achievement levels attained by their Anglo counterparts. For example, achievement tests, which are given totally in the English language, disclose that students at Lindsey are almost a full grade behind children attending other schools in reading, language mechanics and language expression. As the disparity in achievement levels increases between Spanish surnamed and Anglo students, so does the disparity in attendance and school dropout rates.

Expert witnesses explained what effect the Portales school system had on Spanish surnamed students. Henry Pascual, Director of the Communicative Arts Division of the New Mexico Department of Education, stated that a child who goes to a school where he finds no evidence of his language and culture and ethnic group represented becomes withdrawn and nonparticipating. The child often lacks a positive mental attitude. María Gutiérrez Spencer, a longtime teacher in New Mexico, testified that until a child developed a good self image not even teaching English as a second language would be successful. If a child can be made to feel worthwhile in school then he will learn even with a poor English program.

After hearing all evidence, the trial court found that in the Portales schools Spanish surnamed children do not have equal educational opportunity and thus a violation of their constitutional right to equal protection exists. The Portales School District was ordered to [create bilingual-bicultural programs].

In light of the recent Supreme Court decision in *Lau v. Nichols* (1974), however, we need not decide the equal protection issue. *Lau* is a case which appellants admit is almost identical to the present one. Appellees are Spanish surnamed students who prior to this lawsuit were placed in totally English speaking schools. There is substantial evidence that most of these Spanish surnamed students are deficient in the English language; nevertheless no affirmative steps were taken by the Portales school district to rectify these language deficiencies.

[W]hile Spanish surnamed children are required to attend school, and if they attend public schools the courses must be taught in English, Portales school district has failed to institute a program which will rectify language deficiencies so that these children will receive a meaningful education. The Portales school curriculum, which has the effect of discrimination even though probably no purposeful design is present, therefore violates the requisites of Title VI and the requirement imposed by or pursuant to HEW **regulations.** Under these circumstances the trial court had a duty to fashion a program which would provide adequate relief for Spanish surnamed children.

The New Mexico State Board of Education [SEB] stresses the effect the decision will have on the structure of public education in New Mexico. It is suggested that bilingual programs will now be necessitated throughout the state wherever a student is found who does not have adequate facility in the English language. We do not share SEB's fears. As Mr. Justice Blackmun pointed out in his concurring opinion in *Lau,* numbers are at the heart of this case and only when a substantial group is being deprived of a meaningful education will a Title VI violation exist.

We believe the trial court has formulated a just, equitable and feasible plan; accordingly, we will not alter it on appeal. ■

After the decisions in *Lau* and *Serna,* Congress increased funding for bilingual education. Congress also enacted the Equal Educational Opportunity Act (EEOA), which explicitly requires states to take "appropriate action" to address the needs of language-minority children in the public schools. This act specifically provides, "No State shall deny equal educational opportunity to an individual on account of his or her race, color, sex or national origin, by . . . the failure [of] an educational agency to take appropriate action to overcome language barriers that impede equal participation by its students in its instructional programs." Most bilingual education litigation today is decided under the EEOA, but controversy continues over what is required to satisfy the EEOA's requirement of "appropriate action."

■ **Recent Challenges**

In 1998, about 61 percent of California's voters approved Proposition 227, which, with only limited exceptions available to parents, bans bilingual education. Similar measures were also passed in Arizona and Massachusetts but failed in Colorado. Sixty-three percent of Latino voters voted against Proposition 227, as did 52 percent of African American voters. Proposition 227 requires that children with limited English proficiency be placed in structured immersion programs taught only in English. The U.S. Court of Appeals for the Ninth Circuit held that Proposition 227 does not violate the **Equal Protection Clause** of the Fourteenth Amendment.[7] In response to these anti–bilingual education efforts, LULAC, MALDEF, and other organizations concerned with language rights encouraged city councils and other legislative bodies to adopt "English Plus" positions. These efforts stress the learning of English plus an additional language, thereby encouraging multilingualism and multiculturalism.

■ Concluding Thoughts

In many communities in the United States, residents who spoke languages other than English lost their native languages over several generations. For example, few Italian Americans speak proficient Italian, nor do many German Americans speak German. Many Mexican Americans, too, are unable to speak Spanish or do not speak Spanish proficiently. Spanish-speaking Mexican Americans also find it difficult to pass on the language to their children. Some scholars have claimed that without continuing immigration from Mexico and other Latin American countries, Spanish too would slowly die out in the United States within a few generations.[8] The **Chicano Movement** during the 1960s and 1970s encouraged many Mexican Americans to retain or learn Spanish as a reinforcement of cultural pride, and pressed the public schools to provide these services. The increasingly close relationship between Mexico and the United States, with increases in the exchange of goods and people, has also served to strengthen the use of Spanish in the United States. As the cases in this chapter indicate, an increasingly multicultural U.S. society has been met with resistance, hostility, and anti-immigrant sentiment. Accordingly, the U.S. legal system will undoubtedly continue to wrestle with the complex issues raised by the presence of large numbers of persons who speak languages other than English.

■ Discussion Questions

1. Ms. Yñiguez was not asserting an "affirmative right" to have government operations conducted in a foreign tongue. Recall that the English-speaking

Anglo American immigrants to Mexican Texas asserted such a right in the 1820s and 1830s. Should the courts today consider this history in determining whether an affirmative right exists to have government operations conducted in languages other than English?

2. In 1999, the city council of El Cenizo, Texas, a town on the U.S.–Mexico border, adopted an ordinance requiring all city functions and meetings to be conducted in the predominant language of the community: Spanish. The ordinance, which generated great controversy outside of El Cenizo, requires the city to provide English translations if requested within forty-eight hours of the official city meeting or activity. Should such a law promoting the official use of Spanish be permitted in the United States?

3. As construed by the Fifth Circuit in *Gloor v. García,* language discrimination cannot be equated with national origin discrimination for purposes of Title VII litigation. Given that national origin and the Spanish language both contribute to the construction of Mexican American identity, do you think the *Gloor* decision is correct? Should Title VII protect individuals who speak with a Mexican or Spanish accent?

4. Gloor Lumber Company hired Mr. García in part because he spoke Spanish and he could thus assist Gloor's many Spanish-speaking customers, who made up the majority of the surrounding community. Can non-Spanish speakers claim discrimination if an employer requires bilingual skills of its employees in order to better serve its customer base? What effect is such a practice likely to have on non-Spanish speakers?

5. Should the United States foster biculturalism and bilingualism? Do you believe public schools have any obligation to assist children learning English to maintain their native tongue? Do the social and economic costs associated with non–English proficiency make it worthwhile to provide bilingual education?

6. "What do you call a person who speaks three languages? Trilingual. What do you call a person who speaks two languages? Bilingual. What do you call a person who speaks one language? American." This joke reflects the reality that well-educated Americans, unlike their counterparts in the rest of the world, often speak only one language. In 1995, an Amarillo, Texas, state court judge accused a mother of abusing her five-year-old daughter by speaking Spanish to her. The judge asserted that by speaking Spanish, the mother would relegate the young girl to life as a housemaid. After an uproar ensued, the judge reversed his

decision. Should a judge have the authority to issue an order dictating the language in which a mother should speak to her child? How might the fact that most legislators and judges speak only English affect the ways they view language rights?

■ Suggested Readings

Baron, D. *The English-Only Question: An Official Language for Americans?* New Haven: Yale University Press, 1990.

Crawford, J., ed. *Language Loyalties: A Source Book on the Official English Controversy.* Chicago: University of Chicago Press, 1992.

Heath, S. B. "Language Policies: Patterns of Retention and Maintenance." In *Mexican-Americans in Comparative Perspective,* ed. W. Conner, 257–82. Washington, D.C.: Urban Institute Press, 1985.

Juárez, J. R., Jr. "The American Tradition of Language Rights: The Forgotten Right to Government in a Known Tongue." *Law and Inequality Journal* 13 (1995): 443–642.

Perea, J. F. "Demography and Distrust: An Essay on American Languages, Cultural Pluralism, and Official English." *Minnesota Law Review* 77 (1992): 269–373.

■ Notes

1. U.S. Census Bureau, *Profile of Selected Social Characteristics: 2000;* available from factfinder.census.gov (accessed April 3, 2003).

2. *Puerto Rican Organization for Political Action v. Kusper,* 490 F.2d 579, 577 (1973) notes that Illinois' declaration of English as its official language "has never been used to prevent publication of official materials in other languages."

3. J. W. Crawford, *Language Legislation in the U.S.A.* [online]; available from ourworld.compuserve.com/homepages/JWCRAWFORD/langleg.htm (accessed April 5, 2003).

4. Ibid.

5. 998 F.2d 1480.

6. 414 U.S. 563.

7. *Valeria v. Davis,* 307 F.3d 1036 (2002).

8. S. B. Heath, "Language Policies: Patterns of Retention and Maintenance," in *Mexican-Americans in Comparative Perspective,* ed. W. Conner, 257–82 (Washington, D.C.: Urban Institute Press, 1985).

5

Immigration

The likelihood that any given person of Mexican ancestry is an alien is high enough to make Mexican appearance a relevant factor, but standing alone it does not justify stopping all Mexican-Americans to ask if they are aliens.—*U.S. v. Brignoni-Ponce* (1975)

U.S. immigration law and policy have always been influenced by a complex intermingling of exceedingly difficult political, socioeconomic, and racial/ethnic issues. Because of the geographical proximity and unique historical relationship between the United States and Mexico, briefly discussed in chapter 1, immigration policy and law have always been of particular interest and challenge to the Mexican American community. This reality is best illustrated by a few illuminating statistics. According to the U.S. Census Bureau, as of 2000 the U.S. "foreign-born" population—defined as all U.S. residents born outside the United States (including citizens and noncitizens, documented and undocumented)—consisted of 28.4 million individuals. Of this number, 7.8 million, or fully 27.6 percent, were born in Mexico. In short, immigration from Mexico accounted for more than one-quarter of the entire U.S. foreign-born population in 2000. Moreover, this number was approximately six times that of the country with the next highest foreign-born population, China, which has an estimated 1.2 million individuals.[1]

Importantly, despite the competing theories and arguments regarding the causes, effects, costs, and benefits of immigration (both documented and undocumented),[2] almost all immigration experts, activists, and policymakers agree on the importance and significance of two fundamental and corollary principles: the so-called *push* and *pull* factors. Push factors are those factors that cause individuals to leave their country of origin and emigrate to a new country. Such factors in the U.S.–Mexico context began with the **Mexican Revolution** and historically have included the inability to obtain decent-paying jobs in Mexico and Mexico's proximity to the United States. Pull factors, on the other hand, are those factors that make the country of destination an attractive choice for the immigrant. Such factors in the U.S.–Mexico context include availability of relatively well-paying employment in the United States, family reunification, a perception of a higher standard of living, and proximity to Mexico. Perhaps the most difficult and controversial of all pull factors in U.S.–Mexico immigration is U.S. employers' need for a constant supply of cheap labor, which is fueled by Americans' seemingly insatiable desire to have abundant and affordable goods and services, ranging from cheap food and low-cost clothing to low-wage workers such as maids, custodians, and agricultural labor. As has been well documented elsewhere, this demand for labor has caused U.S. immigration law and policy to fluctuate—sometimes dramatically—in direct response to the intolerance Americans have for undocumented immigrants. This labor need has also caused prejudice and discriminatory behavior against the foreign-born and those perceived to be foreign-born. As you read the following cases, consider whether the laws and practices at issue in each of these cases impact or address in any meaningful way the push and pull factors that are at the root of immigration from Mexico to the United States.

■ Securing the U.S.–Mexico Border

One of the more difficult and challenging issues for the Mexican American community, and one that directly implicates the Fourth Amendment of the U.S. **Constitution,** has been U.S. efforts to gain control of and secure the U.S.–Mexico border, an area heavily populated by Mexican Americans. The Fourth Amendment provides that "[t]he right of people to be secure in their persons, houses, papers, and effects, against unreasonable searches and seizures, shall not be violated, and no Warrants shall issue, but upon probable cause . . . and particularly describing the place to be searched, and the persons or things to be seized." In essence, these explicit provisions of the Fourth Amendment make it abundantly clear that before a government actor—such as local police, the FBI, or the U.S. Border Patrol—can stop individuals, detain them, search them, or detain and search them, certain threshold requirements of "probable cause" and "reasonableness" must be met. When and how these threshold requirements can be satisfied has been developed by voluminous Fourth Amendment case law. Indeed, long before "racial profiling" was coined and became part of the American lexicon, Mexican Americans in the southwestern United States commonly experienced unjustified stops, searches, and seizures. In effect, although perhaps unintentionally, the Border Patrol's problematic efforts to control the border also gave rise to Mexican Americans' contribution to the development of significant Fourth Amendment principles. In the landmark case of *U.S. v. Brignoni-Ponce* (1975), for instance, the U.S. Border Patrol's practice of utilizing **roving patrols** as part of its efforts to stem illegal immigration along the U.S.–Mexico border was upheld in a unanimous **decision.** While upholding the practice, the Supreme Court nevertheless issued some clear guidance as to what types of factors would justify stops by roving patrols. Specifically, the Supreme Court held that utilizing "Mexican appearance" alone to justify a roving patrol stop was a violation of the Fourth Amendment.

U.S. v. Brignoni-Ponce

United States Supreme Court
422 U.S. 873 (1975)

Mr. Justice Powell delivered the **opinion** of the Court.

This case raises questions as to the United States Border Patrol's authority to stop automobiles in areas near the Mexican border. [T]he Border Patrol does not claim authority to search cars, but only to question the occupants about their citizenship and immigration status.

The only issue presented for decision is whether a roving patrol may stop a vehicle in an area near the border and question its occupants when the only ground for suspicion is that the occupants appear to be of Mexican ancestry. For the reasons that follow, we affirm the decision of the Court of Appeals.

The Fourth Amendment applies to all seizures of the person, including seizures that involve only a brief detention short of traditional arrest. "(W)henever a police officer accosts an individual and restrains his freedom to walk away, he has 'seized' that person," and the Fourth Amendment requires that the seizure be 'reasonable.' As with other categories of police action subject to Fourth Amendment constraints, the reasonableness of such seizures depends on a balance between the public interest and the individual's right to personal security free from arbitrary interference by law officers.

Against [a] valid public interest we must weigh the interference with individual liberty that results when an officer stops an automobile and questions its occupants. The intrusion is modest. The Government tells us that a stop by a roving patrol 'usually consumes no more than a minute.' There is no search of the vehicle or its occupants, and the visual inspection is limited to those parts of the vehicle that can be seen by anyone standing alongside. According to the Government, "(a)ll that is required of the vehicle's occupants is a response to a brief question or two and possibly the production of a document evidencing a right to be in the United States."

In this case, because of the importance of the governmental interest at stake, the minimal intrusion of a brief stop, and the absence of practical alternatives for policing the border, we hold that when an officer's observations lead him reasonably to suspect that a particular vehicle may contain aliens who are illegally in the country, he may stop the car briefly and investigate the circumstances that provoke suspicion. [T]he stop and inquiry must be 'reasonably related in scope to the justification for their initiation.' The officer may question the driver and passengers about their citizenship and immigration status, and he may ask them to explain suspicious circumstances, but any further detention or search must be based on consent or probable cause.

Any number of factors may be taken into account in deciding whether there is reasonable suspicion to stop a car in the border area. Officers may consider the characteristics of the area in which they encounter a vehicle. Its proximity to the border, the usual patterns of traffic on the particular road, and previous experience with alien traffic are all relevant. They also may consider information about recent illegal border crossings in the area. The driver's behavior may be relevant, as erratic driving or obvious attempts to evade officers can support a reasonable suspicion. Aspects of the vehicle itself may justify suspicion. For instance, officers say that certain station wagons, with large compartments for fold-down seats or spare tires, are frequently used for transporting concealed aliens. The vehicle may appear to be heavily loaded, it may have an extraordinary number of passengers, or the officers may observe persons trying to hide. The Government also points out that trained officers can recognize the characteristic appearance of persons who live in Mexico, relying on such factors as the mode of dress and haircut.

In this case the officers relied on a single factor to justify stopping respondent's car: the apparent Mexican ancestry of the occupants. We cannot conclude that this furnished reasonable grounds to believe that the three occupants were aliens. At best the officers had only a fleeting glimpse of the persons in the moving car, illuminated by headlights. Even if they saw enough to think that the occupants were of Mexican descent, this factor alone would justify neither a reasonable belief that they were aliens, nor a reasonable belief that the car concealed other aliens who were illegally in the country. Large numbers of native-born and naturalized citizens have the physical characteristics identified with Mexican ancestry, and even in the border area a relatively small proportion of them are aliens. The likelihood that any given person of Mexican ancestry is an alien is high enough to make Mexican appearance a relevant factor, but standing alone it does not justify stopping all Mexican-Americans to ask if they are aliens.

The judgment of the Court of Appeals is affirmed. ◼

In *Brignoni-Ponce,* the Supreme Court rejected the notion that roving Border Patrol stops based on "apparent Mexican ancestry" alone could satisfy Fourth Amendment search and seizure requirements, but nevertheless held that "Mexican appearance" was a relevant factor. What the Court did not make clear, however, was the extent to which the Border Patrol could rely on "Mexican appearance" in other areas of border enforcement. That issue gave rise to a great deal of subsequent litigation, culminating in yet another Supreme Court case involving U.S. Border Patrol stops of Mexican Americans and further development of the Fourth Amendment. In *U.S. v. Martínez-Fuerte* (1976), the Supreme Court, by a vote of seven to three, upheld the constitutionality of the U.S. Border Patrol's use of **permanent checkpoints** and its additional practice of subsequently and selectively referring some motorists at the permanent checkpoint to a secondary inspection area—even if the **secondary referral stop** was motivated primarily by "apparent Mexican ancestry."

U.S. v. Martínez-Fuerte

United States Supreme Court
428 U.S. 543 (1976)

Mr. Justice Powell delivered the opinion of the Court.

These cases involve criminal prosecutions for offenses relating to the transportation of illegal Mexican aliens. Each defendant was arrested at a permanent checkpoint operated by the Border Patrol away from the international border with Mexico, and each sought the exclusion of certain evidence on the ground that the operation of the checkpoint was incompatible with the Fourth Amendment. In each instance whether the Fourth Amendment was violated turns primarily on whether a vehicle may be stopped at a fixed checkpoint for brief questioning of its occupants even though there is no reason to believe the particular vehicle contains illegal aliens. We hold today that such stops are consistent with the Fourth Amendment.

The respondents in [this case] are defendants in three separate prosecutions resulting from arrests made on three different occasions at the permanent immigration checkpoint on Interstate 5 near San Clemente, Cal. Interstate 5 is the principal highway between San Diego and Los Angeles, and the San Clemente checkpoint is 66 road miles north of the Mexican border. The "point" agent standing between the two lanes of traffic visually screens all northbound vehicles, which the checkpoint brings to a virtual, if not a complete, halt. Most motorists are allowed to resume their progress without any oral inquiry or close visual examination. In a relatively small number of cases the "point" agent will conclude that further inquiry is in order. He directs these cars to a secondary inspection area, where their occupants are asked about their citizenship and immigration status. The Government informs us that at San Clemente the average length of an investigation in the secondary inspection area is three to five minutes. A direction to stop in the secondary inspection area could be based on something suspicious about a particular car passing through the checkpoint, but the Government concedes that none of the three stops at issue in [these cases] was based on any articulable suspicion.

We turn now to the particulars of the [stop involving Martínez-Fuerte], and the procedural history of the case. Respondent Amado Martínez-Fuerte approached the checkpoint driving a vehicle containing two female passengers. The women were illegal Mexican aliens who had entered the United States at the San Ysidro port of entry by using false papers and rendezvoused with Martínez-Fuerte in San Diego to be transported northward. At the checkpoint their car was directed to the secondary inspection area. Martínez-Fuerte produced documents showing him to be a lawful **resident alien,** but his passengers admitted being present in the country unlawfully. He was charged [among other charges] with two counts of illegally transporting aliens in violation of [U.S. immigration laws]. He moved before trial to suppress all evidence stemming from the stop on the ground that the operation of the checkpoint was in violation of the Fourth Amendment. The motion to suppress was denied, and he was convicted on both counts after a jury trial.

Martínez-Fuerte appealed his conviction. The Court of Appeals held, with one judge dissenting, that [this stop] violated the Fourth Amendment, concluding that a stop for inquiry is constitutional only if the Border Patrol reasonably suspects the presence of illegal aliens on the basis of articulable facts. It reversed Martínez-Fuerte's conviction. We reverse and **remand.**

The Fourth Amendment imposes limits on search-and-seizure powers in order to prevent arbitrary and oppressive interference by enforcement officials with the privacy and personal security of individuals. In delineating the constitutional safeguards applicable in particular contexts, the Court has weighed the public interest against the Fourth Amendment interest of the individual, a process evident in our previous cases dealing with Border Patrol traffic-checking operations.

In *United States v. Brignoni-Ponce* (1975), however, we recognized that other traffic-checking practices involve a different balance of public and private interests and appropriately are subject to less stringent constitutional safeguards. We found that the interference with Fourth Amendment interests involved in such a stop was "modest," while the inquiry served significant law enforcement needs. We held that a roving-patrol stop need not be justified by probable cause and may be undertaken if the stopping officer is "aware of specific articulable facts, together with rational inferences from those facts, that reasonably warrant suspicion" that a vehicle contains illegal aliens.

It is agreed that checkpoint stops are "seizures" within the meaning of the Fourth Amendment. The defendants contend primarily that the routine stopping of vehicles at a checkpoint is invalid because *Brignoni-Ponce* must be read as proscribing any stops in the absence of reasonable suspicion.

While the need to make routine checkpoint stops is great, the consequent intrusion on Fourth Amendment interests is quite limited. The stop does intrude to a limited extent on motorists' right to "free passage without interruption," and arguably on their right to personal security. But it involves only a brief detention of travelers during which " '(a)ll that is required of the vehicle's occupants is a response to a brief question or two and possibly the production of a document evidencing a right to be in the United States.'" Neither the vehicle nor its occupants are searched, and visual inspection of the vehicle is limited to what can be seen without a search.

[T]he reasonableness of the procedures followed in making these checkpoint stops makes the resulting intrusion on the interests of motorists minimal. [And] the purpose of the stops is legitimate and in the public interest. Accordingly, we hold that the stops and questioning at issue may be made in the absence of any individualized suspicion at reasonably located checkpoints.

The defendants arrested at the San Clemente checkpoint suggest that its operation involves a significant extra element of intrusiveness in that only a small percentage of cars are referred to the secondary inspection area, thereby "stigmatizing" those diverted and reducing the assurances provided by equal treatment of all motorists. We think defendants overstate the consequences. Referrals are made for the sole purpose of conducting a routine and limited inquiry into residence status that cannot feasibly be made of every motorist where the traffic is heavy. The objective intrusion of the stop and inquiry thus remains minimal. Selective referral may involve some annoyance, but it remains true that the stops should not be frightening or offensive because of their public and relatively routine nature. Moreover, selective referrals rather than questioning the occupants of every car tend to advance some Fourth Amendment interests by minimizing the intrusion on the general motoring public.

We further believe that it is constitutional to refer motorists selectively to the secondary inspection area at the San Clemente checkpoint on the basis of criteria that would not sustain a roving-patrol stop. Thus, even if it be assumed that such referrals are made largely on the basis of apparent Mexican ancestry, we perceive no constitutional violation. As the intrusion here is sufficiently minimal that no particularized reason need exist to justify it, we think it follows that the Border Patrol officers must have wide discretion in selecting the motorists to be diverted for the brief questioning involved.

In summary, we hold that stops for brief questioning routinely conducted at permanent checkpoints are consistent with the Fourth Amendment and need not be authorized by warrant. The principal protection of Fourth Amendment rights at checkpoints lies in appropriate limitations on the scope of the stop. We have held that checkpoint searches are constitutional only if justified by consent or probable cause to search. And our holding today is limited to the type of stops described in this opinion. "(A)ny further detention . . . must be based on consent or probable cause." None of the defendants in these cases argues that the stopping officers exceeded these limitations. Consequently, we . . . reverse the judgment of the Court of Appeals for the Ninth Circuit and remand the case with directions to affirm the conviction of Martínez-Fuerte. Our holding today, approving routine stops for brief questioning (a type of stop familiar to all motorists) is confined to permanent checkpoints.

It is so ordered.

Mr. Justice Brennan, with whom Mr. Justice Marshall joins, dissenting.

In abandoning any requirement of a minimum of reasonable suspicion, or even articulable suspicion, the Court in every practical sense renders meaningless, as applied to checkpoint stops, the *Brignoni-Ponce* holding that "standing alone (Mexican appearance) does not justify stopping all Mexican-Americans to ask if they are aliens." Since the objective is almost entirely the Mexican illegally in the country, checkpoint officials, uninhibited by any objective standards and therefore free to stop any or all motorists without explanation or excuse, wholly on whim, will perforce target motorists of Mexican appearance. The process will then inescapably discriminate against citizens of Mexican ancestry and Mexican aliens lawfully in this country for no other reason than that they unavoidably possess the same "suspicious" physical and grooming characteristics of illegal Mexican aliens.

Every American citizen of Mexican ancestry and every Mexican alien lawfully in this country must know after today's decision that he travels the fixed checkpoint highways at the risk of being subjected not only to a stop, but also to detention and interrogation, both prolonged and to an extent far more than for non-Mexican appearing motorists. To be singled out for referral and to be detained and interrogated must be upsetting to any motorist . . . [b]ut for the arbitrarily selected motorists who must suffer the delay and humiliation of detention and interrogation, the experience can obviously be upsetting. And that experience is particularly vexing for the motorist of Mexican ancestry who is selectively referred, knowing that the officers' target is the Mexican alien. That deep resentment will be stirred by a sense of unfair discrimination is not difficult to foresee.

Action based merely on whatever may pique the curiosity of a particular officer is the antithesis of the objective standards requisite to reasonable conduct and to avoiding abuse and harassment. Such action, which the Court now permits, has expressly been condemned as contrary to basic Fourth Amendment principles. ■

■ The Challenge of Public Benefits

Another difficult and challenging area of immigration law has been the extent to which public benefits—including education, health care, public assistance, and employment—can be restricted to U.S. citizens and legal residents (see figure 7). Arguably the most significant case dealing with this issue is *Plyler v. Doe* (1982), wherein the U.S. Supreme Court, by a narrow five-to-four majority, held that an attempt to deny the children of undocumented immigrants the benefits of a public education violated the **Equal Protection Clause** of the **Fourteenth Amendment.** Having previously held

MAYBE IF WE REFUSE TO EDUCATE THEIR KIDS THEY'LL GO AWAY.

■ 7. Cartoon responding to efforts denying public education to undocumented immigrants.

that education was not a fundamental constitutional right under the Fourteenth Amendment in *San Antonio Independent School District v. Rodríguez* (1973), discussed in chapter 2, the Supreme Court's controversial holding in *Plyler* was greeted as a welcome surprise and a major victory for immigrants' rights.

Plyler v. Doe

United States Supreme Court
457 U.S. 202 (1982)

Justice Brennan delivered the opinion of the Court.

The question presented by these cases is whether, consistent with the Equal Protection Clause of the Fourteenth Amendment, Texas may deny to undocumented school-age children the free public education that it provides to children who are citizens of the United States or legally admitted aliens.

In May 1975, the Texas Legislature revised its education laws to withhold from local school districts any state funds for the education of children who were not "legally admitted" into the United States. The 1975 revision also authorized local school districts to deny enrollment in their public schools to children not "legally admitted" to the country. These cases involve constitutional challenges to those provisions.

[The case of *Plyler v. Doe*] is a **class action,** filed in the United States District Court for the Eastern District of Texas in September 1977, on behalf of certain school-age children of Mexican origin residing in Smith County, Tex., who could not establish that they had been legally admitted into the United States. The action complained of the exclusion of plaintiff children from the public schools of the Tyler Independent School District. After certifying a class consisting of all undocumented school-age children of Mexican origin residing within the School District, the District Court preliminarily **enjoined** defendants from denying a free education to members of the plaintiff class. In December 1977, the court conducted an extensive hearing on plaintiffs' motion for permanent **injunctive relief.**

The District Court held that illegal aliens were entitled to the protection of the Equal Protection Clause of the Fourteenth Amendment, and that [the state law] violated that Clause. With respect to equal protection, the Court of Appeals affirmed in all essential respects the analysis of the District Court, concluding that [the state law] was "constitutionally infirm."

The Fourteenth Amendment provides that "[n]o State shall . . . deprive any person of life, liberty, or property, without due process of law; nor deny to *any person within its jurisdiction* the equal protection of the laws." (Emphasis added.) Appellants argue at the outset that undocumented aliens, because of their immigration status, are not "persons within the jurisdiction" of the State of Texas, and that they therefore have no right to the equal protection of Texas law. We reject this argument. Whatever his status under the immigration laws, an alien is surely a "person" in any ordinary sense of that term. Aliens, even aliens whose presence in this country is unlawful, have long been recognized as "persons" guaranteed due process of law by the Fifth and Fourteenth Amendments.

That a person's initial entry into a State, or into the United States, was unlawful, and that he may for that reason be expelled, cannot negate the simple fact of his presence within the State's territorial perimeter. Given such presence, he is subject to the full range of obligations imposed by the State's civil and criminal laws.

The more difficult question is whether the Equal Protection Clause has been violated by the refusal of the State of Texas to reimburse local school boards for the education of children who cannot demonstrate that their presence within the United States is lawful, or by the imposition by those school boards of the burden of tuition on those children. It is to this question that we now turn.

Sheer incapability or lax enforcement of the laws barring entry into this country, coupled with the failure to establish an effective bar to the employment of undocumented aliens, has resulted in the creation of a substantial "shadow population" of illegal migrants—numbering in the millions—within our borders. This situation raises the specter of a permanent caste of undocumented resident aliens, encouraged by some to remain here as a source of cheap labor, but nevertheless denied the benefits that our society makes available to citizens and lawful residents. The existence of such an underclass presents most difficult problems for a Nation that prides itself on adherence to principles of equality under law.

The children who are plaintiffs in these cases are special members of this underclass. Persuasive arguments support the view that a State may withhold its beneficence from those whose very presence within the United States is the product of their own unlawful conduct. These arguments do not apply with the same force to classifications imposing disabilities on the minor children of such illegal entrants. Even if the State found it expedient to control the conduct of adults by acting against their children, legislation directing the onus of a parent's misconduct against his children does not comport with fundamental conceptions of justice.

It is thus difficult to conceive of a rational justification for penalizing these children for their presence within the United States. Yet that appears to be precisely the effect of [the state law]. Public education is not a "right" granted to individuals by the Constitution. But neither is it merely some governmental "benefit" indistinguishable from other forms of social welfare legislation. Both the importance of education in maintaining our basic institutions, and the lasting impact of its deprivation on the life of the child, mark the distinction.

These well-settled principles allow us to determine the proper level of deference to be afforded [to the state law which] imposes a lifetime hardship on a discrete class of children not accountable for their disabling status. The stigma of illiteracy will mark them for the rest of their lives. By denying these children a basic education, we deny them the ability to live within the structure of our civic institutions, and foreclose any realistic possibility that they will contribute in even the smallest way to the progress of our Nation. In determining the rationality of [the state law], we may appropriately take into account its costs to the Nation and to the innocent children who are its victims. In light of these countervailing costs, the discrimination contained in [the state law] can hardly be considered rational unless it furthers some substantial goal of the State.

Apart from the asserted state prerogative to act against undocumented children solely on the basis of their undocumented status—an asserted prerogative that carries only minimal force in the circumstances of these cases—we discern three colorable state interests that might support [the state law].

First, appellants appear to suggest that the State may seek to protect itself from an influx of illegal immigrants. While a State might have an interest in mitigating the potentially harsh economic effects of sudden shifts in population, [the state law] hardly offers an effective method of dealing with an urgent demographic or economic problem. There is no evidence in the record suggesting that illegal entrants impose any significant burden on the State's economy. To the contrary, the available evidence suggests that illegal aliens underutilize public services, while contributing their labor to the local economy and tax money to the state. The dominant incentive for illegal entry into the State of Texas is the availability of employment; few if any illegal immigrants come to this country, or presumably to the State of Texas, in order to avail themselves of a free education. Thus . . . we think it clear that "[c]harging tuition to undocumented children constitutes a ludicrously ineffectual attempt to stem the tide of illegal immigration," at least when compared with the alternative of prohibiting the employment of illegal aliens.

Second, while it is apparent that a State may "not . . . reduce expenditures for education by barring [some arbitrarily chosen class of] children from its schools," appellants suggest that undocumented children are appropriately singled out for exclusion because of the special burdens they impose on the State's ability to provide high-quality public education. But the record in no way supports the claim that exclusion of undocumented children is likely to improve the overall quality of education in the State. As the District Court noted, the State failed to offer any "credible supporting evidence that a proportionately small diminution of the funds spent on each child [which might result from devoting some state funds to the education of the excluded group] will have a grave impact on the quality of education." And, after reviewing the State's school financing mechanism, the District Court concluded that barring undocumented children from local schools would not necessarily improve the quality of education provided in those schools [because] undocumented children are "basically indistinguishable" from legally resident alien children.

Finally, appellants suggest that undocumented children are appropriately singled out because their unlawful presence within the United States renders them less likely than other children to remain within the boundaries of the State, and to put their education to productive social or political use within the State. Even assuming that such an interest is legitimate, it is an interest that is most difficult to quantify. The State has no assurance that any child, citizen or not, will employ the education provided by the State within the confines of the State's borders. In any event, the record is clear that many of the undocumented children disabled by this classification will remain in this country indefinitely, and that some will become lawful residents or citizens of the United States. It is difficult to understand precisely what the State hopes to achieve by promoting the creation and perpetuation of a subclass of illiterates within our boundaries, surely adding to the problems and costs of unemployment, welfare, and crime. It is thus clear that whatever savings might be achieved by denying these children an education, they are wholly insubstantial in light of the costs involved to these children, the State, and the Nation.

If the State is to deny a discrete group of innocent children the free public education that it offers to other children residing within its borders, that denial must be justified by a showing that it furthers some substantial state interest. No such showing was made here. Accordingly, the judgment of the Court of Appeals in each of these cases is Affirmed.

Justice Marshall, concurring.

While I join the Court's opinion, I do so without in any way retreating from my opinion in *San Antonio Independent School District v. Rodriguez* (1973) (dissenting opinion). I continue to believe that an individual's interest in education is fundamental, and that this view is amply supported "by the unique status accorded public education by our society, and by the close relationship between education and some of our most basic constitutional values."

Chief Justice Burger, with whom Justice White, Justice Rehnquist, and Justice O'Connor join, dissenting.

Were it our business to set the Nation's social policy, I would agree without hesitation that it is senseless for an enlightened society to deprive any children—including illegal aliens—of an elementary education. I fully agree that it would be folly—and wrong—to tolerate creation of a segment of society made up of illiterate persons, many having a limited or no command of our language. It does not follow, however, that a state should bear the costs of educating children whose illegal presence in this country results from the default of the political branches of the Federal Government. A state has no power to prevent unlawful immigration, and no power to deport illegal aliens; those powers are reserved exclusively to Congress and the Executive. If the Federal Government, properly chargeable with deporting illegal aliens, fails to do so, it should bear the burdens of their presence here. Surely if illegal alien children can be identified for purposes of this litigation, their parents can be identified for purposes of prompt deportation. However, the Constitution does not constitute us as "Platonic Guardians" nor does it vest in this Court the authority to strike down laws because they do not meet our standards of desirable social policy, "wisdom," or "common sense." We trespass on the assigned function of the political branches under our structure of limited and separated powers when we assume a policymaking role as the Court does today.

Moreover, when this Court rushes in to remedy what it perceives to be the failings of the political processes, it deprives those processes of an opportunity to function. When the political institutions are not forced to exercise constitutionally allocated powers and responsibilities, those powers, like muscles not used, tend to atrophy. Today's cases, I regret to say, present yet another example of unwarranted judicial action which in the long run tends to contribute to the weakening of our political processes. ■

The attempted denial of public education that gave rise to *Plyler* was emblematic of an anti-immigrant wave that surfaced in the late 1970s. In the late 1980s and early 1990s, an even more vehement anti-immigrant sentiment swept the country. The driving forces behind this sentiment, virtually mirroring prior periods of history, were the scapegoating of Mexican and other immigrants for the social and economic ills that faced U.S. society. Nowhere in the country was this movement more pronounced than in the state of California, which in the mid-1980s began to attempt to prohibit undocumented immigrant students from qualifying as California residents for tuition purposes in state colleges and universities. Several state legislatures had already begun to struggle with the difficult issue of providing access to higher education for undocumented students who had graduated from the state's high schools but because of their undocumented status had to pay much higher out-of-state tuition in state colleges and universities. The net effect was to make higher education prohibitively expensive for these individuals.

In California, this issue was raised in a series of cases that resulted in largely negative outcomes for undocumented immigrant students.[3] Given the judicial response, Mexican Americans and others working on this issue began to turn their energies away from the courts and instead focus on legislative remedies. In 2000, Texas was the first state, although others have since followed, to enact legislation allowing higher-education students to pay in-state tuition if they are graduates of a Texas high school and have been resident in the state for at least three years, irrespective of their legal status.

8. Protesters marching against California's Proposition 187.

California's most recent wave of anti-immigrant sentiment culminated in 1994, when in an effort spearheaded largely by an openly anti-immigrant governor, voters in the state passed Proposition 187 (see figure 8). Among other prohibitions, this proposition sought to deny undocumented immigrants a host of public benefits, including public education for their children, despite the U.S. Supreme Court's clear and unequivocal holding in *Plyler* that such a denial was unconstitutional. Proposition 187 also attempted to deny postsecondary education to undocumented individuals. In a legal challenge to this **statute,** *League of United Latin American Citizens v. Wilson* (1997), the trial court concluded that *Plyler* and a relevant federal law superseded Proposition 187's provisions relating to public and postsecondary education. Much of the holding in *Wilson* was based on a constitutional law principle known as the Supremacy Clause, which holds that in areas whose regulation pertains exclusively to the federal government (such as immigration) federal law will always take precedence over state law, a concept commonly referred to as **preemption.**

League of United Latin American Citizens v. Wilson

United States District Court for
the Central District of California
997 F.Supp. 1244 (1997)

Pfaelzer, District Judge.

Proposition 187 is an initiative measure which was submitted to the voters of the State of California in the November 8, 1994, general election. The stated purpose of Proposition 187 is to "provide for cooperation between [the] agencies of state and local government with the federal government, and to establish a system of required notification by and between such agencies to prevent illegal aliens in the United States from receiving benefits or public services in the State of California." The initiative's provisions require law enforcement, social services, health care and public education personnel to (i) verify the immigration status of persons with whom they come in contact; (ii) notify certain defined categories of persons of their immigration status; (iii) report those persons to state and federal officials; and (iv) deny those persons social services, health care and education.

After Proposition 187 was passed, several actions challenging the constitutionality of the initiative were commenced in state and federal courts in California. Ultimately, five actions filed in the United States District Court were consolidated in this Court for purposes of pre-trial proceedings and trial (collectively, the "consolidated actions").

The plaintiffs in the consolidated actions filed suit for **declaratory** and injunctive relief seeking to bar California Governor Pete Wilson ("Wilson"), Attorney General Dan Lungren ("Lungren"), and other state actors (collectively, "defendants") from enforcing the provisions of Proposition 187. On May 1, 1995, the League of United Latin American Citizens ("LULAC") and Gregorio T., plaintiffs, brought motions . . . in which they contended that Proposition 187 is unconstitutional on the sole ground that the initiative is preempted by the federal government's exclusive constitutional authority over the regulation of immigration, Congress' exercise of that power through the **Immigration and Nationality Act** ("INA"), and other federal statutes. Defendants opposed the

LULAC and Gregorio T. motions on the grounds that Proposition 187 is not preempted and, alternatively, that if any portion of the initiative is preempted, the remaining portions are valid and must be upheld. On November 20, 1995, the Court granted in part and denied in part the plaintiffs' motions. The Court held that section 7's denial of primary and secondary education conflicted with the decision reached by the Supreme Court in *Plyler v. Doe* (1982), and should be enjoined. The Court denied plaintiffs' motions with respect to sections 2 and 3. The Court also denied plaintiffs' motions . . . regarding the benefits denial provisions in sections 5, 6 and 8. The benefits denial provisions in sections 5 and 6 deny public social services and publicly-funded health care to "an alien in the United States in violation of federal law."

On August 22, 1996, the President signed the PRA [Personal Responsibility and Work Opportunity Reconciliation Act]. The PRA creates a comprehensive statutory scheme for determining aliens' eligibility for federal, state and local benefits and services. It categorizes all aliens as "qualified" or not "qualified" and then denies public benefits based on that categorization. In the PRA, Congress expressly stated a national policy restricting the availability of public benefits to aliens. This Memorandum [opinion] will discuss whether the PRA preempts any of these provisions of Proposition 187.

The intention of Congress to occupy the field of regulation of government benefits to aliens is declared throughout Title IV of the PRA. Whatever the level of government extending the benefits and whatever the source of the funding for the benefits—federal, state or local—they are all included within the expansive reach of the PRA. Together, these provisions both demarcate a field of comprehensive federal regulation within which states may not legislate, and define federal objectives with which states may not interfere.

[I]n enacting the PRA, Congress has made it clear that it is the immigration policy of the United States to deny public benefits to all but a narrowly defined class of immigrants which does not include illegal immigrants. In a sweeping statement, Congress has announced that there is a "compelling government interest to remove the incentive for illegal immigration provided by the availability of public benefits." This policy statement concerning the relationship between welfare and immigration leaves no doubt that the federal government has taken full control of the field of regulation of public benefits to aliens. Congress has ousted state power in the field of regulation of public benefits to immigrants by enacting legislation that denies federal, state and local health, welfare and postsecondary education benefits to aliens who are not "qualified."

Federal, state or local public benefits, as defined in the PRA, include social services and health services, which are the same benefits covered by sections 5 and 6 of Proposition 187. Because the PRA is a comprehensive regulatory scheme that restricts alien eligibility for all public benefits, however funded, the states have no power to legislate in this area. Congress has expressly exercised its authority to establish the procedure that must be followed in verifying immigrant eligibility for federal, state and local benefits. The states have no power to effectuate a scheme parallel to that specified in the PRA, even if the parallel scheme does not conflict with the PRA.

Section 7 of Proposition 187 denies public elementary and secondary education to any child not "a citizen of the United States, an alien lawfully admitted as a permanent resident, or a person who is otherwise authorized under federal law to be present in the United States." The Court found section 7 invalid on the ground that in *Plyler*, the Supreme Court held that a state cannot deny basic public education to children based on their immigration status.

As stated, the PRA is a comprehensive statutory scheme regulating alien eligibility for government benefits. It does not deny public elementary and secondary education to aliens, but it does specifically deal with the subject of basic public education. Section 1643 provides, "Nothing in this chapter may be construed as addressing alien eligibility for a basic public education as determined by the Supreme Court of the United States under *Plyler*." Thus, although basic public education clearly must be classified as a government benefit, just as health care is, the PRA does not purport to deny it to non-qualified aliens.

Section 8 of Proposition 187 denies public postsecondary education to anyone not a "citizen of the United States, an alien lawfully admitted as a permanent resident in the United States, or a person who is otherwise authorized under federal law to be present in the United States." For all practical purposes, the preemption analysis with respect to section 8 of Proposition 187 is the same as the analysis for sections 5 and 6 [because] Congress has occupied the field of regulation of public postsecondary education benefits to aliens. On September 30, 1996, Congress enacted the Illegal Immigration Reform and Immigrant Responsibility Act of 1996 ("IRA"). The IRA regulates alien eligibility for postsecondary education benefits on the basis of residence within a state. Because the IRA defines alien eligibility for postsecondary education, it also manifests Congress' intent to occupy this field [thereby preempting California's efforts with respect to this issue].

After the Court's November 20, 1995 Opinion, Congress enacted the PRA, a comprehensive statutory scheme regulating alien eligibility for public benefits. The PRA states that it is the immigration policy of the United States to restrict alien access to substantially all public benefits. Further, the PRA ousts state power to legislate in the area of public benefits for aliens. When President Clinton signed the PRA, he effectively ended any further debate about what the states could do in this field. As the Court pointed out in its prior Opinion, California is powerless to enact its own legislative scheme to regulate immigration. It is likewise powerless to enact its own legislative scheme to regulate alien access to public benefits. It can do what the PRA permits, and nothing more. Federal power in these areas was always exclusive and the PRA only serves to reinforce the Court's prior conclusion that substantially all of the provisions of Proposition 187 are preempted. ■

■ **Other Important Developments**

As illustrated throughout this chapter, the issue of immigration law and policy will always have a particular importance and significance to the Mexican American community. As decided in the *Wilson* case, due to the concept of preemption, regulation of immigration is exclusively the province of the federal government, which means changes to immigration law and policy cannot be undertaken by any of the fifty states. Rather, such changes can be made only at the federal level and will be binding throughout the United States. Unlike many other areas of the law discussed in this book, therefore, immigration law and policy can be, and have been, quickly changed through federal congressional and executive actions. Such changes have often been driven largely by the country's level of anti-immigrant sentiment. As noted, this tolerance or intolerance for immigrants can fluctuate wildly (as illustrated in the changes to immigration statutes enacted almost immediately following the September 11, 2001, terrorist attacks) and is influenced by the push and pull factors discussed throughout this chapter. The impact of such changes can be positive or negative for the Mexican American community.

Among the more harmful pieces of legislation for Mexican immigrants and Mexican Americans are two statutes passed by Congress in 1996: the Antiterrorism and Effective Death Penalty Act, and the Illegal Immigration and Immigrant Responsibility Act. The net effect of these two statutes was (1) stricter enforcement of previously unenforced or minimally enforced immigration statutes and a dramatic increase in the size of the U.S. Border Patrol, (2) an increase in the number and type of crimes for which an immigrant may be deported, and (3) new barriers for immigrants seeking to challenge detention and deportation proceedings in the courts. Thus, following the enactment of these two statutes, even if an immigrant has been a legal resident of the United States for a number of years and has deep historical and familial ties to his or her community, upon the commission of one of the newly identified criminal offenses, such an immigrant is now vulnerable to being deported without recourse.

These two restrictive statutes have been successfully challenged by numerous individuals on various grounds. In June 2001, the U.S. Supreme Court handed down two rulings involving challenges to these statutes, *INS v. St. Cyr* (2001)[4] and *Calcano-Martínez v. INS* (2001),[5] holding that despite the provisions of these two statutes, immigrants must be accorded their rights under the **Due Process Clause** before being deported. And, in a subsequent case challenging the practice of indefinitely detaining deportable immigrants, *Zadvydas v. Davis* (2001),[6] the Supreme Court once again emphasized, "It is well established that certain constitutional protections available to persons inside the United States are unavailable to [noncitizens] outside our geographic borders. But once an [undocumented individual] enters the country, the legal circumstance changes, for the Due Process Clause applies to all persons within the United States, whether their presence is lawful, unlawful, temporary or permanent."

Among the more positive legislation for Mexican immigrants and Mexican Americans are the Violence Against Women Acts of 1994 and 2000 (VAWA I and VAWA II, respectively), both of which contain provisions addressing the rights of battered immigrant women. Prior to the passage of these two statutes, Mexican and other immigrant women who were victims of domestic violence had a very difficult time obtaining legal residence status in the United States independent of their abusive husbands. As a result, many of these domestic violence victims simply stayed with their abusive spouses, who often used the threat of deportation as yet another form of abuse. As a result of these two statutes, immigrant women who are victims of domestic violence may now seek legal residency on their own, independent of their abusive spouse. As illustrated in the discussion of *Aguirre-Cervantes v. INS* in chapter 3, Mexican immigrant women who have been victims of domestic violence have been at the forefront of developing this area of law.

■ Concluding Thoughts

The cases in this chapter illustrate how Mexican Americans have challenged various policies, such as roving patrols, checkpoint stops, denial of public benefits, and efforts to quickly deport unwanted immigrants. As long as the push and pull factors that drive both legal and illegal immigration from Mexico to the United States continue to exist, U.S. efforts to control immigration will have only limited success. As further illustrated in this chapter, the reasons why individuals leave Mexico, or any country of origin, and emigrate to the United States are many and complex. Accordingly, while immigration control efforts may have great popular appeal, insofar as they continue to fail to account for this reality, such efforts will continue to be challenged in the courts by Mexican Americans and others.

■ Discussion Questions

1. Given the geographical proximity and unique historical relationship between Mexico and the United States, do you agree with the holding in *Brignoni-Ponce* that "[t]he likelihood that any given person of Mexican ancestry is an alien is high enough to make Mexican appearance a relevant factor," for purposes of Border Patrol stops? What are potential problems or dangers in randomly

stopping individuals who possess a "Mexican appearance" if they are near the U.S.–Mexico border?

2. Do the U.S. Border Patrol's practices at issue in both *Brignoni-Ponce* and *Martínez-Fuerte* address the push or pull factors present in immigration from Mexico to the United States?

3. Do you believe the availability or withholding of public assistance and health and educational benefits has any impact on the decision of an individual to immigrate to the United States? Are the policies reflected in statutes such as the one at issue in *Plyler* and Proposition 187 in *Wilson,* an effective mechanism for addressing the push and pull factors that drive undocumented immigration?

4. Despite the Supremacy Clause, the principle of preemption, and *Wilson's* holding that states cannot regulate immigration, is it fair that border states such as Arizona, California, New Mexico, and Texas are not permitted to regulate immigration, specifically in light of dramatically changing demographics in these states?

■ Suggested Readings

Johnson, K. R. "The Case against Race Profiling in Immigration Enforcement." *Washington University Law Quarterly* 78 (2000): 675–736.

——. "The End of 'Civil Rights' As We Know It: Immigration and Civil Rights in the New Millennium." *University of California Los Angeles Law Review* 49 (2002): 1481–1511.

Martínez, G. A. "Race and Immigration Law: A Paradigm Shift." *University of Illinois Law Review* (2000): 517–24.

Moran, R. F. "Demography and Distrust: The Latino Challenge to Civil Rights and Immigration Policy in the 1990s and Beyond." *La Raza Law Journal* 8 (1995): 1–24.

Romero, V. C. "Postsecondary School Education Benefits for Undocumented Immigrants: Promises and Pitfalls." *North Carolina Journal of International Law and Commercial Regulation* 27 (2002): 393–418.

Terán, L. J. "Barriers to Protection at Home and Abroad: Mexican Victims of Domestic Violence and the Violence Against Women Act." *Boston University International Law Journal* 17 (1999): 1–77.

■ Notes

1. A. D. Schmidley, "Profile of the Foreign-Born Population in the United States: 2000," in U.S. Census Bureau, *Current Population Reports,* Series P23-206 (Washington, D.C.: U.S. Government Printing Office, 2001).

2. Although immigration law and policy are without a doubt major issues for Mexican Americans, a thorough treatment of the entire area of immigration law and policy is beyond the scope and focus of this book. Moreover, a great deal of careful and thoughtful scholarly attention has been devoted to the general area of immigration law. For some definitive works in this area, consult the suggested readings for this chapter as well as the following: T. A. Aleinikoff, D. A. Martin, and H. Motomura, eds., *Immigration and Citizenship: Process and Policy* (St. Paul, Minnesota: West Publishing Co., 1998).

3. See discussion in *American Association of Women v. Board of Trustees of the California State University (Leticia "A")*, 31 Cal.App. 4th 702, 38 Cal.Rptr. 2d 15 (1995).

4. 533 U.S. 289.

5. 533 U.S. 348.

6. 121 S. Ct. 2491.

Voting Rights

[T]here can be no doubt that lack of political participation by . . . Chicanos is affected by a cultural incompatibility which has been fostered by a deficient educational system.—*Graves v. Barnes* (1972)

Contemporary election laws generally, and voting rights specifically, are the direct result of decades of litigation brought by Mexican Americans and other racial minorities. During the first part of the nineteenth century, politicians created a plethora of barriers to the political participation of Mexican Americans and African Africans. For example, between 1865 and 1906, the Texas state legislature either refused to recognize that a problem existed or passed bills overtly denying the franchise (i.e., the right to vote) or implementing a **poll tax. Racial gerrymandering** and **all-white primaries** were also prevalent means of ensuring that African Americans could not achieve electoral success. Although many of the nineteenth-century **disenfranchisement** efforts were directed toward African Americans, Mexican Americans were equally targeted for electoral discrimination, particularly after the Mexican War. Specifically, restrictive registration laws and laws prohibiting interpreters at the polls were passed in order to minimize the Mexican American franchise.

■ Voting Rights Litigation

Voting rights litigation has successfully eliminated numerous barriers that had hampered or completely prohibited Mexican Americans and other racial minorities from exercising their right to vote (see figure 9). Among the practices and barriers ultimately struck down as a result of litigation are the poll tax, the all-white primary, excessive restrictions on voter registration, systems that required annual registration, absolute prohibitions on the use of interpreters by non-English-speaking persons, and high candidate filing fees.[1] In each of these cases, the plaintiffs were either Mexican American or another racial or ethnic minority, and the court rulings

■ 9. Su Voto Es Su Voz (your vote is your voice), the slogan of the Southwest Voter Registration Education Project.

enabled these communities to participate more effectively and fully in the political process.

The major effort aimed at eradicating voting barriers for Mexican Americans was the passage of the **Voting Rights Act of 1965.** This new federal law was concerned principally with protecting the voting rights of African Americans. As mentioned in chapter 1, it was not until 1972 that legislative changes finally clarified that Mexican Americans and other racial or ethnic groups were protected classes under the **statute.** After 1972, the Voting Rights Act allowed Mexican Americans to bring lawsuits attacking the discriminatory election laws and structures pervasive in various states throughout the Southwest. These legal challenges were based on two very important sections of the Voting Rights Act: Section 2 and Section 5. Section 2 allows Mexican Americans to challenge a jurisdiction with barriers, such as racial gerrymandering or maintenance of **at-large election systems** that result in dilution of the Mexican American community's voting strength—a process or practice more commonly referred to as **vote dilution.** Section 5, in turn, prohibits jurisdictions identified in the act as having a history of constructing voting barriers against racial minorities from implementing certain voting changes without federal authorization.

In addition to successfully challenging many of the most pernicious voting barriers by alleging race discrimination under the Voting Rights Act of 1965, Mexican Americans also succeeded in challenging other election obstacles, sometimes even without explicit findings of racial discrimination. For instance, in a Texas state court case, *Gonzáles v. Stevens* (1968), plaintiff H. C. Gonzáles challenged a Texas law authorizing only certain persons to deliver a voter registration application to the county assessor-collector. In another Texas case, *Garza v. Smith* (1970), the plaintiff, Anita Garza, argued that the articles of the Texas election code prohibiting illiterate citizens from having assistance in the voting booth violated the **Equal Protection Clause** of the **Fourteenth Amendment** to the U.S. **Constitution.** In the *Gonzáles* case, the court held against H. C. Gonzáles, but the issue became so politicized that the law was subsequently changed to loosen the requirements for becoming a voting registrar and delivering completed registration forms to the appropriate agency. In contrast, in the *Garza* case, the court found for plaintiff Anita Garza and ruled that anyone who has difficulty reading a ballot should be allowed personal assistance in the booth. This right was extended to include the use of interpreters for those voters who spoke Spanish and needed the assistance of an interpreter. Both *Gonzáles* and *Garza* were brought by Mexican Americans, but the rights secured benefited all voters.

■ Reapportionment and Redistricting

Gonzáles and *Garza* notwithstanding, the preeminent case concerning the voting rights of Mexican Americans, and indeed all racial minorities, is the U.S. Supreme Court ruling in *White v. Regester* (1973)—which for technical legal reasons had a different name, *Graves v. Barnes* (1972),[2] at the federal trial court level. *White* challenged the reapportionment and redistricting that followed the 1970 U.S. Census.

Article I, Section 2, Clause 3 of the U.S. Constitution outlines the specific manner in which the census is to be taken and stipulates, "Representatives . . . shall be apportioned among the several States . . . according to their respective Numbers." This article further provides, "The actual Enumeration shall be made within three Years after the first Meeting of the Congress of the United States, and within every subsequent Term of ten Years, in such Manner as they shall by Law direct." Section 2 of the Fourteenth Amendment similarly provides, "Representatives shall be apportioned among the several States according to their respective numbers, counting the whole number of persons in each State." The national census, taken every ten years, reveals shifts in population among the states. The loss and gain of population within the various states are then used to determine the ratio upon which congressional seats are allotted, resulting in some states gaining additional seats and others losing a seat or two. State legislatures are then left with the difficult task of drawing congressional, state legislative, and board of education districts based on the statewide population distribution.

The trial court's **opinion** in *Graves* actually provided a better and more complete understanding of the facts and legal arguments in this historic and pathbreaking case than did the Supreme Court opinion in *White.* In *Graves,* the federal trial court consolidated four separate actions that challenged the 1970 Texas state legislative redistricting process. In one of these cases, the plaintiff challenged the multimember state house districts in Béxar County (San Antonio), and also alleged that the senatorial districts in Béxar County were "politically and racially gerrymandered."

The trial court, citing the landmark *Hernández v. Texas* (1954) **decision** discussed in chapter 1, reiterated that "Chicanos, as well as Blacks, require the protective intervention of the Federal Courts" when they have been identified as a distinct class and the laws, as written or as applied, single out that class for different and unreasonable treatment. The trial court then went on to point out that the Chicano community in San Antonio, Texas, was indeed easily identifiable because it was marked by geographical isolation, undereducated children due to poorly funded schools (see *San Antonio v. Rodríguez* [1973], discussed in chapter 2), and low income levels with correspondingly high poverty rates. The court observed that the Mexican American population in Texas had suffered historically "long-standing educational, social, legal, economic, political and other widespread and prevalent restrictions, customs, traditions, biases and prejudices." The trial court also pointed out that language differences may affect the ability of Mexican Americans to interact with and receive services from various public agencies. In doing so, the trial court emphasized that language competency is essential if one is to play a significant role in the public and political life of a society. The trial court concluded "there can be no doubt that lack of political participation by Texas Chicanos is affected by a cultural incompatibility which has been fostered by a deficient educational system." The history of discrimination and disparate treatment of Chicanos caused the Supreme Court in *White,* by a six-to-three vote, to strike down the use of **multimember districts** and impose a legal remedy known as **single-member districts** in Béxar County. *Graves v. Barnes,* renamed

White v. Regester on appeal, opened the door for Mexican Americans and others successfully to challenge redistricting processes that had denied them the opportunity to achieve meaningful results with respect to voting.

White v. Regester

United States Supreme Court
412 U.S. 755 (1973)

Mr. Justice White delivered the opinion of the Court.

This case raises two questions concerning the validity of the reapportionment plan for the Texas House of Representatives adopted in 1970 by the State Legislative Redistricting Board: First, whether there were unconstitutionally large variations in population among the districts defined by the plan; second, whether the multimember districts provided for Béxar and Dallas Counties were properly found to have been **invidiously discriminatory** against cognizable racial or ethnic groups in those counties.

The Texas Constitution requires the state legislature to reapportion the House and Senate at its first regular session following the decennial census. On October 15, 1971, the [Legislative] Redistricting Board's plan for the reapportionment of the Senate was released, and, on October 22, 1971, the House plan was promulgated. Only the House plan remains at issue in this case. That plan divided the 150-member body among 79 single-member and 11 multimember districts.

A three-judge District Court sustained the Senate plan, but found the House plan unconstitutional. *Graves v. Barnes* (1972). The House plan was held to contain constitutionally impermissible deviations from population equality, and the multimember districts in Béxar and Dallas Counties were deemed constitutionally invalid.

The reapportionment plan for the Texas House of Representatives provides for 150 representatives selected from 79 single-member and 11 multimember districts. The ideal district is 74,645 persons. The districts range from 71,597 to 78,943 in population per representative, or from 5.8% overrepresentation to 4.1% underrepresentation. The total variation between the largest and smallest district is thus 9.9%.

The District Court read our prior cases to require any deviations from equal population among districts to be justified by "acceptable reasons" grounded in state policy. Noting the single fact that the total deviation from the ideal between District 3 and District 85 was 9.9%, the District Court concluded that justification by appellants was called for and could discover no acceptable state policy to support the deviations. The District Court was also critical of the actions and procedures of the Legislative Reapportionment Board and doubted "that [the] board did the sort of deliberative job . . . worthy of judicial abstinence." It also considered the combination of single-member and multimember districts in the House plan "haphazard," particularly in providing single-member districts in Houston and multimember districts in other metropolitan areas, and that this "irrationality, without reasoned justification, may be a separate and distinct ground for declaring the plan unconstitutional." Finally, the court specifically invalidated the use of multimember districts in Dallas and Béxar Counties as unconstitutionally discriminatory against a racial or ethnic group.

The District Court's ultimate conclusion was that "the apportionment plan for the State of Texas is unconstitutional as unjustifiably remote from the ideal of '**one-man, one-vote**,' and the multimember districting schemes for the House of Representatives as they relate specifically to Dallas and Béxar Counties are unconstitutional in that they dilute the votes of racial minorities."

Only 23 districts, all single-member, were overrepresented by more than 3%, and only three of those districts by more than 5%. We are unable to conclude from these deviations alone that appellees satisfied the threshold requirement of proving a **prima facie** case of invidious discrimination under the Equal Protection Clause. Because the District Court had a contrary view, its judgment must be reversed in this respect.

We affirm the District Court's judgment, however, insofar as it invalidated the multimember districts in Dallas and Béxar Counties and [we] order those districts to be redrawn into single-member districts.

Consistently with *Hernández v. Texas* (1954), the District Court considered the Mexican-Americans in Béxar County to be an identifiable class for Fourteenth Amendment purposes and proceeded to inquire whether the impact of the multimember district on this group constituted invidious discrimination. Surveying the historic and present condition of the Béxar County Mexican-American community, which is concentrated for the most part on the west side of the city of San Antonio, the court observed, based upon prior cases and the record before it, that the Béxar County community, along with other Mexican-Americans in Texas, had long "suffered from, and continues to suffer from, the results and effects of invidious discrimination and treatment in the fields of education, employment, economics, health, politics and others."

Based on the totality of the circumstances, the District Court evolved its ultimate assessment of the multimember district, overlaid, as it was, on the cultural and economic realities of the Mexican-American community in Béxar County and its relationship with the rest of the county. Its judgment was that Béxar County Mexican-Americans "are effectively removed from the political processes of Béxar [County], . . . whatever their absolute numbers may total in that County." Single-member districts were thought required to remedy "the effects of past and present discrimination against Mexican-Americans," and to bring the community into the full stream of political life of the county and State by encouraging their further registration, voting, and other political activities.

On the record before us, we are not inclined to overturn these findings. *Affirmed in part, reversed in part, and* **remanded.**

Redistricting after *White*

The *White* decision remained the guiding authority on redistricting practices for the next twenty years until the 1990 census redistricting. During the 1980s numerous cases were filed in heavily Mexican American areas seeking to vindicate the voting rights of Mexican Americans. One of the most visible, controversial, and complex of these lawsuits was a challenge to the districting plan for, and an attempt to increase the size of, the Board of Supervisors in Los Angeles, California, brought in August 1985. This case dramatically overhauled the system for electing the L.A. Board of Supervisors, resulting in the first ever Latina/o presence on the board.

In 1990, Texas was allotted three additional congressional districts because of its significant population growth between 1980 and 1990. This required the Texas legislature to redraw its state legislative districts, which it did following the guidance in *White*. Political tensions immediately arose regarding the location of these three new districts. If these districts were drawn as **majority-minority districts,** Mexican Americans felt they had an opportunity to increase the number of Hispanic congressional representatives. Republicans also saw an opportunity to increase their number of seats in Congress. Meanwhile both Democrats and African Americans positioned themselves to ensure that the redistricting process would not diminish their existing congressional representation. The political tension fueled by all these competing interests resulted in the filing of a record number of redistricting lawsuits.

In one of these cases, several individuals, including a Houston-area businessman named Luis Vera, filed suit in federal district court alleging that race was the predominant factor used to determine the boundaries of the congressional districts under the 1990 Texas redistricting plan. This suit, *Bush v. Vera* (1996), followed a series of redistricting cases filed in North Carolina, Florida, Georgia, and Louisiana subsequent to the 1990 redistricting cycle. All of these cases also argued that traditional redistricting criteria were abandoned and that race was used as the predominant factor in drawing congressional district lines. Of these cases, *Vera* was the only case where Mexican Americans defended their status as an identifiable protected group under the Voting Rights Act in order to retain a "new majority-Hispanic district." Although the other cases focused on African American voting rights, the **precedents** they established ultimately prevented Mexican Americans from using race as a factor in their own efforts to influence the redrawing of districts. The best known and arguably most controversial case in this series was the U.S. Supreme Court decision in *Shaw v. Reno* (1994),[3] a North Carolina redistricting case challenging the creation of a new majority-minority congressional district for African Americans. In this case, the court concluded that race could no longer be used as the "predominant factor" when deciding where to draw congressional district lines. The net effect of this holding was to encourage further challenges to majority-minority districts.

Ultimately, by a five-to-four vote, the Supreme Court affirmed in *Bush v. Vera* that race could not be a predominant factor in redistricting. Moreover, the Court also held that race could not be considered among the "traditional" factors that inform redistricting decisions, such as **compactness, contiguity, incumbency protection,** or other social variables. In this regard, the *Vera* decision followed the same formula that the Supreme Court had created in the *Shaw* decision and refined in its subsequent decisions. Unfortunately because of its outcome, *Vera* proved to be a barrier to continued Latino progress in voting-rights litigation. Additionally, *Vera* dictated the strategies Latinos could use in voting-rights litigation until the 2001 redistricting round, when the Supreme Court modified the *Shaw* decision and further clarified the proper use of race as a redistricting factor.

Bush v. Vera

United States Supreme Court
517 U.S. 952 (1996)

Justice O'Connor announced the judgment of the court.

The present case is a mixed motive case. The appellants concede that one of Texas' goals in creating the three districts at issue was to produce majority[-]minority districts, but they also cite evidence that other goals, particularly incumbency protection (including protection of "functional incumbents," i.e., sitting members of the Texas legislature who had declared an intention to run for open congressional seats), also played a role in the drawing of the district lines.

The means that Texas used to make its redistricting decisions provides further evidence of the importance of race. The primary tool used in drawing district lines was a computer program called "REDAPPL." REDAPPL permitted redistricters to manipulate district lines on computer maps, on which racial and other socioeconomic data were superimposed. The availability and use of block to block racial data was unprecedented; before the 1990 census, data were not broken down beyond the census tract level. By providing uniquely detailed racial data, REDAPPL enabled redistricters to make more intricate refinements on the basis of race than on the basis of other demographic information.

These findings—that the State substantially neglected traditional districting criteria such as compactness, that it was committed from the outset to creating majority[-]minority districts, and that it manipulated district lines to exploit unprecedentedly detailed racial data—together weigh in favor of the application of **strict scrutiny.** For strict scrutiny to apply, traditional districting criteria must be subordinated to race. [T]he decision to create a majority[-]minority district [is not] objectionable in and of itself.

Several factors other than race were at work in the drawing of the districts. Traditional districting criteria were not entirely neglected.

The population of District 30 is 50% African American and 17.1% Hispanic. Fifty percent of the district's population is located in a compact, albeit irregularly shaped, core in South Dallas, which is 69% African American. But the remainder of the district consists of narrow and bizarrely shaped tentacles—the State identifies seven "segments"—extending primarily to the north and west. Over 98% of the district's population is within Dallas County, but it crosses two county lines at its western and northern extremities. Its western excursion into Tarrant County grabs a small community that is 61.9% African American, its northern excursion into Collin County occupies a hook-like shape mapping exactly onto the only area in the southern half of that county with a combined African American and Hispanic percentage population in excess of 50%.

In some circumstances, incumbency protection might explain as well as, or better than, race a State's decision to depart from other traditional districting principles, such as compactness, in the drawing of bizarre district lines. If district lines merely correlate with race because they are drawn on the basis of political affiliation, which correlates with race, there is no racial classification to justify, just as racial disproportions in the level of prosecutions for a particular crime may be unobjectionable if they merely reflect racial disproportions in the commission of that crime.

Finally, and most significantly, the objective evidence provided by the district plans and demographic maps suggests strongly the preponderance of race. [T]hat the districting software used by the State provided only racial data at the block by block level . . . suggests that racial criteria predominated over other districting criteria in determining the district's boundaries.

The combination of these factors compels us to agree with the District Court that "the contours of Congressional District 30 are unexplainable in terms other than race." It is true that District 30 does not evince a consistent, single minded effort to "segregate" voters on the basis of race, and does not represent "apartheid." But the fact that racial data were used in complex ways, and for multiple objectives, does not mean that race did not predominate over other considerations. The record discloses intensive and pervasive use of race both as a proxy to protect the political fortunes of adjacent incumbents, and for its own sake in maximizing the minority population of District 30 regardless of traditional districting principles.

A State's interest in remedying discrimination is compelling when two conditions are satisfied. First, the discrimination that the State seeks to remedy must be specific, "identified discrimination"; second, the State "must have had a 'strong basis in evidence'" to conclude that remedial action was necessary, "before it embarks on an **affirmative action** program." Here, the only current problem that appellants cite as in need of remediation is alleged vote dilution as a consequence of **racial bloc voting.** We have indicated that such problems will not justify race based districting unless "the State employ[s] sound districting principles, and . . . the affected racial group's residential patterns afford the opportunity of creating districts in which they will be in the majority."

Legislators and district courts have modified their practices—or, rather, reembraced the traditional districting practices that were almost universally followed before the 1990 census—in response to *Shaw I.* Those practices and our precedents, which acknowledge voters as more than mere racial statistics, play an important role in defining the political identity of the American voter. Our Fourteenth Amendment jurisprudence evinces a commitment to eliminate unnecessary and excessive governmental use and reinforcement of racial stereotypes. We decline to retreat from that commitment today.

The judgment of the District Court is affirmed.

Justice Stevens, with whom Justice Ginsburg and Justice Breyer join, dissenting.

The 1990 census revealed that Texas' population had grown, over the past decade, almost twice as fast as the population of the country as a whole. As a result, Texas was entitled to elect three additional Representatives to the United States Congress, enlarging its delegation from 27 to 30. Because Texas' growth was concentrated in South Texas and the cities of Dallas and Houston, the state legislature concluded that the new congressional districts should be carved out of existing districts in those areas. The consequences of the political battle that produced the new map are some of the most oddly shaped congressional districts in the United States.

Today, the Court strikes down three of Texas' majority[-]minority districts, concluding, *inter alia,* that their odd shapes reveal that the State impermissibly relied on predominantly racial reasons when it drew the districts as it did. For two reasons, I believe that the Court errs in striking down those districts.

First, I believe that the Court has misapplied its own tests for racial gerrymandering, both by applying strict scrutiny to all three of these districts, and then by concluding that none can meet that scrutiny. In asking whether strict scrutiny should apply, the Court improperly ignores the "complex interplay" of political and geographical considerations that went into the creation of Texas' new congressional districts and focuses exclusively on the role that race played in the State's decisions to adjust the shape of its districts. A quick comparison of the unconstitutional majority-minority districts with three equally bizarre majority-Anglo districts . . . demonstrates that race was not necessarily the predominant factor contorting the district lines. I would follow the fair implications of the District Court's findings, and conclude that Texas' entire map is a political, not a racial, gerrymander.

Even if strict scrutiny applies, I would find these districts constitutional, for each considers race only to the extent necessary to comply with the State's responsibilities under the Voting Rights Act while achieving other race-neutral political and geographical requirements. The **plurality's** finding to the contrary unnecessarily restricts the ability of States to conform their behavior to the Voting Rights Act while simultaneously complying with other race-neutral goals.

Second, even if I concluded that these districts failed an appropriate application of this still-developing law to appropriately read facts, I would not uphold the District Court decision. The decisions issued today serve merely to reinforce my conviction that the Court has, with its "analytically distinct" jurisprudence of racial gerrymandering, struck out into a jurisprudential wilderness that lacks a definable constitutional core and threatens to create harms more significant than any suffered by the individual plaintiffs challenging these districts. Though we travel ever farther from it with each passing decision, I would return to the well-traveled path that we left in *Shaw I*.

The history of race relations in Texas and throughout the South demonstrates overt evidence of discriminatory voting practices lasting through the 1970s. Even in recent years, Texans have elected only two black candidates to statewide office; majority-white Texas districts have never elected a minority to either the State Senate or the United States Congress. One recent study suggests that majority-white districts throughout the South remain suspiciously unlikely to elect black representatives. And nationwide, fewer than 15 of the hundreds of legislators that have passed through Congress since 1950 have been black legislators elected from majority-white districts. In 1994, for example, 36 of the Nation's 39 black Representatives were elected from majority-minority districts, while only 3 were elected from majority-white districts.

Perhaps the state of race relations in Texas and, for that matter, the Nation, is more optimistic than might be expected in light of these facts. If so, it may be that the plurality's exercise in redistricting will be successful. Perhaps minority candidates, forced to run in majority-white districts, will be able to overcome the long history of stereotyping and discrimination that has heretofore led the vast majority of majority-white districts to reject minority candidacies. Perhaps not. I am certain only that bodies of elected federal and state officials are in a far better position than anyone on this Court to assess whether the Nation's long history of discrimination has been overcome, and that nothing in the Constitution requires this unnecessary intrusion into the ability of States to negotiate solutions to political differences while providing long-excluded groups the opportunity to participate effectively in the democratic process. I respectfully dissent. ■

■ Combining Forces with African Americans

As the preceding discussion illustrates, historically the voting rights of Mexican Americans were often determined in conjunction with, or as a corollary to, the determination of African American voting rights. It was not long before civil and voting rights activists came to believe that in communities in which Mexican Americans or African Americans were few in number, combining the forces of these groups for purposes of voting-rights litigation would prove beneficial. This strategy was in direct response to the U.S. Supreme Court's holding in *Thornburg v. Gingles* (1986)[4] and was successfully used in *Campos v. Baytown* (1988),[5] a decision from the U.S. Court of Appeals for the Fifth Circuit.

As previously mentioned, Section 2 of the Voting Rights Act makes it illegal for any jurisdiction to create or maintain any election structure that "dilutes" the voting strength of a protected racial or language group. In *Gingles,* the Supreme Court ruled that at-large systems were not in and of themselves discriminatory. However, the Court ruled that under certain circumstances these systems could "operate to impair minority voters' ability to elect representatives of their choice." The Court articulated three factors to consider in determining the existence of such vote dilution: (1) "the minority group must be able to demonstrate that it is sufficiently large and geographically compact to constitute a majority in a single-member district"; (2) "the minority group must be able to show that it is politically cohesive"; and (3) "the white majority [must vote] sufficiently as a bloc to enable it . . . to defeat the minority's preferred candidates."

Arguably the most important challenge for racial or ethnic minority groups attempting to prove vote dilution is the first requirement that such groups constitute a large and compact majority. In the *Campos* litigation, which challenged the Baytown, Texas, redistricting plan, the plaintiffs theorized that if Mexican Americans and African Americans combined their populations, they would possess adequate numbers to satisfy the first *Gingles* requirement. The *Campos* plaintiffs hoped that by replacing the at-large system with a new system that included single-member districts, they would ultimately increase their chances of electing representatives of their choice.

The Supreme Court's requirements in *Gingles* were clearly articulated with the mindset that a single racial minority group would have to constitute a majority of a single-member district. The plaintiffs' innovative argument in *Campos,* however, postulated that Mexican Americans and African Americans satisfied the "one minority group" requirement because both experienced similar forms of discrimination and as a result "voted in a cohesive manner for minority candidates." The *Campos* court found a history of Anglo voting patterns similar to those the Supreme Court had found in *Gingles*. On that basis it concluded that the at-large election system was a discriminatory structure that diluted the voting strength of both Mexican Americans and African Americans. This dilution, the *Campos* court held, inhibited both Mexican Americans and African Americans from electing the representatives of their choice. Ultimately, because the redistricting plan at issue in *Campos* had not been preapproved by the Department of Justice in accordance with Section 5 of the Voting Rights Act, the court dismissed the case.

Nevertheless, *Campos* contributed in several important ways to the development of Mexican American voting rights. First, it was proven to the court's satisfaction that Mexican Americans and African Americans in some instances may vote similarly enough to be considered as one minority group for proving a vote-dilution case. Most important, the expert evidence documented that both groups had been subjected to a history of similar types of discriminatory activities, thus providing another strategy for future collaboration between the two largest minority groups in the United States, African Americans and Latinos, on voting-rights issues.

■ The Unrealized Hope of Statistical Sampling

The most recent case directly implicating the voting rights of Mexican Americans centered on the use of a controversial technique known as statistical sampling. Although Mexican Americans were not a party in the case, the implications of this decision nevertheless weigh heavily against Mexican Americans and other racial minority groups' ability to expand their representational presence in state legislatures and the U.S. Congress.

Given the sheer size and increasingly transitory nature of the U.S. population, counting each individual within the time allotted every ten years for the census has become virtually impossible. Due to these and similarly complex challenges, it became increasingly clear during the late 1990s that census results were plagued with a systemic problem of undercounting, and that Mexican Americans were traditionally among the most severely undercounted groups. One of the most important factors prohibiting an accurate enumeration of Mexican Americans is their high migratory rates in connection with seeking employment such as agricultural work. This mobility has led to growing communities of Mexican Americans in parts of the United States, such as the Midwest, Northeast, and Southeast, that historically have not had a large Mexican American presence. In addition, undercounting is exacerbated by language differences and the suspicion that many Mexican Americans have of government officials.

Because of these and similar undercounting issues with respect to other populations, the U.S. Census Bureau, a division of the Department of Commerce, began to use statistical sampling as a data-gathering technique. Statistical sampling involves counting a proportion of the overall population and from that count projecting mathematically the overall population numbers. By using statistical sampling for the 2000 census, the Census Bureau hoped to project more accurately the overall U.S. population and the proportions of various racial and ethnic groups within it. The ultimate goal was to derive better and more accurate estimates of Mexican American, African American, and other minority populations.

In *Department of Commerce v. United States House of Representatives* (1999),[6] plaintiffs—which included a number of members of the U.S. House of Representatives—filed suit against the Department of Commerce over its use of statistical sampling as a way of compensating for the traditional undercounting of members of racial minority groups. The record in the case indicated that the Census Bureau had been tracking the undercounting of large segments of the American population since 1940, but it was unclear whether the bureau had been aware of this problem before 1940. The record was also unclear regarding whether the undercount was an artifact of the post–World War II population explosion and increasing mobility of Americans, or rather an unintended consequence of new technologies designed to make the census more accurate, but which in fact had the opposite effect—or perhaps a combination of both factors. Nevertheless, the record indicated that the Census Bureau had determined that using statistical sampling was necessary during the census enumeration process to measure more accurately the historically undercounted segments of the population.

Throughout the case, the Census Bureau maintained that it did not consider statistical sampling as violative of the constitutional provisions in Article I, Section 2, Clause 3, or in Section 2 of the Fourteenth Amendment. The plaintiffs in the case argued that statistical sampling violated the section of the Fourteenth Amendment that requires "counting the whole number of persons in each State." In short, the plaintiffs alleged that if the Census Bureau was allowed to continue using statistical sampling, rather than the constitutionally mandated actual enumeration of whole persons, then the plaintiffs would be vulnerable to losing apportioned seats. The plaintiffs also argued that statistical sampling violated the **one person, one vote** principle articulated by the Supreme Court in its landmark *Baker v. Carr* (1962) decision.[7] The federal trial court ruled against the use of statistical sampling and the Supreme Court agreed.

The ultimate effect of this decision on Mexican Americans is difficult to measure. It certainly has the potential, however, to limit Mexican American representation in the U.S. Congress. Another consequence of this Supreme Court decision is that Latinos and other racial and ethnic groups will likely continue to be undercounted in future censuses. For instance, although the federal government undertook unprecedented and widespread efforts, including print and broadcast media blitzes, to ensure a complete and accurate population count in the 2000 census, virtually all experts agree that the undercount persisted.

The Court did stipulate, however, that sampling was prohibited only in the gathering of data necessary for determining how many federal congressional seats a given state should be allotted after each census. It did not prohibit the use of statistical sampling in the reapportionment of state legislative and local seats or in the allocation of monies for government services. Accurate population data are particularly important in the context of government services provided to the Mexican American community, because these services encompass many issues ranging from bilingual education to Spanish-language ballots. However, since almost all state and local redistricting efforts are based upon the national census, the effects of a national undercount undoubtedly will continue to be felt even at the local levels of government.

▉ Concluding Thoughts

As the cases summarized in this chapter illustrate, voting-rights litigation has challenged various issues ranging from discriminatory redistricting plans to the enumeration techniques employed by the Census Bureau. The voting rights of Mexican Americans have been established through hard-fought battles resulting in legal decisions and codification of new rules in federal statutes. Nevertheless, these voting rights are still evolving and are subject to redefinition with each new census. Accordingly, reapportionment and redistricting issues will continue to arise. Indeed, even before completion of the most recent 2000 census, numerous lawsuits had been prepared and were ready for filing in anticipation of the new population data. It is safe to assume that Mexican Americans will continue to file voting-rights lawsuits against jurisdictions ranging from state legislatures to school districts across the United States. In the future, as the Mexican American and Latino vote increases in importance across the country, these lawsuits will take on more and more significance and visibility. For example, one recent and highly visible redistricting controversy occurred in Texas. Because the Texas Legislature was unable to pass redistricting legislation following the 2000 census, redistricting in Texas for this cycle was actually done pursuant to a legal settlement of federal court litigation alleging that the voting rights of Mexican Americans had been violated. Then, in the summer of 2003, during an unprecedented third Special Session, the Republican-dominated Texas State Legislature chose yet again to redraw Texas' thirty-two federal congressional districts in an off-cycle year. The argument set forth by the Republican majority was that since most Texans voted Republican in statewide elections, redistricting was necessary in order to assure an increase following the 2004 election of the number of Republicans in the Texas congressional delegation. Accordingly, the Texas Legislature passed legislation that caused the federal court-approved redistricting plan to become moot. In doing so, the Republican majority failed to recognize that a parallel argument could also be made on behalf of Latinos—namely, that since Latinos make up more than 38 percent of the Texas population, they deserve a similar proportion of majority-Latino districts. As of fall 2003, MALDEF was contemplating filing a lawsuit concerning this very issue.

Although three of the four cases discussed in this chapter focused on Mexican Americans, the holdings in these decisions are important and relevant to every Latino national-origin group and to all racial minorities. The complex legal issues addressed in *White, Vera, Campos,* and *Department of Commerce* will affect all Latinos equally and will have to be reargued, redefined, and refined in future decades.

■ Discussion Questions

1. Following the decision in *White,* which resulted in the increased use of single-member districts, record numbers of Mexican Americans were elected to various local, state, and federal offices. Does the sheer increase in the number of Mexican Americans elected to office ensure the effective representation of this community?

2. What assumptions are being made about Mexican Americans' voting cohesiveness and candidate preference when a majority-Hispanic, single-member district is drawn? Can such a district be adequately represented by a non–Mexican American?

3. Dramatic population increases are anticipated for both Latinos and African Americans. What do you think the political landscape will look like in five years, in ten years, and in twenty years, assuming these groups are allowed and continue to combine forces for Section 2 litigation purposes?

4. Given the increasing population of Latinos in many parts of the United States, do you agree that Latinos should bring litigation seeking proportional representation to their population?

■ Suggested Readings

Davidson, C. *Race and Class in Texas Politics*. Princeton: Princeton University Press, 1992.

Davidson, C., and B. Grofman. *Quiet Revolution in the South: The Impact of the Voting Rights Act, 1965–1990*. Princeton: Princeton University Press, 1994.

Grofman, K., ed. *Race and Redistricting in the 1990s*. New York: Agathon Press, 1998.

Guinier, L., and G. Torres. *The Miner's Canary: Enlisting Race, Resisting Power, Transforming Democracy*. Cambridge: Harvard University Press, 2002.

Key, V. O. Jr. *Southern Politics in State and Nation: A New Edition*. Knoxville: University of Tennessee Press, 1984.

Kousser, J. M. *Colorblind Injustice: Minority Voting Rights and the Undoing of the Second Reconstruction*. Chapel Hill: University of North Carolina Press, 1999.

■ Notes

1. Poll taxes were struck down in *United States v. Texas*, 252 F. Supp. 234 (W.D. Tex. 1966), *affirmed in* 384 U.S. 155 (1966); all-white primaries in *Smith v. Allwright*, 321 U.S. 649 (1944); voter registration restrictions in *Gonzáles v. Stevens*, 427 S.W.2d 694 (Tex. Civ. App.—Corpus Christi 1968); annual registration in *Beare v. Smith*, 321 F. Supp. 1100 (S.D. Tex. 1971); prohibitions on interpreters in *Garza v. Smith*, 320 F. Supp. 131 (W.D. Tex. 1970); and high filing fees in *Bullock v. Carter*, 405 U.S. 134 (5th Cir. 1973).

2. 343 F. Supp. 704.

3. 509 U.S. 630.

4. 478 U.S. 30

5. 840 F.2d 1240.

6. 525 U.S. 316.

7. 396 U.S. 186.

Affirmative Action

> [T]he [district] court approved of the non-remedial goal of having a diverse student body, reasoning that "obtaining the educational benefits that flow from a racially and ethnically diverse student body remains a sufficiently compelling interest to support the use of racial classifications."—*Hopwood v. Texas* (1996)

Affirmative action has generated great controversy throughout the United States, particularly within the legal system. Proponents of affirmative action argue that governmental entities, employers, and educational institutions should be permitted to consider the race, ethnicity, and gender of candidates in order to ensure that members of previously excluded groups, such as Mexican Americans, are brought into the mainstream of U.S. society. In considering how the legal system should handle affirmative action programs, it is important to understand the history of the development of these programs.

Immediately after the Civil War, three amendments to the U.S. **Constitution** were adopted to ensure equal rights for African Americans. The Thirteenth Amendment bans slavery in the United States. The **Fourteenth Amendment** guarantees U.S. citizenship to all persons born in the United States; prohibits state and local governments from depriving any person of life, liberty, or property without due process of law; and guarantees everyone **equal protection** under the law. The Fifteenth Amendment guarantees the voting rights of all citizens. Congress used the power granted to it under these amendments to enact civil rights **statutes** protecting the rights of the newly freed slaves. Within twenty years of the Civil War, however, the U.S. Supreme Court limited the protections afforded under these constitutional provisions and statutes. As a result, African Americans continued to experience discrimination throughout many sectors of society, including in the legal system. In many areas of the Southwest, Mexican Americans suffered similar discrimination.

■ Brief History of Affirmative Action

Historically, Mexican Americans, like African Americans and other minorities, have actively resisted discrimination. This resistance culminated in the 1960s with the **Civil Rights Movement** and the **Chicano Movement.** President John F. Kennedy was elected with substantial support from Mexican American and African American voters. He issued **Executive Order** 10925, which created the Presidential Commission on Equal Employment Opportunity and for the first time mandated that federal contractors take "affirmative action" to ensure they did not discriminate on the basis of race, creed, color, or **national origin.** After President Kennedy's assassination, President Lyndon B. Johnson successfully urged Congress to enact new civil rights statutes. But President Johnson argued that prohibiting discrimination was not enough: "You do not take a person who for years has been hobbled by chains, and liberate him, bring him up to the starting line of a race, and then say, 'You are free to compete with all the others,' and still justly believe that you have been completely fair. Thus, it is not enough just to open the gates of opportunity; all our citizens must have the ability to walk through those gates."[1] As a complement to Executive Order 10925, President Johnson issued Executive Order 11246, requiring federal contractors to take "affirmative action" to recruit, hire, and promote more minorities. Two years later, he added women to the previously covered groups.

In 1971, President Richard M. Nixon unveiled a program, which for the first time required federal contractors to prepare annual affirmative action plans with goals and timetables for hiring minorities. Affirmative action plans were widely adopted in major U.S. corporations. In turn, federal courts began requiring employers sued for employment discrimination to adopt affirmative action plans with goals and timetables for workplace diversification. In *Local 28, Sheet Metal Workers International Association v. EEOC* (1986),[2] the U.S. Supreme Court approved the use of court-ordered affirmative action plans in hiring for employers who are found to have violated federal employment discrimination statutes. Under the ruling in *United States v. Paradise* (1987),[3] federal courts may also order employers who have violated federal employment discrimination statutes to institute affirmative action in promotions. Affirmative action plans involving Mexican Americans have regularly been implemented as one of the remedies in employment discrimination lawsuits. Affirmative action plans are not automatically ordered by the courts, however. In *Pérez v. Federal Bureau of Investigation* (1988), discussed in chapter 1, for instance, the court found that the class of Latino FBI agents had been discriminated against but nevertheless declined to order adoption of an affirmative action plan as a remedy.

Criticism of affirmative action programs arose soon after they were established. Critics of affirmative action programs have argued that such programs (1) discriminate against innocent white males; (2) benefit middle class minorities and women, not those who are "truly disadvantaged"; (3) are unnecessary because state and federal laws have eradicated discrimination; (4) heighten race consciousness instead of promoting a color-blind society; and (5) result in the selection and promotion of "underqualified" minorities and women.

Proponents of affirmative action argue that such programs (1) temporarily "discriminate" to remedy well-entrenched discrimination that will otherwise never be remedied, or will not be remedied for many, many years; (2) are necessary to integrate minorities and women into the economic mainstream of U.S. society; (3) are required to maintain the economic competitiveness of the United States by ensuring that the talents of individuals from underrepresented groups are no longer wasted; (4) benefit everyone in society, including white males, by ensuring diversity in classrooms and workplaces and the economic productivity of all sectors of society; (5) are fair because the persistence of racial and gender discrimination requires affirmative steps to remedy such discrimination. Ultimately, opponents and proponents of affirmative action come to different conclusions about the fairness of affirmative action programs.

In addition to all the historical and traditional objections, some critics of affirmative action have argued that affirmative action is unnecessary for Mexican Americans and other Latinos because, unlike African Americans, these groups were never enslaved and never experienced an equivalent level of oppression. Another argument against affirmative action for Mexican Americans is that while Mexican immigrants have lower educational and income levels than native-born Americans, it is expected that as the children of these immigrants assimilate into U.S. society, their educational and income levels will rise dramatically, as has been true in the past with European immigrants to the United States. In other words, assert these critics, affirmative action is thus unnecessary because the problem of underrepresentation of Mexican Americans in the major institutions of our society will take care of itself over time. Finally, one of the more unusual arguments against affirmative action for Mexican American and other Latinos is a reactionary, anti-immigrant stance to the large proportion of recent immigrants within the Latino community. More specifically, critics of affirmative action argue that recent immigrants, who did not experience the blatant discrimination of the past, should not benefit from affirmative action.

Proponents of affirmative action have not been persuaded by these arguments. Affirmative action programs have never required the beneficiaries of such programs to prove that they individually have suffered discrimination, so why require such evidence from Mexican Americans? Affirmative action programs are instead designed to address historical and systematic discrimination against particular groups in U.S. society. Moreover, immigrants in the United States often encounter discrimination based solely on the fact that they are not native-born citizens. The cases highlighted in this chapter demonstrate that the courts continue to debate these questions and the legal permissibility of affirmative action.

■ Legal Standards for Reviewing Affirmative Action Programs

We begin with a review of the very particularized legal standards that are discussed in the following **opinions.** Much of the debate in the area of affirmative action revolves around what should be the appropriate legal standard for reviewing affirmative action programs; depending on the standard chosen, affirmative action programs are likely to be approved or disapproved by the courts.

This area of case law involves affirmative action programs implemented by state or federal government actors, including public institutions of higher learning and in the workforce. The **Equal Protection Clause** of the Fourteenth Amendment to the U.S. Constitution requires that all state and local governments provide the "equal protection of the laws" to all persons. Although there is no text in the Constitution that requires the federal government to provide equal protection of the laws, the **Due Process Clause** of the **Fifth Amendment** provides that the federal government cannot deprive any person of life, liberty, or property "without due process of law." The Due Process Clause of the Fifth Amendment has been interpreted by the U.S. Supreme Court as requiring the federal government to provide equal protection of the laws in a manner similar to what is required of state and local governments in the Fourteenth Amendment.

The Equal Protection Clause of the Fourteenth Amendment has been invoked in many lawsuits challenging discriminatory treatment by state or local governments. If the alleged discrimination is based on race or ethnicity, the courts ordinarily review the evidence under the **strict scrutiny** standard, the highest and toughest standard of review under the Fourteenth Amendment. Recall that the Fourteenth Amendment was adopted after the Civil War to guarantee the equality of the newly freed slaves and, as interpreted by the U.S. Supreme Court in *Hernández v. Texas* (1954), also protects Mexican Americans from racial or ethnic discrimination. The strict scrutiny standard is intended to implement that guarantee. Under the strict scrutiny standard, any classification based on race or ethnicity must (1) serve a compelling governmental interest; and (2) be narrowly tailored and use the least restrictive means to serve that governmental interest. Most classifications based on race will not survive application of the strict scrutiny standard because usually the government is unable to show a "compelling governmental interest" in racial or ethnic classifications. For example, the government has no compelling interest in maintaining racially segregated public schools. Hence, the often-heard refrain is that strict scrutiny review is "strict in theory but fatal in fact."

Advocates of affirmative action argue that such programs should not be evaluated under the strict scrutiny standard because the programs are intended to remedy racial discrimination. Furthermore, if strict scrutiny is applied, the need to remedy past racial discrimination and societal injustices, and the interests in a diverse workforce and diverse classrooms, provide the compelling governmental interest required to meet the strict scrutiny standard. Opponents, on the other hand, demand that all affirmative action programs be evaluated under the strict scrutiny standard. Moreover, they argue that neither remedying past discrimination nor achieving diversity is a compelling governmental interest, and thus affirmative action programs do not satisfy the strict scrutiny standard.

For classifications not based on race, the courts will often apply a less rigorous standard of intermediate scrutiny. Under intermediate scrutiny, a classification will be permitted if (1) it serves an important governmental interest; and (2) there is a substantial relationship between the classification and the governmental purpose. Intermediate scrutiny is primarily applied to classifications based on gender. Under intermediate scrutiny, most but not all classifications based on gender are impermissible. Advocates of affirmative action have sometimes argued that a level of scrutiny below strict scrutiny, such as intermediate scrutiny, should be applied to affirmative action programs.

The final, and lowest, level of scrutiny for Fourteenth Amendment purposes is the rational relationship test. Under this form of scrutiny, if a government classification has at least some rational relationship to the ultimate governmental goal, it will be ruled constitutional.

Besides the appropriate level of scrutiny, the other underlying legal issue debated in this area of case law is whether the same standards should be applied to federal affirmative action programs as are applied to state and local programs. In essence, the debate centers around whether affirmative action programs adopted by the federal government (reviewable under the Fifth Amendment's Due Process Clause), should receive the same level of scrutiny as affirmative action programs adopted by state and local entities (reviewable under the Fourteenth Amendment's Equal Protection Clause).

■ Affirmative Action in Institutions of Higher Learning

Prior to the late 1960s, few Mexican Americans attended institutions of higher education. Colleges and universities voluntarily adopted affirmative action plans in the late 1960s and early 1970s to remedy the net effects of past purposeful discrimination. Admissions committees at undergraduate, graduate, and professional schools began considering race as a factor in admissions to enhance the likelihood that racial and ethnic minorities would be admitted. In using race-conscious processes, admissions committees that historically had excluded racial and ethnic minorities began to broaden the factors they considered in determining eligibility for admission. Under these programs, record numbers of Mexican Americans and other minorities were admitted to higher education.

Resistance against these policies quickly appeared by the early 1970s, leading to the landmark **decision** in *Regents of the University of California v. Bakke* (1978),[4] in which the U.S. Supreme Court struck down an affirmative action policy at the University of California, Davis, medical school. In order to increase historically underrepresented racial and ethnic minorities in the medical profession, the uc Davis medical school had adopted a policy that set aside sixteen out of one hundred seats for "disadvantaged" applicants in its entering class. Bakke, a white applicant who was not admitted, challenged the policy as a form of reverse discrimination. He argued that because whites were essentially blocked from competing for the sixteen seats, the medical school's admissions program guaranteed a quota for minority applicants that discriminated against whites. The U.S. Supreme Court, in a **plurality decision,** meaning that a majority of the court did not endorse any of the various opinions written by the justices, agreed that quotas violate the Fourteenth Amendment's Equal Protection Clause. Yet, the Court also held that race could still be used as one factor among other factors in deciding the admission of applicants to universities and professional schools. Furthermore, Justice Powell, who served as the deciding vote on this issue, concluded that UC Davis has a compelling interest in achieving diversity in the student body that justifies affirmative action policies, so long as these policies are not in the form of quotas. Almost immediately following the *Bakke* decision, institutions of higher education adopted Justice Powell's diversity rationale to guide their admissions policies.

After the *Bakke* decision, the U.S. Supreme Court did not hear a case dealing specifically with affirmative action in institutions of higher learning until *Grutter v. Bollinger* and *Gratz v. Bollinger*[5] in the spring of 2003. Both these cases, dealing with admissions policies at the University of Michigan, will be discussed later. In the interim between 1978 and 2003, however, the U.S. Supreme Court did restrict affirmative action policies with respect to federal and local contracting. At the same time, the Court upheld some affirmative action plans in the workplace, especially if there had been a history of purposeful discrimination and if the plans were narrowly tailored.

Over the twenty-five years without guidance from the U.S. Supreme Court between *Bakke* and the *Grutter* and *Gratz* cases, controversy continued in the lower federal courts regarding the use of affirmative action in higher education admissions policies. Some of the lower federal courts have relied primarily on other Supreme Court cases not dealing with university admissions such as *Adarand Constructors, Inc., v. Peña* (1995),[6] discussed later, rather than the *Bakke* case. These courts have inferred from these decisions that affirmative action is no longer constitutional and that achieving diversity is no longer a compelling interest justifying affirmative action in university admissions policies. A case from the U.S. Court of Appeals for the Fifth Circuit, one of the most conservative circuit courts in

■ 10. Society of American Law Teachers marching in Washington, D.C., in connection with University of Michigan affirmative action cases.

the country, *Hopwood v. Texas* (1996), excerpted later, exemplifies this reasoning. Other courts, however, relying on *Bakke* as binding **precedent,** have upheld university affirmative action policies.

On April 1, 2003, the U.S. Supreme Court heard oral arguments in the aforementioned *Grutter* and *Gratz* appeals from the United States Court of Appeals for the Sixth Circuit (see figure 10). The *Grutter* case involved a challenge to the use of affirmative action at the University of Michigan School of Law, while the *Gratz* case challenged the University of Michigan's affirmative action program for undergraduate admissions.

The Court's willingness to hear the *Grutter* and *Gratz* cases stemmed from a history of conflicting courts of appeals decisions on affirmative action in admissions. The decision of the U.S. Court of Appeals for the Fifth Circuit in *Hopwood* was the first to question the *Bakke* precedent allowing the use of affirmative action in admissions. The *Hopwood* case, in turn, relied heavily on the U.S. Supreme Court's decision in *Adarand,* which examined whether the Fourteenth Amendment prohibited Congress from using voluntary incentive programs to encourage contracting opportunities for minority, women-owned, and other disadvantaged businesses.

Adarand centered on the Gonzáles Construction Company, a minority-owned business. Gonzáles was hired as a subcontractor by the Mountain Gravel & Construction Company to work on a highway construction project. As part of a federal affirmative action program, general contractors such as Mountain Gravel received financial incentives to subcontract work to minority-owned businesses. When Adarand, the Anglo owner of Adarand Constructors, Inc., did not win the contract, he sued then–Secretary of Transportation, Federico Peña (the first Mexican American to hold this position and a former governor of Colorado), because the highway construction project was funded by the Department of Transportation. Adarand claimed that the government's use of race in identifying minority-owned businesses and the use of financial incentives were discriminatory. In a five-to-four decision, the Supreme Court held that with respect to federal contracting, unless there was a "compelling justification," affirmative action programs that provide financial incentives to hire minority-owned businesses are not constitutional. *Adarand* is especially significant in that the Court held that courts would have to apply *strict scrutiny* to review affirmative action plans or programs, irrespective of whether the state or federal government adopted the plan or program and despite the fact that these programs benefited, rather than disadvantaged, racial and ethnic minorities. The *Adarand* Court concluded,

> [A]ll racial classifications, imposed by whatever federal, state, or local governmental actor, must be analyzed by a reviewing court under strict scrutiny. In other words, such classifications are constitutional only if they are narrowly tailored measures that further compelling governmental interests. . . . We think that requiring strict scrutiny is the best way to ensure that courts will consistently give racial classifications that kind of detailed examination, both as to ends and as to means.

In so holding, the Court made it difficult to use affirmative action plans in federal contracting, a decision that mirrored an earlier holding involving state and local contracting. The *Adarand* Court also refused to distinguish racial classifications that historically have been used to discriminate against racial minorities (**invidious racial classifications**) from racial classifications that have been adopted to make up for the past effects of racial discrimination, to aid rather than disadvantage minorities, and to foster equality (**benign racial classifications**). On this point, in particular, the Justices in *Adarand* differed sharply. In his concurring opinion, for instance, Justice Thomas stated that "there can be no doubt that racial paternalism and its unintended consequences can be as poisonous and pernicious as any other form of discrimination. So-called 'benign' discrimination teaches many that because of chronic and apparently immutable handicaps, minorities cannot compete with [whites] without their patronizing indulgence. These programs stamp minorities with a badge of inferiority and may cause them to develop dependencies or to adopt an attitude that they are 'entitled' to preferences." By contrast, Justice Stevens in his dissenting opinion argued that "there is no moral or constitutional equivalence between a policy that is designed to perpetuate a caste system and one that seeks to eradicate racial subordination. Invidious discrimination is an engine of oppression, subjugating a disfavored group to enhance or maintain the power of the majority. Remedial race-based preferences reflect the opposite impulse: a desire to foster equality in society."

Adarand dealt with affirmative action in contracting, not admissions in higher education. Nevertheless, in *Hopwood,* the U.S. Court of Appeals for the Fifth Circuit relied on *Adarand* to strike down the affirmative action program of the University of Texas School of Law. The following opinion illustrates how the Fifth Circuit essentially ignored the *Bakke* decision.

Hopwood v. State of Texas

United States Court of Appeals for the Fifth Circuit
78 F.3d 932 (1996)

Jerry E. Smith, Circuit Judge:

With the best of intentions, in order to increase the enrollment of certain favored classes of minority students, the University of Texas School of Law ("the law school") discriminates in favor of those applicants by giving substantial racial preferences in its admissions program. The beneficiaries of this system are blacks and Mexican Americans, to the detriment of whites and non-preferred minorities. The question we decide today is whether the Fourteenth Amendment permits the school to discriminate in this way. We hold that it does not. The law school has presented no compelling justification, under the Fourteenth Amendment or Supreme Court precedent, that allows it to continue to elevate some races over others, even for the wholesome purpose of correcting perceived racial imbalance in the student body. As a result of its diligent efforts in this case, the district court concluded that the law school may continue to impose racial preferences. We reverse and **remand,** concluding that the law school may not use race as a factor in law school admissions.

The University of Texas School of Law is one of the nation's leading law schools, consistently ranking in the top twenty. Accordingly, admission to the law school is fiercely competitive, with over 4,000 applicants a year competing to be among the approximately 900 offered admission to achieve an entering class of about 500 students.

In the early 1990s, the law school largely based its initial admissions decisions upon an applicant's so-called Texas Index ("TI") number, a composite of undergraduate grade point average ("GPA") and Law School Aptitude Test ("LSAT") score. The law school used this number as a matter of administrative convenience in order to rank candidates and to predict, roughly, one's probability of success in law school. Of course, the law school did not rely upon numbers alone. The admissions office necessarily exercised judgment in interpreting the individual scores of applicants, taking into consideration factors such as the strength of a student's undergraduate education, the difficulty of his major, and significant trends in his own grades and the undergraduate grades at his respective college (such as grade inflation). Admissions personnel also considered what qualities each applicant might bring to his law school class. Thus, the law school could consider an applicant's background, life experiences, and outlook. Not surprisingly, these hard-to-quantify factors were especially significant for marginal candidates.

Because of the large number of applicants and potential admissions factors, the TI's administrative usefulness was its ability to sort candidates. For the class entering in 1992—the admissions group at issue in this case—the law school placed the typical applicant in one of three categories according to his TI scores: "presumptive admit," "presumptive deny," or a middle "discretionary zone." An applicant's TI category determined how extensive a review his application would receive. Most, but not all, applicants in the presumptive admit category received offers of admission with little review. Applicants in the presumptive denial category also received little consideration. Applications in the middle range were subjected to the most extensive scrutiny. For all applicants other than blacks and Mexican Americans, the files were bundled into stacks of thirty, which were given to admissions subcommittees consisting of three members of the full admissions committee. Subject to the chairman's veto, if a candidate received two or three votes, he received an offer; if he garnered one vote, he was put on the waiting list; those with no votes were denied admission.

Blacks and Mexican Americans were treated differently from other candidates, however. First, compared to whites and non-preferred minorities, the TI ranges that were used to place them into the three admissions categories were lowered to allow the law school to consider and admit more of them. In March 1992, for example, the presumptive TI admission score for resident whites and non-preferred minorities was 199. Mexican Americans and blacks needed a TI of only 189 to be presumptively admitted. The difference in the presumptive-deny ranges is even more striking. The presumptive denial score for "nonminorities" was 192; the same score for blacks and Mexican Americans was 179. While these cold numbers may speak little to those unfamiliar with the pool of applicants, the results demonstrate that the difference in the two ranges was dramatic. According to the law school, 1992 resident white applicants had a *mean* GPA of 3.53 and an LSAT of 164. Mexican Americans scored 3.27 and 158; blacks scored 3.25 and 157. The category of "other minority" achieved a 3.56 and 160. These disparate standards greatly affected a candidate's chance of admission. The stated purpose of this lowering of standards was to meet an "aspiration" of admitting a class consisting of 10 percent Mexican Americans and 5 percent blacks, proportions roughly comparable to the percentages of those races graduating from Texas colleges.

In addition to maintaining separate presumptive TI levels for minorities and whites, the law school ran a segregated application evaluation process. Upon receiving an application form, the school color-coded it according to race. Thus, race was always an overt part of the review of any applicant's file. The law school reviewed minority candidates within the applicable discretionary range differently from whites. Instead of being evaluated and compared by one of the various discretionary zone sub-committees, black and Mexican American applicants' files were reviewed by a minority subcommittee of three, which would meet and discuss every minority candidate. Finally, the law school maintained segregated waiting lists, dividing applicants by race and residence. Thus, even many of those minority applicants who were not admitted could be set aside in "minority-only" waiting lists.

Cheryl Hopwood, Douglas Carvell, Kenneth Elliott, and David Rogers (the "plaintiffs") applied for admission to the 1992 entering law school class. All four were white residents of Texas and were rejected. The plain-tiffs were considered as discretionary zone candidates. [For instance], Hopwood, with a GPA of 3.8 and an LSAT of 39 (equivalent to a three-digit LSAT of 160), had a TI of 199, a score barely within the presumptive-admit category for resident whites, which was 199 and up. She was dropped into the discretionary zone for resident whites (193 to 198).

The plaintiffs sued primarily under the Equal Protection Clause of the Fourteenth Amendment. The plaintiffs' central claim is that they were subjected to unconstitutional racial discrimination by the law school's evaluation of their admissions applications.

The central purpose of the Equal Protection Clause "is to prevent the States from purposefully discriminating between individuals on the basis of race." It seeks ultimately to render the issue of race irrelevant in governmental decisionmaking. Hence, "[p]referring members of any one group for no reason other than race or ethnic origin is discrimination for its own sake. This the Constitution forbids." *Regents of Univ. of Cal. v. Bakke* (1978). These equal protection maxims apply to all races. *Adarand Constructors v. Peña* (1995). In order to preserve these principles, the Supreme Court recently has required that any governmental action that expressly distinguishes between persons on the basis of race be held to the most exacting scrutiny. Furthermore, there is now absolutely no doubt that courts are to employ strict scrutiny when evaluating all racial classifications, including those characterized by their proponents as "benign" or "remedial." Under the strict scrutiny analysis, we ask two questions: (1) Does the racial classification serve a compelling government interest, and (2) is it narrowly tailored to the achievement of that goal?

[W]e turn to the specific issue of whether the law school's consideration of race as a factor in admissions violates the Equal Protection Clause. The district court found both a compelling remedial and a non-remedial justification for the practice. First, the court approved of the non-remedial goal of having a diverse student body, reasoning that "obtaining the educational benefits that flow from a racially and ethnically diverse student body remains a sufficiently compelling interest to support the use of racial classifications." Second, the court determined that the use of racial classifications could be justified as a remedy for the "present effects at the law school of past discrimination in both the University of Texas system and the Texas educational system as a whole."

Justice Powell's separate opinion in *Bakke* provided the original impetus for recognizing diversity as a compelling state interest in higher education. Justice Powell reasoned that diversity is a sufficient justification for limited racial classification. "[The attainment of a diverse student body] clearly is a constitutionally permissible goal for an institution of higher education." In sum, Justice Powell found the school's program to be an unconstitutional "quota" system, but he intimated that the Constitution would allow schools to continue to use race in a wide-ranging manner.

Here, the plaintiffs argue that diversity is not a compelling governmental interest under superseding Supreme Court precedent. The law school maintains, on the other hand, that Justice Powell's formulation in *Bakke* is law and must be followed—at least in the context of higher education. We agree with the plaintiffs that any consideration of race or ethnicity by the law school for the purpose of achieving a diverse student body is not a compelling interest under the Fourteenth Amendment. Justice Powell's view in *Bakke* is not binding precedent on this issue. No case since *Bakke* has accepted diversity as a compelling state interest under a strict scrutiny analysis. Indeed, recent Supreme Court precedent shows that the diversity interest will not satisfy strict scrutiny. Foremost, the Court appears to have decided that there is essentially only one compelling state interest to justify racial classifications: remedying past wrongs. While the use of race *per se* is proscribed, state-supported schools may reasonably consider a host of factors—some of which may have some correlation with race—in making admissions decisions. Schools may even consider factors such as whether an applicant's parents attended college or the applicant's economic and social background. In sum, the use of race to achieve a diverse student body . . . as a proxy for permissible characteristics, simply cannot be a state interest compelling enough to meet the steep standard of strict scrutiny. These latter factors may, in fact, turn out to be substantially correlated with race, but the key is that race itself not be taken into account.

We now turn to the district court's determination that "the remedial purpose of the law school's affirmative action program is a compelling government objective." The plaintiffs argue that the court erred by finding that the law school could employ racial criteria to remedy the present effects of past discrimination in Texas's primary and secondary schools. The plaintiffs contend that the proper unit for analysis is the law school, and the state has shown no recognizable present effects of the law school's past discrimination. The law school, in response, notes Texas's well-documented history of discrimination in education and argues that its effects continue today at the law school, both in the level of educational attainment of the average minority applicant and in the school's reputation. Generally, "In order to justify an affirmative action program, the State must show there are 'present effects of past discrimination.'"

The Supreme Court has "insisted upon some showing of prior discrimination by the governmental unit involved before allowing limited use of racial classifications in order to remedy such discrimination." [W]e conclude that the district court erred in expanding the remedial justification to reach all public education within the State of Texas. No one disputes that in the past, Texas state actors have discriminated against some minorities in public schools. But the very program at issue here shows how remedying such past wrongs may be expanded beyond any reasonable limits.

We further reject the proposition that the University of Texas System, rather than the law school, is the appropriate governmental unit for measuring a constitutional remedy. The law school operates as a functionally separate unit within the system. Thus, for much the same reason that we rejected the educational system as the proper measure—generally ensuring that the legally imposed racially discriminatory program is remedial—we conclude that the University of Texas System is itself too expansive an entity to scrutinize for past discrimination. In order for any of these entities to direct a racial preference program at the law school, it must be because of past wrongs at that school.

Next, the relevant governmental discriminator must prove that there are present effects of past discrimination of the type that justify the racial classifications at issue. [A]s part of showing that the alleged present effects of past discrimination in fact justify the racial preference program at issue, the law school must show that it adopted the program specifically to remedy the identified present effects of the past discrimination. Here, according to the district court: ". . . those effects include the law school's lingering reputation in the minority community, particularly with prospective students, as a 'white' school; an underrepresentation of minorities in the student body; and some perception that the law school is a hostile environment for minorities." Plaintiffs now argue that these three alleged effects are at most examples of societal discrimination, which the Supreme Court has found not to be a valid remedial basis. As a legal matter, the district court erred in concluding that the first and third effects it identified—bad reputation and hostile environment—were sufficient to sustain the use of race in the admissions process.

There was simply no showing of action by the university that contributed to any racial tension. Similarly, one cannot conclude that the law school's *past* discrimination has created any *current* hostile environment for minorities. While the school once did practice *de jure* discrimination in denying admission to blacks, the Court in *Sweatt v. Painter* 339 U.S. 629 (1950), struck down the law school's program. Any other discrimination by the law school ended in the 1960s. By the late 1960s, the school had implemented its first program designed to recruit minorities, and it now engages in an extensive minority recruiting program that includes a significant amount of scholarship money. The vast majority of the faculty, staff, and students at the law school had absolutely nothing to do with any discrimination that the law school practiced in the past. Any racial tension at the law school is most certainly the result of present societal discrimination and, if anything, is contributed to, rather than alleviated by, the overt and prevalent consideration of race in admissions. Even if the law school's alleged current lingering reputation in the minority community—and the perception that the school is a hostile environment for minorities—were considered to be the present effects of past discrimination, rather than the result of societal discrimination, they could not constitute compelling state interests justifying the use of racial classifications in admissions.

In sum, the law school has failed to show a compelling state interest in remedying the present effects of past discrimination sufficient to maintain the use of race in its admissions system. Accordingly, it is unnecessary for us to examine the district court's determination that the law school's admissions program was not narrowly tailored to meet the compelling interests that the district court erroneously perceived. In summary, we hold that the University of Texas School of Law may not use race as a factor in deciding which applicants to admit in order to achieve a diverse student body, to combat the perceived effects of a hostile environment at the law school, to alleviate the law school's poor reputation in the minority community, or to eliminate any present effects of past discrimination by actors other than the law school.

The judgment is REVERSED and REMANDED for further proceedings in accordance with this opinion.

Judge Wiener, filed a specially concurring opinion.

As to present effects, I concur in the panel opinion's analysis. . . . As to diversity, however, I respectfully disagree . . . that diversity can never be a compelling government interest in a public graduate school. . . . I would assume arguendo that diversity can be a compelling interest but conclude that the admissions process here under scrutiny was not narrowly tailored to achieve diversity. ■

Because *Hopwood* questioned the holding in *Bakke,* and ultimately struck down the use of affirmative action in higher education in the three states governed by the Fifth Circuit—Texas, Louisiana, and Mississippi— the case received national attention and was immediately controversial, despite the fact that it was not a U.S. Supreme Court case. Controversy over the *Hopwood* decision continued and escalated when then–State Attorney General Dan Morales, a Mexican American, interpreted the court's ruling to require the elimination of race-based financial aid scholarships and outreach programs. Six years later, Morales lost his bid to become governor of Texas in the Democratic primary to Tony Sánchez, who made Morales' actions around the *Hopwood* decision an issue in the campaign.

Ultimately, the Fifth Circuit denied the University of Texas School of Law's request to rehear the case **en banc.** The U.S. Supreme Court also denied the ut School of Law's appeal on the grounds that the case was **moot** because during the course of the case, the law school had stopped the admissions practices originally challenged in the case and was now operating under a new admissions system. In December 2000, a different Fifth Circuit panel in *Hopwood III* found that none of the plaintiffs had a realistic chance of being offered admission to the ut School of Law even under a "race-blind system," ruled on attorneys' fees, and granted an **injunction** prohibiting the use of race in the ut School of Law admissions process.

Although the U.S. Supreme Court refused to hear the case on appeal, and although the case directly affected only the states in the Fifth Circuit, *Hopwood* began a firestorm of controversy and encouraged challenges against affirmative action all over the country. The challenges resulted in conflicting opinions in the lower federal courts. In a finding similar to that in *Hopwood,* the Eleventh Circuit Court of Appeals, for instance, declared the University of Georgia's affirmative action plan unconstitutional in *Johnson v. Board of Regents of University of Georgia* (2001),[7] because the Georgia plan was not narrowly tailored. In contrast, the U.S. Court of Appeals for the Ninth Circuit, in *Smith v. University of Washington Law School* (2000),[8] upheld the University of Washington's affirmative action program and ruled that *Bakke*'s holding that diversity is a compelling governmental interest for affirmative action in higher education is still binding precedent. Finally, the Sixth Circuit Court of Appeals in the previously mentioned *Grutter* case upheld the University of Michigan Law School's admissions program. This line of conflicting circuit court cases prompted the Supreme Court to agree to hear the *Grutter* and *Gratz* appeals from the University of Michigan and presumably settle this matter.

On June 23, 2003, the United States Supreme Court issued its rulings in the University of Michigan cases. In *Grutter,* the Court, in a 5-4 opinion, affirmed the Sixth Circuit's decision upholding the law school's affirmative action policy whereby race was one of several factors considered in the admissions process. The Court held that "student body diversity is a compelling state interest that can justify the use of race in university admissions," and "that the Law School has a compelling interest in attaining a diverse student body." Concurrently, in a 6-3 opinion in the *Gratz* case, the Court ruled that the affirmative action program utilized in the university's undergraduate admission process, whereby certain underrepresented racial and ethnic minority applicants received an automatic 20-point increase in the application process, was unconstitutional. The Court concluded that "because the University's use of race in its current freshman admissions policy is not narrowly tailored to achieve respondents' asserted compelling interest in diversity, the admissions policy violates the Equal Protection Clause of the Fourteenth Amendment." Through these decisions, the United States Supreme Court explicitly affirmed the principle that diversity in higher education does constitute a constitutionally protected compelling governmental interest, but continued to make clear that affirmative action policies must always be narrowly tailored, otherwise they will be ruled unconstitutional.

■ State Initiatives

Before the *Grutter* and *Gratz* cases, opponents to affirmative action garnered enough support to place propositions on the California and Washington state ballots that eliminated affirmative action in admissions policies for state universities, state contracting, and state employment policies. Both measures passed. California's Proposition 209 also placed limitations on race-based financial aid and scholarships. Proposition 209, which was passed by 54 percent of voters in 1996, was quickly challenged in the state and federal courts. Mexican American and other Latino civil rights organizations played very active roles in challenging Proposition 209. As the following opinion demonstrates, the U.S. Court of Appeals for the Ninth Circuit upheld the constitutionality of Proposition 209.

Coalition for Economic Equity v. Wilson

United States Court of Appeals for the Ninth Circuit
110 F.3d 1431 (1997)

O'Scannlain, Circuit Judge:

We must decide whether a provision of the California Constitution prohibiting public race and gender preferences violates the Equal Protection Clause of the United States Constitution.

On November 5, 1996, the people of the State of California adopted the California Civil Rights Initiative as an amendment to their Constitution. The initiative, which appeared on the ballot as Proposition 209, provides in relevant part that "[t]he state shall not discriminate against, or grant preferential treatment to, any individual or group on the basis of race, sex, color, ethnicity, or national origin in the operation of public employment, public education, or public contracting." The California Legislative Analyst's Office portrayed Proposition 209 to the voters as a measure that would eliminate public race-based and gender-based affirmative action programs. Proposition 209 passed by a margin of 54 to 46 percent; of nearly 9 million Californians casting ballots, 4,736,180 voted in favor of the initiative and 3,986,196 voted against it.

On the day after the election, November 6, 1996, several individuals and groups ("plaintiffs") claiming to represent the interests of racial minorities and women filed a complaint in the Northern District of California against several officials and political subdivisions of the State of California ("the State"). The complaint alleges that Proposition 209 denies racial minorities and women the equal protection of the laws guaranteed by the Fourteenth Amendment. As relief, plaintiffs seek a declaration that Proposition 209 is unconstitutional and a permanent injunction **enjoining** the State from implementing and enforcing it. With their complaint, plaintiffs filed an application for a temporary restraining order ("TRO") and a preliminary injunction. The district court entered a TRO on November 27, 1996, and granted a preliminary injunction on December 23, 1996. The preliminary injunction enjoins the State, pending trial or final judgment, "from implementing or enforcing Proposition 209 insofar as said amendment to the Constitution of the State of California purports to prohibit or affect affirmative action programs in public employment, public education or public contracting."

On February 10, 1997, we heard oral argument.

As a matter of "conventional" equal protection analysis, there is simply no doubt that Proposition 209 is constitutional. The Equal Protection Clause provides that "[n]o State shall . . . deny to any person within its jurisdiction the equal protection of the laws." The central purpose of the Equal Protection Clause "is the prevention of official conduct discriminating on the basis of race." The ultimate goal of the Equal Protection Clause is "to do away with all governmentally imposed discrimination based on race." Therefore, "whenever the government treats any person unequally because of his or her race, that person has suffered an injury that falls squarely within the language and spirit of the Constitution's guarantee of equal protection." *Adarand Constructors v. Peña* (1995).

Any governmental action that classifies persons by race is presumptively unconstitutional and subject to the most exacting judicial scrutiny. To be constitutional, a racial classification, regardless of its purported motivation, must be narrowly tailored to serve a compelling governmental interest, an extraordinary justification. Proposition 209 provides that the State of California shall not discriminate against, or grant preferential treatment to, any individual or group on the basis of race or gender. Rather than classifying individuals by race or gender, Proposition 209 *prohibits* the State from classifying individuals by race or gender. Proposition 209's ban on race and gender preferences, as a matter of law and logic, does not violate the Equal Protection Clause in any conventional sense.

Assuming all facts alleged in the complaint and found by the district court to be true, and drawing all reasonable inferences in plaintiffs' favor, we must conclude that, as a matter of law, Proposition 209 does not violate the United States Constitution. For the foregoing reasons, we **vacate** the preliminary injunction . . . and remand to [the] district court for further proceedings consistent with this opinion. Preliminary injunction VACATED; stay DENIED as moot; REMANDED. ■

■ Concluding Thoughts

The cases in this chapter illustrate the deep factions among judges about the legal permissibility of affirmative action programs and reflect the general underlying conflict within U.S. society about the value of affirmative action. As illustrated throughout this book, racial discrimination against Mexican Americans persists, and such discrimination does not distinguish between recent immigrants and the descendants of those who, in 1848, became the first Mexican Americans when the United States annexed their lands. Attempts by opponents of affirmative action to divide the Mexican American community should therefore be viewed with skepticism.

The U.S. Supreme Court's decisions in the University of Michigan affirmative action cases do not resolve the underlying policy disagreements. So long as Mexican Americans, other minorities, and women continue to be underrepresented in the major institutions of our society, and in particular in higher education, affirmative action programs are a necessary tool to attain a more equitable and just society.

■ Discussion Questions

1. Do you agree with Justice Powell's opinion in the *Bakke* case (referred to in the *Hopwood* case and relied upon in the *Grutter* case) that "diversity" remains a compelling justification for affirmative action today? Why or why not?

2. What do you think about using other factors, such as an applicant's status as the first family member to attend college, or the applicant's hometown and socioeconomic background, in deciding admission to postsecondary education? These factors may have some overlap with being Mexican American. Why would it be acceptable to consider these factors, but not whether the applicant self-identifies as Mexican American, in admissions decisions?

3. Following the *Hopwood* and *Wilson* decisions, some states—including Texas, Florida, and California—enacted policies that would automatically grant admission to the top 10 percent, 20 percent, and 4 percent, respectively, of students graduating from high school into any state university. Opponents claim that these efforts are a means to achieve racial diversity without using explicit race-based remedies. Proponents argue that this is an inadequate replacement for race-conscious affirmative action programs, and that these alternatives have

failed to restore the numbers of racial minorities, including Mexican Americans, being admitted to universities, particularly in professional schools. What is your opinion?

4. In the University of Michigan cases, the U.S. Supreme Court reviewed the constitutionality of admissions policies at both the undergraduate and law school levels. Should the constitutionality of such policies be dependent on the level of higher education, particularly since racial and ethnic minorities are more severely underrepresented at the postbaccalaureate level?

■ Suggested Readings

Acuña, R. *Sometimes There Is No Other Side: Chicanos and the Myth of Equality.* Notre Dame: University of Notre Dame Press, 1998.

Bowen, W. G., D. Bok, and G. C. Loury. *The Shape of the River.* Princeton: Princeton University Press, 2000.

Brest, P., and M. Oshige. "Affirmative Action for Whom?" *Stanford Law Review* 47 (1995): 855–900.

Delgado, R., and J. Stefancic. "California's Racial History and Constitutional Rationales for Race-Conscious Decision Making in Higher Education." *University of California at Los Angeles Law Review* 47 (2000): 1521–1614.

Morán, R. F. "Diversity and Its Discontents: The End of Affirmative Action at Boalt Hall." *California Law Review* 88 (2000):. 2241–2352.

Padilla, L. M. "Intersectionality and Positionality: Situating Women of Color in the Affirmative Action Dialogue." *Fordham Law Review* 66 (1997): 843–930.

Treviño, D. J. "The Currency of Reparations: Affirmative Action in College Admissions." *The Scholar: St. Mary's Law Review on Minority Issues* 4 (2002): 439–71.

■ Notes

1. M. I. Urofsky. *A Conflict of Rights: The Supreme Court and Affirmative Action* (New York: Charles Scribner's Sons, 1991): 17 (quoting President Johnson's speech at Howard University). Our brief summary of the history of affirmative action is derived from chapter 2 of Professor Urofsky's book.

2. 478 U.S. 421.

3. 480 U.S. 149.

4. 438 U.S. 265.

5. 2003 WL 21433492 (2003) and 2003 WL 21434002 (2003), respectively.

6. 515 U.S. 200.

7. 263 F.3d 1234.

8. 233 F.3d 1188.

The Criminal Justice System

The exclusion of otherwise eligible persons from jury service solely because of their ancestry or national origin is discrimination prohibited by
the Fourteenth Amendment.—*Hernández v. Texas* (1954)

Numerous studies continue to document that Mexican Americans
and other Latinos are disproportionately arrested, charged, and
jailed in comparison to their numbers in the overall population. For
example, while Latinos constituted approximately 11 percent of the total
U.S. population in 2000, they constituted a full 16 percent of the total
prison population. Moreover, Mexican Americans and other Latinos continue to receive harsher penalties, including longer sentences, for crimes in
comparison to non-Latino whites, particularly with respect to drug offenses. While the factors contributing to this disturbing overrepresentation
of Latinos in the criminal justice system are complex, some of the more
challenging of these issues include racial profiling, prosecutorial discretion,
the "war on drugs," mandatory sentencing, the death penalty, the dearth of
properly trained and qualified court interpreters, and the ever-persistent
problem of inadequate counsel.

As illustrated in chapter 1, Mexican Americans' problems in the American criminal justice system are not new. Rather, such problems have a long
and well-documented history. Indeed, in 1967 and 1968, the U.S. Commission on Civil Rights conducted a comprehensive study of the relationship
between the criminal justice system and residents in the southwestern
United States. Professors Leo Romero and Luis Stelzner summarize the
commission's findings as follows:

A bleak picture was painted of the relationship between Mexican-
Americans and Southwestern criminal justice systems. The commission
found that Mexican-Americans viewed criminal justice agencies with distrust, fear, and hostility; that they were being subjected to unduly harsh
treatment by police; that they were often arrested on insufficient grounds,
abused physically and verbally, and subjected to disproportionately severe

11. Cartoon satirizing the U.S. criminal justice system.

penalties; that they were being denied proper use of bail and adequate representation by counsel; and that they were substantially underrepresented on grand and petit juries. Mexican-Americans were underrepresented as employees in law enforcement agencies, especially in supervisory positions. The language barrier between Spanish-speaking citizens and English-speaking officials further aggravated the problem.[1]

Against this background, Mexican Americans, perhaps quite unintentionally, began to play an important role in the historical development of important constitutional rights within the framework of the U.S. criminal justice system (figure 11). Indeed, the Fourth Amendment right to be free from unreasonable searches and seizures discussed in chapter 5, the right to be apprised of one's constitutional rights during interrogation (**Fifth Amendment**), the right to counsel (Sixth Amendment), and the right to serve on juries (**Fourteenth Amendment**) were all secured or significantly advanced in large part because of Mexican Americans' involvement with and challenges to the criminal justice system. As with the voting rights issues discussed in chapter 6, Mexican Americans' contribution to the development of this body of law has been both direct and indirect. That is, in the cases and legal principles discussed in this chapter, Mexican Americans played a crucial role in securing and developing legal rights for all Americans, not specifically Mexican Americans.

Moreover, although the numbers of Mexican American lawyers, judges, and elected officials have grown dramatically since many of these cases were litigated, Mexican Americans remain severely underrepresented in all these areas. As of 2001, for instance, the State Bar of Texas had a membership in excess of 67,500 lawyers. Of this number, only approximately 3,400, or 6 percent, were Latino—in a state in which Latinos (overwhelmingly Mexican American) constituted more than 30 percent of the total population.[2] This underrepresentation of Latino attorneys exists throughout the southwestern United States and in all other states with high concentrations of Latinos. In 2001, for instance, only 3.5 percent and 3.7 percent of all lawyers in Arizona and California, respectively, were Latino. The state with the highest percentage of Latino lawyers was New Mexico at 17 percent. Yet, given that Latinos constitute more than 40 percent of the total population of New Mexico, they remain severely underrepresented in the legal profession in that state as well.

■ Fourteenth Amendment Equal Protection and Jury Exclusion

As discussed in chapter 1, the first case involving Mexican Americans ever to reach the U.S. Supreme Court, *Hernández v. Texas* (1954), centered on criminal justice issues. In this landmark case, the Mexican American defendant challenged his state court conviction for murder on the basis that Mexican Americans had been unconstitutionally excluded from jury service in violation of the **Equal Protection Clause** of the Fourteenth Amendment. In short, Hernández argued that without Mexican Americans on his jury, he was denied his constitutional right to be judged by a jury of his peers. Interestingly, *Hernández* was handed down on May 3, 1954, only two weeks before the monumental *Brown v. Board of Education* **decision** discussed in chapter 2. Like *Brown,* the *Hernández* **opinion** was unanimous and authored by Chief Justice Earl Warren. As evidenced in this chapter, the Warren Court of the 1960s was much more liberal than subsequent Supreme Courts. Finally, it bears repeating here that *Hernández* was also historic as the first time that Mexican American lawyers (Carlos Cadena and Gus García) argued a case before the U.S. Supreme Court.

Hernández v. Texas

United States Supreme Court
347 U.S. 475 (1954)

Mr. Chief Justice Warren delivered the opinion of the Court.

The petitioner, Pete Hernández, was indicted for the murder of one Joe Espinosa by a grand jury in Jackson County, Texas. He was convicted and sentenced to life imprisonment. The Texas Court of Criminal Appeals affirmed the judgment of the trial court. Prior to the trial, the petitioner, by his counsel, offered timely motions to quash the indictment and the jury panel. He alleged that persons of Mexican descent were systematically excluded from service as jury commissioners, grand jurors, and petit jurors, although there were such persons fully qualified to serve residing in Jackson County. The petitioner asserted that exclusion of this class deprived him, as a member of the class, of the equal protection of the laws guaranteed by the Fourteenth Amendment of the **Constitution.** After a hearing, the trial court denied the motions.

[Note: The portions of the Court's opinion wherein the Court rejected the State of Texas' assertion that the Fourteenth Amendment's protections applied only to "whites" and "Negroes," not to Mexican Americans, is contained in the chapter 1 treatment of this case.]

The exclusion of otherwise eligible persons from jury service solely because of their ancestry or **national origin** is discrimination prohibited by the Fourteenth Amendment. The Texas **statute** makes no such discrimination, but the petitioner alleges that those administering the law do.

The State of Texas stipulated that 'for the last twenty-five years there is no record of any person with a Mexican or Latin American name having served on a jury commission, grand jury or petit jury in Jackson County.' The parties also stipulated that 'there are some male persons of Mexican or Latin American descent in Jackson County who, by virtue of being citizens, freeholders, and having all other legal prerequisites to jury service, are eligible to serve as members of a jury commission, grand jury and/or petit jury.'

> Circumstances or chance may well dictate that no persons in a certain class will serve on a particular jury or during some particular period. But it taxes our credulity to say that mere chance resulted in there being no members of this class among the over six thousand jurors called in the past 25 years. The result bespeaks discrimination, whether or not it was a conscious decision on the part of any individual jury commissioner. The judgment of conviction must be reversed.
>
> Reversed. ■

A more recent case involving Latinos' selection for jury service is *Hernández v. New York,* a 1991 U.S. Supreme Court decision involving the exclusion of Spanish-speaking jurors from a New York state court jury. As discussed in chapter 4, the issue of Spanish language ability has oftentimes presented Mexican American and other Latinos with unexpected and unanticipated legal ramifications. In *Hernández,* a six-to-three decision, the defendant, Dionisio Hernández, a Puerto Rican, alleged that the prosecutor exercised his **peremptory challenges,** which unlike **challenges for cause** require no justification, "to exclude Latinos from the jury by reason of their ethnicity." Under relevant governing law, the prosecutor in the case had to provide a "race-neutral" reason for dismissing the jurors. The prosecution in the case argued that exclusion of the Latino jurors in question was race neutral because the jurors in question were excluded not by reason of their race but because of their ability to speak Spanish, as well as the concern that the jurors would not be able to adhere to the official court interpreter's version of the court proceedings. The court held that the prosecutor's actions were race neutral and did not violate the Fourteenth Amendment.

Hernández v. New York

United States Supreme Court
500 U.S. 352 (1991)

Mr. Justice Kennedy announced the judgment of the Court.

Petitioner argues that Spanish-language ability bears a close relation to ethnicity, and that, as a consequence, it violates the Equal Protection Clause to exercise a peremptory challenge on the ground that a Latino potential juror speaks Spanish. He points to the high correlation between Spanish-language ability and ethnicity in New York, where the case was tried. We need not address that argument here, for the prosecutor did not rely on language ability without more, but explained that the specific responses and the demeanor of the two individuals during [jury selection] caused him to doubt their ability to defer to the official translation of Spanish-language testimony.

The prosecutor here offered a race-neutral basis for these peremptory strikes. As explained by the prosecutor, the challenges rested neither on the intention to exclude Latino or bilingual jurors, nor on stereotypical assumptions about Latinos or bilinguals. The prosecutor's articulated basis for these challenges divided potential jurors into two classes: those whose conduct during [jury selection] would persuade him they might have difficulty in accepting the translator's rendition of Spanish-language testimony and those potential jurors who gave no such reason for doubt. Each category would include both Latinos and non-Latinos. While the prosecutor's criterion might well result in the disproportionate removal of prospective Latino jurors, that disproportionate impact does not turn the prosecutor's actions into a *per se* violation of the Equal Protection Clause.

We would face a quite different case if the prosecutor had justified his peremptory challenges with the explanation that he did not want Spanish-speaking jurors. It may well be, for certain ethnic groups and in some communities, that proficiency in a particular language, like skin color, should be treated as a surrogate for race under an equal protection analysis. And, as we make clear, a policy of striking all who speak a given language, without regard to the particular circumstances of the trial or the individual responses of the jurors, may be found by the trial judge to be a pretext for racial discrimination. But that case is not before us.

The state courts came to the proper conclusion that the prosecutor offered a race-neutral basis for his exercise of peremptory challenges. The trial court did not commit clear error in choosing to believe the reasons given by the prosecutor.

Affirmed. ■

Voluntary Confessions and the Fifth Amendment Right against Self-Incrimination

Perhaps the best-known rights in the American system of criminal justice are the "Miranda rights," or "Miranda warnings," which stem from the Fifth Amendment guarantee that no person shall "be compelled in any criminal case to be a witness against himself." American popular culture is replete with references to the Miranda warnings, which must be provided to criminal suspects before interrogation. What is not as well known are the facts and contextual underpinnings of this legal decision, or the fact that the decision in *Miranda v. Arizona* (1966) was an extremely close five-to-four vote. Before the *Miranda* decision, it was not unusual for the nation's courts to hear defendants' challenges to arrests and confessions on the basis of alleged psychological and physical coercion by law enforcement officers, and in too many instances such allegations were often fully substantiated. After *Miranda,* however, if the arresting officer can document that the warnings were provided, the likelihood of a defendant successfully challenging his or her arrest or confession is markedly decreased. Furthermore, both court decisions and practical application subsequent to *Miranda* have made it clear that the warnings must be given in a manner understandable to the suspects taken into custody, including presentation in a language other than English when applicable.

Miranda v. Arizona

United States Supreme Court
384 U.S. 436 (1966)

Mr. Chief Justice Warren delivered the opinion of the Court.

On March 13, 1963, petitioner, Ernesto Miranda, was arrested at his home and taken in custody to a Phoenix police station. He was there identified by the complaining witness. The police then took him to "Interrogation Room No. 2" of the detective bureau. There he was questioned by two police officers. The officers admitted at trial that Miranda was not advised that he had a right to have an attorney present. Two hours later, the officers emerged from the interrogation room with a written confession signed by Miranda. At the top of the statement was a typed paragraph stating that the confession was made voluntarily, without threats or promises of immunity and 'with full knowledge of my legal rights, understanding any statement I make may be used against me.'

We have concluded that without proper safeguards the process of in-custody interrogation of persons suspected or accused of crime contains inherently compelling pressures which work to undermine the individual's will to resist and to compel him to speak where he would not otherwise do so freely. In order to combat these pressures and to permit a full opportunity to exercise the privilege against self-incrimination, the accused must be adequately and effectively apprised of his rights and the exercise of those rights must be fully honored.

At the outset, if a person in custody is to be subjected to interrogation, he must first be informed in clear and unequivocal terms that he has the right to remain silent. For those unaware of the privilege, the warning is needed simply to make them aware of it—the threshold requirement for an intelligent decision as to its exercise. More important, such a warning is an absolute prerequisite in overcoming the inherent pressures of the interrogation atmosphere. It is not just the subnormal or woefully ignorant who succumb to an interrogator's imprecations, whether implied or expressly stated, that the interrogation will continue until a confession is obtained or that silence in the face of accusation is itself damning and will bode ill when presented to a jury. Further, the warning will show the individual that his interrogators are prepared to recognize his privilege should he choose to exercise it.

The warning of the right to remain silent must be accompanied by the explanation that anything said can and will be used against the individual in court. This warning is needed in order to make him aware not only of the privilege, but also of the consequences of forgoing it. It is only through an awareness of these consequences that there can be any assurance of real understanding and intelligent exercise of the privilege. Moreover, this warning may serve to make the individual more acutely aware that he is faced with a phase of the adversary system—that he is not in the presence of persons acting solely in his interest.

The circumstances surrounding in-custody interrogation can operate very quickly to overbear the will of one merely made aware of his privilege by his interrogators. Therefore, the right to have counsel present at the interrogation is indispensable to the protection of the Fifth Amendment privilege under the system we delineate today. Our aim is to assure that the individual's right to choose between silence and speech remains unfettered throughout the interrogation process.

Accordingly we hold that an individual held for interrogation must be clearly informed that he has the right to consult with a lawyer and to have the lawyer with him during interrogation under the system for protecting the privilege we delineate today. As with the warnings of the right to remain silent and that anything stated can be used in evidence against him, this warning is an absolute prerequisite to interrogation.

If an individual indicates that he wishes the assistance of counsel before any interrogation occurs, the authorities cannot rationally ignore or deny his request on the basis that the individual does not have or cannot afford a retained attorney. The financial ability of the individual has no relationship to the scope of the rights involved here. In fact, were we to limit these constitutional rights to those who can retain an attorney, our decisions today would be of little significance.

In order fully to apprise a person interrogated of the extent of his rights under this system then, it is necessary to warn him not only that he has the right to consult with an attorney, but also that if he is indigent a lawyer will be appointed to represent him. Without this additional warning, the admonition of the right to consult with counsel would often be understood as meaning only that he can consult with a lawyer if he has one or has the funds to obtain one. The warning of a right to counsel would be hollow if not couched in terms that would convey to the indigent—the person most often subjected to interrogation—the knowledge that he too has a right to have counsel present.

Once warnings have been given, the subsequent procedure is clear. If the individual indicates in any manner, at any time prior to or during questioning, that he wishes to remain silent, the interrogation must cease. If the individual states that he wants an attorney, the interrogation must cease until an attorney is present. At that time, the individual must have an opportunity to confer with the attorney and to have him present during any subsequent questioning. If the individual cannot obtain an attorney and he indicates that he wants one before speaking to police, they must respect his decision to remain silent.

Under the system of warnings we delineate today or under any other system which may be devised and found effective, the safeguards to be erected about the privilege must come into play. Our decision is not intended to hamper the traditional function of police officers in investigating crime.

To summarize, we hold that when an individual is taken into custody or otherwise deprived of his freedom by the authorities in any significant way and is subjected to questioning, the privilege against self-incrimination is jeopardized. Procedural safeguards must be employed to protect the privilege and unless other fully effective means are adopted to notify the person of his right of silence and to assure that the exercise of the right will be scrupulously honored, the following measures are required. He must be warned prior to any questioning that he has the right to remain silent, that anything he says can be used against him in a court of law, that he has the right to the presence of an attorney, and that if he cannot afford an attorney one will be appointed for him prior to any questioning if he so desires. Opportunity to exercise these rights must be afforded to him throughout the interrogation. After such warnings have been given, and such opportunity afforded him, the individual may knowingly and intelligently waive these rights and agree to answer questions or make a statement. But unless and until such warnings and waiver are demonstrated by the prosecution at trial, no evidence obtained as a result of interrogation can be used against him.

At his trial before a jury, the written confession was admitted into evidence over the objection of defense counsel, and the officers testified to the prior oral confession made by Miranda during the interrogation. Miranda was found guilty of kidnapping and rape. He was sentenced to 20 to 30 years' imprisonment on each count, the sentences to run concurrently. On appeal, the Supreme Court of Arizona held that Miranda's constitutional rights were not violated in obtaining the confession and affirmed the conviction. In reaching its decision, the court emphasized heavily the fact that Miranda did not specifically request counsel.

From the testimony of the officers and by the admission of respondent, it is clear that Miranda was not in any way apprised of his right to consult with an attorney and to have one present during the interrogation, nor was his right not to be compelled to incriminate himself effectively protected in any other manner. Without these warnings the statements were inadmissible. The mere fact that he signed a statement which contained a typed-in clause stating that he had 'full knowledge' of his 'legal rights' does not approach the knowing and intelligent waiver required to relinquish constitutional rights.

We reverse.

Mr. Justice Harlan, with whom Mr. Justice Stewart and Mr. Justice White join, dissenting.

I believe the decision of the Court represents poor constitutional law and entails harmful consequences for the country at large. How serious these consequences may prove to be only time can tell. There can be little doubt that the Court's new code would markedly decrease the number of confessions. To warn the suspect that he may remain silent and remind him that his confession may be used in court are minor obstructions. To require also an express waiver by the suspect and an end to questioning whenever he demurs must heavily handicap questioning. And to suggest or provide counsel for the suspect simply invites the end of the interrogation. How much harm this decision will inflict on law enforcement cannot fairly be predicted with accuracy.

On March 3, 1963, an 18-year-old girl was kidnapped and forcibly raped near Phoenix, Arizona. Ten days later, on the morning of March 13, petitioner Miranda was arrested and taken to the police station. At this time Miranda was 23 years old, indigent, and educated to the extent of completing half the ninth grade. He had 'an emotional illness' of the schizophrenic type, according to the doctor who eventually examined him; the doctor's report also stated that Miranda was 'alert and oriented as to time, place, and person,' intelligent within normal limits, competent to stand trial, and sane within the legal definition. At the police station, the victim picked Miranda out of a lineup, and two officers then took him into a separate room to interrogate him, starting about 11:30 a.m. Though at first denying his guilt, within a short time Miranda gave a detailed oral confession and then wrote out in his own hand and signed a brief statement admitting and describing the crime. All this was accomplished in two hours or less without any force, threats or promises and— I will assume this though the record is uncertain—without any effective warnings at all.

Mr. Justice White, with whom Mr. Justice Harlan and Mr. Justice Stewart join, dissenting.

The rule announced today will measurably weaken the ability of the criminal law. It is a deliberate calculus to prevent interrogations, to reduce the incidence of confessions and pleas of guilty and to increase the number of trials. I have no desire whatsoever to share the responsibility for any such impact on the present criminal process. In some unknown number of cases the Court's rule will return a killer, a rapist or other criminal to the streets and to the environment which produced him, to repeat his crime whenever it pleases him. ■

■ Sixth Amendment Right to Legal Counsel

As discussed in *Miranda,* one of the most significant rights criminal suspects have is the Sixth Amendment right to counsel. Indeed, two of the four required Miranda warnings—notification of the right to counsel and notification of the right to have counsel provided at no cost if one is indigent—are derived directly from this important Sixth Amendment guarantee. In requiring these two warnings, the Supreme Court in *Miranda* relied on and built upon its holding in an extremely significant predecessor case, *Escobedo v. Illinois* (1964), which helped set the stage for *Miranda*. Like *Miranda*, *Escobedo* also involved a criminal defendant described as "of Mexican extraction," and was decided by a very close five-to-four majority. Rather than the Fifth Amendment right against self-incrimination at issue in *Miranda*, *Escobedo* involved a criminal defendant's Sixth Amendment right to counsel.

Escobedo v. Illinois

United States Supreme Court
378 U.S. 478 (1964)

Mr. Justice Goldberg delivered the opinion of the Court.

The critical question in this case is whether, under the circumstances, the refusal by the police to honor petitioner's request to consult with his lawyer during the course of an interrogation constitutes a denial of "the Assistance of Counsel" in violation of the Sixth Amendment to the Constitution as 'made obligatory upon the States by the Fourteenth Amendment,' and thereby renders inadmissible in a state criminal trial any incriminating statement elicited by the police during the interrogation.

On the night of January 19, 1960, petitioner's brother-in-law was fatally shot. In the early hours of the next morning, at 2:30 a.m., petitioner was arrested without a warrant and interrogated. Petitioner made no statement to the police and was released at 5 that afternoon pursuant to a state court writ of habeas corpus obtained by Mr. Warren Wolfson, a lawyer who had been retained by petitioner.

On January 30, Benedict DiGerlando, who was then in police custody and who was later indicted for the murder along with petitioner, told the police that petitioner had fired the fatal shots. Between 8 and 9 that evening, petitioner and his sister, the widow of the deceased, were arrested and taken to police headquarters. En route to the police station, the police "had handcuffed the defendant behind his back," and "one of the arresting officers told defendant that DiGerlando had named him as the one who shot" the deceased. Petitioner testified, without contradiction, that the "detective said they had us pretty well, up pretty tight, and we might as well admit to this crime," and that he replied, "I am sorry but I would like to have advice from my lawyer." A police officer testified that although petitioner was not formally charged, "he was in custody" and "couldn't walk out the door." Shortly after petitioner reached police headquarters, his retained lawyer arrived. The lawyer described the ensuing events in the following terms: "On that day I received a phone call (from 'the mother of another defendant') and pursuant to that phone call I went to the Detective Bureau at 11th and State. The first person I talked to was the Sergeant on duty at the Bureau Desk, Sergeant Pidgeon. I asked Sergeant Pidgeon for permission to speak to my client, Danny Escobedo. Sergeant Pidgeon made a call to the Bureau lockup and informed me that the boy had been taken from the lockup to the Homicide Bureau. This was between 9:30 and 10:00 in the evening. Before I went anywhere, he called the Homicide Bureau and told them there was an attorney waiting to see Escobedo. He told me I could not see him. Then I went upstairs to the Homicide Bureau. There were several Homicide Detectives around and I talked to them. I identified myself as Escobedo's attorney and asked permission to see him. They said I could not. The police officer told me to see Chief Flynn who was on duty. I identified myself to Chief Flynn and asked permission to see my client. He said I could not. I think it was approximately 11:00 o'clock. He said I couldn't see him because they hadn't completed questioning. (F)or a second or two I spotted him in an office in the Homicide Bureau. The door was open and I could see through the office. I waved to him and he waved back and then the door was closed, by one of the officers at Homicide. There were four or five officers milling around the Homicide Detail that night. As to whether I talked to Captain Flynn any later that day, I waited around for another hour or two and went back again and renewed by (sic) request to see my client. He again told me I could not. I filed an official complaint with Commissioner Phelan of the Chicago Police Department. I had a conversation with every police officer I could find. I was told at Homicide that I couldn't see him and I would have to get a writ of habeas corpus. I left the Homicide Bureau and from the Detective Bureau at 11th and State at approximately 1:00 A.M. (Sunday morning) I had no opportunity to talk to my client that night. I quoted to Captain Flynn the Section of the Criminal Code which allows an attorney the right to see his client."

Petitioner testified that during the course of the interrogation he repeatedly asked to speak to his lawyer and that the police said that his lawyer "didn't want to see" him. The testimony of the police officers confirmed these accounts in substantial detail.

Notwithstanding repeated requests by each, petitioner and his retained lawyer were afforded no opportunity to consult during the course of the entire interrogation. At one point, as previously noted, petitioner and his attorney came into each other's view for a few moments but the attorney was quickly ushered away. Petitioner testified "that he heard a detective telling the attorney the latter would not be allowed to talk to (him) 'until they were done'" and that he heard the attorney being refused permission to remain in the adjoining room. A police officer testified that he had told the lawyer that he could not see petitioner until "we were through interrogating" him.

There is testimony by the police that during the interrogation, petitioner, a 22-year-old of Mexican extraction with no record of previous experience with the police, "was handcuffed" in a standing position and that he "was nervous, he had circles under his eyes and he was upset" and was "agitated" because "he had not slept well in over a week."

It is undisputed that during the course of the interrogation Officer Montejano, who "grew up" in petitioner's neighborhood, who knew his family, and who uses "Spanish language in (his) police work," conferred alone with petitioner "for about a quarter of an hour." Petitioner testified that the officer said to him "in Spanish that my sister and I could go home if I pinned it on Benedict DiGerlando," that "he would see to it that we would go home and be held only as witnesses, if anything, if we had made a statement against DiGerlando, that we would be able to go home that night." Petitioner testified that he made the statement in issue because of this assurance. Officer Montejano denied offering any such assurance.

Petitioner moved both before and during trial to suppress the incriminating statement, but the motions were denied. Petitioner was convicted of murder and he appealed the conviction.

The Supreme Court of Illinois, in its original opinion of February 1, 1963, held the statement inadmissible and reversed the conviction. The State petitioned for, and the court granted, rehearing. The court then affirmed the conviction. We granted a writ of certiorari to consider whether the petitioner's statement was constitutionally admissible at his trial. We conclude, for the reasons stated below, that it was not and, accordingly, we reverse the judgment of conviction.

The interrogation here was conducted before petitioner was formally indicted. But in the context of this case, that fact should make no difference. When petitioner requested, and was denied, an opportunity to consult with his lawyer, the investigation had ceased to be a general investigation of 'an unsolved crime.' Petitioner had become the accused, and the purpose of the interrogation was to 'get him' to confess his guilt despite his constitutional right not to do so. At the time of his arrest and throughout the course of the interrogation, the police told petitioner that they had convincing evidence that he had fired the fatal shots. Without informing him of his absolute right to remain silent in the face of this accusation, the police urged him to make a statement.

Petitioner, a layman, was undoubtedly unaware that under Illinois law an admission of 'mere' complicity in the murder plot was legally as damaging as an admission of firing of the fatal shots. The 'guiding hand of counsel' was essential to advise petitioner of his rights in this delicate situation. This was the 'stage when legal aid and advice' were most critical to petitioner. What happened at this interrogation could certainly 'affect the whole trial,' since rights 'may be as irretrievably lost, if not then and there asserted.'

We hold, therefore, that where, as here, the investigation is no longer a general inquiry into an unsolved crime but has begun to focus on a particular suspect, the suspect has been taken into police custody, the police carry out a process of interrogations that lends itself to eliciting incriminating statements, the suspect has requested and been denied an opportunity to consult with his lawyer, and the police have not effectively warned him of his absolute constitutional right to remain silent, the accused has been denied 'The Assistance of Counsel' in violation of the Sixth Amendment to the Constitution as 'made obligatory upon the

States by the Fourteenth Amendment,' and that no statement elicited by the police during the interrogation may be used against him at a criminal trial.

We hold only that when the process shifts from investigatory to accusatory—when its focus is on the accused and its purpose is to elicit a confession—our adversary system begins to operate, and, under the circumstances here, the accused must be permitted to consult with his lawyer.

The judgment of the Illinois Supreme Court is reversed and the case **remanded** for proceedings not inconsistent with this opinion.

Reversed and remanded.

Mr. Justice Harlan, dissenting.

I think the rule announced today is most ill-conceived and that it seriously and unjustifiably fetters perfectly legitimate methods of criminal law enforcement.

Mr. Justice White, with whom Mr. Justice Clark and Mr. Justice Stewart join, dissenting.

I do not suggest for a moment that law enforcement will be destroyed by the rule announced today. The need for peace and order is too insistent for that. But it will be crippled and its task made a great deal more difficult, all in my opinion, for unsound, unstated reasons, which can find no home in any of the provisions of the Constitution. ■

■ Concluding Thoughts

Throughout history, the American system of criminal justice has presented Mexican Americans and other Latinos with definite and difficult challenges. Viewed in this light, many contemporary challenges facing Mexican Americans and the criminal justice system are simply new variants of the same historically difficult and troublesome issues. Thus, the war on drugs, racial profiling, police brutality, **hate crimes,** death penalty disparities, inadequate or unavailable court interpreters, and inadequate assistance of counsel are all merely new catch phrases for the perplexing problems that have always challenged this community. Indeed, as recently as its spring 2003 term, the U.S. Supreme Court heard a challenge to the alleged "formal policy" of the Dallas County District Attorney's office of excluding racial and ethnic minorities from jury service. The defendant in *Miller-El v. Cockrell*, 2003 WL 431659 (2003), who was convicted of murder and sentenced to death by the trial court, alleged that potential African American jurors had been illegally and systematically excluded by the prosecutors at his trial. As evidence of this, the defendant offered a "1963 circular by the District Attorney's Office [which] instructed its prosecutors to exercise peremptory strikes against minorities." The language of the circular specifically stated, "Do not take Jews, Negroes, Dagos, Mexicans, or a member of any minority race on a jury, no matter how rich or how well educated." The defendant asserted that this circular and other similar practices and policies continued to be in effect at the time of his murder trial in 1986, and the Supreme Court remanded the case for further consideration of these issues.

Given the complex interaction between historical discrimination against Mexican Americans and this community's contemporary linguistic, cultural, and class differences, such challenges in the criminal justice system will in all likelihood continue and, in fact, increase in both number and magnitude. Unless and until the United States becomes more sensitive to the differences and needs of Mexican Americans, true change cannot be expected or realized with respect to the area of criminal justice.

■ Discussion Questions

1. In *Hernández v. New York,* the Supreme Court noted, "It may well be, for certain ethnic groups and in some communities, that proficiency in a particular language, like skin color, should be treated as a surrogate for race" for purposes of certain types of discrimination claims. Do you agree? Why or why not?

2. The Court in *Hernández v. New York* further noted that "a policy of striking all who speak a given language, without regard to the particular circumstances of the trial or the individual responses of the jurors, may be found by the trial judge to be a pretext for racial discrimination. But that is not the case before us." If dismissing jurors on the basis of language ability is not a pretext for racial discrimination, can you think of circumstances that might satisfy the Court's test?

3. What, if anything, should be done when a Mexican American suspect is given the Miranda warnings in English but would understand them better and more thoroughly in Spanish?

4. In *Miranda v. Arizona*, do the facts provided about defendant Ernesto Miranda's past criminal history, psychological challenges, and limited educational background convince you that such defendants are more deserving of protection from the American criminal justice system, or do these factors make no difference?

5. Officer Montejano, who spoke Spanish and was from Escobedo's neighborhood, played a key role in *Escobedo v. Illinois*. Do you believe the presence of Mexican American or Latino law enforcement officers changes the dynamics of the arrest of a Mexican American suspect?

6. Although the landmark *Escobedo* and *Miranda* decisions are now more than forty years old, Mexican Americans continue to be overrepresented in the criminal justice system. Why do you suppose this continues to be true? Do you believe that it is appropriate to highlight or celebrate the significant contributions of Mexican Americans such as Ernesto Miranda and Danny Escobedo to the positive development of the rights of criminal defendants?

■ Suggested Readings

Escobar, E. J. *Race, Police, and the Making of Political Identity: Mexican Americans and the Los Angeles Police Department, 1900–1945*. Berkeley: University of California Press, 1999.

García, R. "Latinos and the Criminal Justice System." *Chicano-Latino Law Review* 14 (1994): 6–19.

Lopez, A. S., ed. "Criminal Justice and Latino Communities." In *Latinos in the United States: History, Law, and Perspective*, vol. 3. New York: Garland Publishing, 1995.

Mendez, M. A., and Martinez, L. P. "Toward a Statistical Profile of Latina/os in the Legal Profession." *Berkeley La Raza Law Journal* 13 (2002): 59–86.

Mirendé, A. *Gringo Justice*. Notre Dame: University of Notre Dame Press, [1987] 1990.

Romero, M. "State Violence, and the Social and Legal Construction of Latino Criminality: From El Bandido to Gang Member." *Denver University Law Review* 78 (2001): 1081–1118.

Valencia, R. A. "Latinos and the Criminal Justice System: An Overview of the Invisible/Visible Minority." *Harvard Latino Law Review* 1 (1994): 27–120.

Villareal, F. A. et al. *Donde Está la Justicia?: A Call to Action on Behalf of Latino and Latina Youth in the U.S. Justice System.* East Lansing: Michigan State University, Institute for Children, Youth and Families, 2002.

■ Notes

1. L. Romero and L. Stelzner, "Hispanics and the Criminal Justice System," in *Hispanics in the United States,* ed. P. San Juan Cafferty, and W. C. McCready (Somerset: Transaction Publishers, 1985), 218 (commenting on the U.S. Commission on Civil Rights 1967–1968 study of discrimination by court agencies and police in Arizona, California, Colorado, New Mexico, and Texas).

2. C. L. Cannon and K. J. Priestner, *Annual Report on the Status of Racial/Ethnic Minorities in the State Bar of Texas 2000–01* (Austin: State Bar of Texas Department of Research & Analysis, June 2001).

■ GLOSSARY

The legal definitions and terms in this glossary were constructed largely by consulting some of the more popular legal dictionaries, including J. S. Lynton, *Ballentine's Legal Dictionary/Thesaurus* (Independence, Ky.: Delmar Learning, 1995); B. A. Garner, ed., *Black's Law Dictionary,* 6th ed. (St. Paul, Minn.: West Group, 1990); and S. Gifis, *Law Dictionary,* 4th ed. (Hauppauge, N.Y., 1996).

affirmative action: Any program adopted by an employer, governmental entity, or private or public educational institution to increase the representation of minorities, women, and other historically underrepresented groups. While civil rights statutes prohibit discrimination, the enactment of such statutes does not automatically increase the representation of previously excluded groups. In contrast, an affirmative action program requires the entity to take *affirmative* steps to increase the representation of previously excluded groups. Affirmative action programs may include relatively uncontroversial efforts, such as increased outreach to and recruitment of previously underrepresented groups. A more controversial process is to set goals with timetables for increasing the representation of previously underrepresented groups; for example, seeking to enroll a student body that is 10 percent Mexican American within two years. Quotas, which require the entity to hire, award contracts to, or admit fixed numbers of minorities and women, have been found unconstitutional by the U.S. Supreme Court.

all-white primaries: Restrictions in many southern states prior to the 1960s allowing only white voters to vote in Democratic primary elections. After the Civil War, white voters in the southern states overwhelmingly voted for Democratic Party candidates. The Democratic primaries in these states became the only truly contested elections: Whoever won the Democratic primary ordinarily won the general election automatically. Many southern states attempted to justify all-white primaries on the basis that the Democratic Party was a private organization and therefore not subject to the nondiscrimination requirements of the Fourteenth and Fifteenth Amendments to the U.S. Constitution. The U.S. Supreme Court rejected this argument and invalidated the practice in *Smith v. Allwright,* 321 U.S. 649 (1944).

American GI Forum: As millions of World War II veterans returned home, many sought assistance under the GI Bill of Rights, which guaranteed educational, medical, housing, and other basic benefits. But these benefits were largely denied to Mexican American and other Latino veterans throughout the United States. This aroused a young army major veteran, Dr. Hector P. García, from Corpus Christi, Texas, to rally his former comrades in arms in 1948. Thus was born the American GI Forum, dedicated to addressing problems of discrimination and inequities endured by Mexican American veterans. For more information about the forum, refer to the websites listings.

Anti–Vietnam War Movement: A wave of protests and actions by individuals who opposed U.S. involvement in the Vietnam War. As the war expanded during the 1960s, increasing numbers of Mexican Americans were drafted and sent to fight on the front lines. College students were exempt from the draft, but since Mexican Americans rarely attended college, few qualified for this exemption. As a result, Mexican Americans and other minorities were overrepresented among Vietnam War casualties. Chicano Movement activists protested against the Vietnam War, including calling for a moratorium on the draft and the war. For these activists, the war was another facet of the continuing discrimination against Chicanos (*see also* Chicano Movement).

at-large election system: A system under which elected officials are chosen by the voters of a jurisdiction as a whole rather than from separate districts within the jurisdiction (*see also* multimember districts, single-member districts).

benign racial discrimination: A temporary difference in treatment among various groups of people intended to benefit racial and ethnic minorities as a compensatory measure for past discrimination.

bias crime or **hate crime:** An offense where the person acted, at least in part, with ill will, bias, or hatred toward, and with a purpose to intimidate, an individual or group because of race, color, ethnicity, religion, or sexual orientation. The perpetrator of offenses such as harassment, assault, intimidation, or criminal mischief may have an enhanced sentence imposed if the act is proved to have been a bias crime.

business necessity: Describes a practice that is necessary in order to operate a business and that has no less discriminatory alternative. When an employment or educational practice is challenged under the disparate impact standard, the plaintiff is required to prove that the challenged practice has a discriminatory effect on some protected group (such as Mexican Americans). Once that discriminatory effect is shown, the defendant in the lawsuit will be ordered to stop the practice unless business necessity is shown. For example, an employer cannot require job applicants to pass a written test if the test has a discriminatory effect on Mexican Americans and the test is not necessary for the operation of the employer's business. If, however, the employer can show that the employee must read and write English in order to conduct his or her job, the test may be upheld as a business necessity (*see also* disparate impact).

challenge for cause: A request from a party in a criminal proceeding that the judge not allow a prospective juror to be a member of the jury for specified reasons or causes. There is no set number of such challenges allowed when selecting a jury (*see also* peremptory challenge).

Chicano Movement: A political movement prominent during the 1960s and early 1970s, in which large numbers of Mexican Americans demanded equal treatment with other U.S. citizens. Inspired by the Civil Rights Movement, the Chicano Movement relied on many similar tactics, such as protests, demonstrations, boycotts, and walkouts.

Civil Rights Act of 1964: A federal statute intended to implement and give further force to basic personal rights guaranteed by the Constitution. This act prohibits any public or private agency from actions that discriminate on the basis of race, color, national origin, religion, or age.

Civil Rights Movement: A political movement spearheaded by African Americans to secure racial equality in the United States. The Civil Rights Movement enjoyed its highest public profile during the late 1950s and 1960s. While movement supporters sought assistance from the courts in their fight for equality, they also mounted political pressure through protests, demonstrations, boycotts, walkouts, and other tactics.

class action: A lawsuit brought by a representative member or members of a large group of individuals on behalf of all the members of the group; see, e.g., the discussions of *Pérez v. Federal Bureau of Investigation* in chapter 1.

common law: The legal system used in forty-nine of the fifty states of the United States—all except Louisiana. Under the common law system, a court looks to the prior decisions of other courts to identify the rules of law that will be applied in a lawsuit. While written laws such as constitutions, statutes, and regulations are also applied, common law courts rely heavily on the use of precedents both within and from other courts.

compactness: The quality of being closely or firmly united or packed. Under U.S. Supreme Court precedents, an electoral district, such as a congressional district or a city council ward, must be compact.

constitution: The fundamental law. The U.S. Constitution organizes the federal government, sets out the powers of that government, and establishes the rights and freedoms guaranteed to each person in the United States. Each state also has its own constitution, which performs similar functions for that state. Whereas federal protections in the U.S. Constitution are binding on all states, state constitutions may nevertheless include additional or higher protections (*see also* statute).

contiguity: A situation where tracts of land physically adjoin. Electoral districts are required to be contiguous. A state legislative district, for example, cannot consist of two tracts of land several miles apart.

decision: A judge's written explanation of why he, she, or a group of judges issued a particular ruling. This written explanation is referred to as the decision or the opinion in the case (*see also* opinion, plurality).

declaratory relief: A court action brought not for the purpose of requesting monetary rewards but simply to have the court determine a party's rights. For example, if a school were to ban the speaking of Spanish, the students could ask a court for declaratory relief in order to determine whether such a rule is legal, rather than risking punishment by violating the rule and subsequently challenging the application of the rule in court.

de facto segregation: Segregation that is due to economic, social, and other determinants. In theory it is inadvertent, without direct assistance of authorities, and is not caused by any state action, but in reality it is often the result of concomitant de jure segregation (*see also* de jure segregation).

de jure segregation: Generally, segregation directly mandated or intended by law.

desegregation: A process eliminating a person's race or ethnicity as a basis for disqualification to attend the school of his or her choice.

disenfranchisement: The act of removing an individual's ability to participate in the democratic voting process.

disparate impact: The finding that an employment or educational practice has a discriminatory and disproportionate effect on Mexican Americans or some other legally protected group. Ordinarily, a plaintiff who alleges discrimination is required to prove that the defendant intentionally or purposefully discriminated against him or her. Because this is often difficult to do, under some civil rights statutes, a plaintiff can prevail simply by showing a discriminatory effect. Once disparate impact is shown, the defendant in the lawsuit will be ordered to stop the practice unless business necessity is shown (*see also* business necessity).

Due Process Clause: A guarantee that no person may be deprived of life, liberty, or property without due process, meaning a formal proceeding to establish a legal basis for the action. There are two aspects of due process: procedural, which guarantees a person fair procedures, and substantive, which protects a person from actions that are unfair, arbitrary, or unreasonable. Two such clauses are found in the U.S. Constitution, one in the Fifth Amendment pertaining to the federal government, the other in the Fourteenth Amendment, which protects persons from state actions. Similar clauses can be found in most state constitutions.

en banc: A review of the decision of an appellate court panel by the entire court of appeals. Ordinarily, an appeal in a lawsuit is heard by a panel of three appellate judges of that circuit court of appeals. If the lawsuit raises very important issues, however, the parties can seek a review by the entire court, which is an en banc review.

enjoin: A person who is enjoined by a court is required to obey the court's order, which in this context is referred to as an injunction. An injunction, in turn, may require the person to perform an act or prohibit the person from performing an act. An employer, for example, may be enjoined by a court from discriminating against Mexican American job applicants (*see also* injunctive relief).

Equal Employment Opportunity Commission (EEOC): A commission created by Title VII of the Civil Rights Act of 1964. The purposes of the EEOC are to end discrimination based on race, color, religion, age, sex, or national origin in hiring, promotion, firing, wages, and all other conditions of employment; and to promote voluntary action programs by employers, unions, and community organizations to put equal employment opportunity into practice (for more information see the websites list).

Equal Protection Clause: The provision in the Fourteenth Amendment to the U.S. Constitution that prohibits a state from denying to any person within its jurisdiction the equal protection of the laws. This clause requires that any person be given equal protection as others in the same circumstances with regard to the enjoyment of personal rights and the prevention and redress of wrongs. The Equal Protection Clause is usually invoked by plaintiffs who are alleging discrimination on the basis of race, gender, or national origin.

executive order: An order issued by the president of the United States that has the force of law and is binding on all federal agencies unless invalidated by Congress or by a court. As head of the executive branch of the U.S. government, the president has the authority to issue and enforce executive orders.

Fifth Amendment: An amendment to the U.S. Constitution that protects individuals against self-incrimination and requires the federal government to provide them with due process (*see also* Due Process Clause).

First Amendment: Amendment to the U.S. Constitution guaranteeing basic freedoms of speech, religion, press, and assembly and the right to petition the government for redress of grievances. The various freedoms and rights protected by the First Amendment have been held applicable to the states through the Due Process Clause of the Fourteenth Amendment (*see also* Due Process Clause).

Fourteenth Amendment: Ratified in 1868, the Fourteenth Amendment creates, or at least recognizes, a citizenship of the United States, distinct from state citizenship; forbids any state from making or enforcing any law abridging the privileges and immunities of citizens of the United States; and secures all persons against any state action that would result in deprivation of life, liberty, or property without due process of law or in denial of the equal protection of the law (*see also* Due Process Clause, Equal Protection Clause).

fundamental right: A fundamental right, such as the right to privacy, is a right or value inferred by the courts under the Due Process Clause; a right or value that is not directly found in the constitutional text or history. When a fundamental right is at issue, the government's actions are reviewed under the strict scrutiny test (*see also* strict scrutiny).

hate crime or **bias crime:** An offense where the person acted, at least in part, with ill will, bias, or hatred toward, and with a purpose to intimidate, an individual or group because of race, color, ethnicity, religion, or sexual orientation. The perpetrator of offenses such as harassment, assault, intimidation, or criminal mischief may have an enhanced sentence imposed if the act is proved to have been a bias crime.

Immigration and Nationality Act (INA): A comprehensive federal law that deals with immigration, naturalization, and exclusion of aliens.

incumbency protection: The redrawing of electoral districts in a way that benefits the current, or incumbent, elected officials. Because incumbent state legislators are responsible for redistricting, it is not particularly surprising that their first priority is often to draw electoral districts that will assist in their reelection and maximize partisan advantage. Protection of incumbents poses problems for those seeking to create majority-minority legislative and congressional districts, since quite often the incumbents are white. The U.S. Supreme Court has upheld the use of incumbency protection as a factor in drawing electoral districts.

injunctive relief (injunction): An order by a court requiring a party to engage in an act or prohibiting a party from engaging in an act. Injunctive relief is issued only when compensatory damages, such as monetary awards, are inadequate (*see also* enjoin).

invidious discrimination or **invidious racial classification:** A difference in treatment among various groups of people that is irrational, arbitrary, and not reasonably related to a legitimate purpose. One example is segregation of public schools on the basis of race (*see also* benign racial discrimination).

League of United Latin American Citizens (LULAC): The first political advocacy organization for Latinos. LULAC was founded by Mexican Americans in Texas in 1929 and quickly spread nationwide. Its aims are to promote and protect the rights of Latinos and facilitate their integration into U.S. society (for more information see the websites list).

legal/lawful resident or **resident alien:** Describes the "status of having been lawfully accorded the privilege of residing permanently in the United States as an immigrant in accordance with the immigration laws" under the Immigration and Nationality Act.

majority-minority districts: Electoral districts in which a majority of the population consists of racial or ethnic minorities such as Mexican Americans, Native Americans, African Americans, or Asian Americans.

Mexican American Legal Defense and Educational Fund (MALDEF): Founded as a legal aid organization patterned after the National Association for the Advancement of Colored People, MALDEF became a major force in litigating important issues such as education, immigration, employment, and voting rights and the recognition of Latinos as a protected class. MALDEF's primary founder, Pete Tijerina, passed away in 2003. (For more information see the websites list.)

Mexican Revolution: A revolution that began in 1910 and largely centered on land reform issues. Two central figures leading the fight, which pitted peasants against the government, were Emiliano Zapata and Pancho Villa. The Mexican Revolution caused great turmoil in Mexico for more than a decade and led hundreds of thousands of Mexicans to emigrate to the United States in an effort to escape the violence and unrest. Many Mexican Americans trace their ancestry to one or more refugees from the Mexican Revolution.

moot: Describes an issue or controversy that no longer exists for the courts to review. For example, if a lawsuit is filed challenging the qualifications of a candidate for elected office but by the time the appeal is heard the candidate's term of office has ended, the court will typically dismiss the case as moot.

multimember district: An electoral district that elects more than one legislator. Prior to the enactment of the Voting Rights Act, multimember districts were often used to deprive racial and ethnic minority voters of representation in a legislature or other elected body. For example, imagine that Mexican Americans constitute 40 percent of the population of a county that is entitled to elect three legislators. If everyone in the county votes for all three legislators, and racially polarized bloc voting is a factor, as is typical, then all three legislators elected are likely to reflect the will of the 60 percent non–Mexican American voting population. In contrast, if the county is divided into three single-member districts, then a district that contains a majority of Mexican Americans is more likely to be able to elect a representative—typically but not necessarily a Mexican American—sensitive to its needs and concerns (*see also* racial bloc voting, single-member districts, Voting Rights Act of 1965).

National Association for the Advancement of Colored People (NAACP): An interracial advocacy organization formed in 1909 to remove barriers of discrimination and segregation for African Americans, to protect their constitutional rights, and to abolish racism (for more information see the websites list).

national origin: With respect to equal employment opportunities under the Civil Rights Act, the term "national origin" on its face refers to the country where a person was born, or, more broadly, the country from which his or her ancestors came, and is not intended to embrace a requirement of U.S. citizenship (*see also* Civil Rights Act of 1964).

nativist: A person who dislikes people who are not from his or her native land. Nativist sentiments appear regularly among some segments of the U.S. population, frequently causing problems for Mexican Americans, who may be perceived by nativists as foreigners, even if they are native-born citizens of the United States.

one man, one vote or **one person, one vote:** Expression used to describe state legislative districting that gives equal legislative representation to all persons from all locations within the district. Prior to the U.S. Supreme Court decision in *Reynolds v. Sims,* 377 U.S. 533 (1964), some state legislatures had very unequal numbers of voters in their electoral districts. If one electoral district has 10,000 people and a second electoral district has 100,000 people, the voters in the first district have much greater influence over who will be elected to the state legislature. As a result of *Sims,* the population of each legislative district must be approximately equal, so that each person casts a vote of nearly equal weight.

opinion: A written explanation prepared by a judge giving his, her, or a group of judges' reasons for making a particular ruling on a legal issue; also referred to as the decision in the case (*see also* the discussion of decisions and opinions in the introduction).

ordinance: A law passed by a local government, such as that of a county or city. An ordinance is law only in the local jurisdiction that enacts it.

peremptory challenge: A request from a party in a criminal proceeding that a judge not allow a certain prospective juror to be a member of the jury. No reason or "cause" need be stated for this type of challenge. Unlike a "challenge for cause," the number of peremptory challenges afforded each party is normally limited by statute or court rule (*see also* challenge for cause).

permanent checkpoints: Permanent U.S. Border Patrol roadblocks on major highways leading from the U.S.–Mexico border. At these checkpoints, cars must stop and the occupants are questioned about their legal right to be in the United States. The occupants and the vehicle may also be searched for illegal contraband, such as drugs. Mexican Americans and other Latinos have often challenged the use of such checkpoints, arguing that only persons of Mexican or Latino appearance are searched and that such searches occur even when there is no additional evidence that the person is not a U.S. citizen.

plurality decision: An opinion of an appellate court in which a majority of the court does not join in any of the opinions issued; distinguished from a majority opinion, in which a majority of the panel court does concur (*see also* decision, opinion).

poll tax: A tax assessed before a citizen is allowed to vote. Poll taxes were used in many states to prevent African Americans throughout the South, and Mexican Americans in Texas, from voting. Poll taxes as a prerequisite to voting in federal elections were prohibited by the Twenty-Fourth Amendment to the U.S. Constitution and were held unconstitutional in state elections in *Harper v. Virginia Board of Elections,* 383 U.S. 663 (1966).

precedent: A prior decision issued by a court. Under the common law system, the courts use precedents to identify the rules and principles of law that are to be applied in a lawsuit.

preemption: A legal principle that state and local governments have no authority to act in any area where the U.S. Constitution or federal law gives the federal government sole authority. For example, the U.S. Constitution gives the federal government sole authority to regulate immigration, meaning that state and local governments cannot interfere in immigration in any way.

prima facie case: Producing sufficient evidence to require the defendant to proceed with his case. If a prima facie case is established, the plaintiff wins the lawsuit unless the defendant can present evidence to the contrary.

racial bloc voting: A phenomenon existing in many areas of the country in which voters of a particular race or ethnicity vote in the same way. Where racial bloc voting exists, most Anglo voters, for example, will vote for one candidate, typically a white candidate, while most Mexican American voters will support a different candidate. If racial bloc voting exists and Mexican Americans are a minority of the voters, Mexican Americans are unlikely ever to be able to elect the representative of their choice. Single-member districts are one common solution for this problem (*see also* single-member districts).

racial gerrymandering: A process wherein congressional, state, and local district boundaries are established largely on the basis of race or ethnicity. Historically, racial gerrymandering was used to dilute the voting strength of racial and ethnic minorities. More recently, racial gerrymandering has been used to create majority-minority districts.

regulation: A rule issued by an administrative agency such as the EEOC, INS, or SBA. If the administrative agency has been authorized to issue binding regulations, such a regulation has the force of law, similar to the force of a statute passed by the legislature.

remand: The act of an appellate court when it sends a case back to the trial court and orders the trial court to conduct limited new hearings or an entirely new trial, or to take some other further action.

resident alien or legal/lawful resident: Describes the "status of having been lawfully accorded the privilege of residing permanently in the United States as an immigrant in accordance with the immigration laws" under the Immigration and Nationality Act.

roving patrols: Patrols by the U.S. Border Patrol through the countryside along the U.S.–Mexico border, intended to apprehend undocumented immigrants. Such roving patrols are controversial because documented Mexican immigrants and Mexican American citizens are more likely than other U.S. citizens and residents to be questioned about their legal right to be in the United States.

secondary referral stop: A location at a U.S. Border Patrol permanent checkpoint where certain cars are referred for a more detailed search of the vehicle and occupants (*see also* permanent checkpoint).

single-member district: An electoral district that elects only one representative to the legislature or other elected body. The establishment of a single-member district in an area with a high percentage of Mexican American voters is one remedy that courts frequently award in voting-rights lawsuits (*see also* at-large districts, multimember districts).

Small Business Administration (SBA):   A federally sponsored organization that aids, counsels, assists, and protects the interests of small business owners; ensures that small businesses receive a fair proportion of government purchases, contracts and subcontracts (for more information see websites list).

statute: A law passed by a state or federal legislature. Statutes are binding law and must be followed by the courts, unless the statute is in violation of the U.S. Constitution or relevant state constitution (*see also* constitution).

strict scrutiny test or **strict scrutiny standard:** A constitutional legal requirement and standard of review that any classification based on race must (1) serve a compelling governmental interest; and (2) be narrowly tailored to serve that compelling governmental interest.

suspect class: An identifiable class of individuals, such as a racial or ethnic group, deserving of heightened constitutional review and protection. When such a suspect classification is at issue, the courts will review the policy or practice under the strict scrutiny test (*see also* strict scrutiny).

test case: A lawsuit brought to establish an important legal principle or right or to bring about a change in policy (*see also* precedent).

Treaty of Guadalupe Hidalgo: A treaty signed on February 2, 1948 to end the U.S.–Mexican War (for more information, see the websites list).

vacate: To annul; to set aside; to cancel or rescind; to render an act void in terms of a judgment.

vote dilution: A claim in a voting rights lawsuit that a particular electoral practice has the effect of rendering less effective the votes of racial or ethnic minority voters. For example, the use of multimember districts often leads to claims of Mexican American vote dilution (*see also* at-large district, multimember district).

Voting Rights Act of 1965: Federal law that guarantees the right of citizens to vote without discrimination based on race, color, or previous condition of servitude. The U.S. attorney general is authorized to file proper proceedings for preventive relief to protect this right.

■ LIST OF WEBSITES

American GI Forum: A national veterans' organization since 1948, dedicated to addressing problems of discrimination and inequities endured by Mexican American veterans. The forum soon became an advocate for all Hispanics and broadened its activities throughout the states to promote civic affairs. For more information on the GI Forum, and for its history, see the following websites: www.va.gov/vso/agif.htm, www.agif.org, www.justiceformypeople.com/drhector3.html

Handbook of Texas Online: An online resource for historical information regarding Texas. This website has particularly useful information regarding Gus C. García, one of this book's dedicatees, and regarding the seminal case of *Hernandez v. Texas*. www.tsha.utexas.edu

League of United Latin American Citizens (LULAC):   The first political advocacy organization for Latinos. LULAC was founded by Mexican Americans in Texas in 1929 and quickly spread nationwide. Its aims are to promote and protect the rights of Latinos and facilitate their integration into U.S. society. www.lulac.org

Mexican American Legal Defense and Educational Fund (MALDEF): Founded as a legal aid organization patterned after the National Association for the Advancement of Colored People, MALDEF became a major force in litigating important issues such as immigration, employment, and voting rights and the recognition of Latinos as a protected class. www.maldef.org

Mexican American Student Organization (MASO):   A student organization similar to MAYO. For examples of student MASO organizations and a brief history of MASO see the following site: www.uhv.edu/student'org/maso/index.htm

Mexican American Youth Organization (MAYO):   An organization founded in San Antonio in 1967 that was for a decade the major political organization of Mexican American youth in Texas. For information on MAYO, see the following site: www.tsha.utexas.edu/handbook/online/articles/view/MM/wem1.html

Movimiento Estudiantil Chicano de Aztlán (MEChA):   A Chicano organization founded at a conference held in Santa Barbara, California, in April 1968. Concerned Raza and community members gathered at this conference to draw attention to the needs and concerns of Chicanos, both in the educational system and in the community. For a history of MEChA and related student organizations, such as MAYO and MASO, see the following site: www.utexas.edu/ftp/student/mecha/archive/research.html For three examples of student MEChA organizations see the following sites: www-rohan.sdsu.edu/dept/mecha/index.html/, www.stanford .edu/group/MEChA/, http://gladstone.uoregon.edu/~mecha/

National Association for the Advancement of Colored People (NAACP): An organization striving to ensure the political, educational, social, and economic equality of minority citizens of the United States: www .naacp.org

National Association of Latino Elected and Appointed Officials (NALEO): An organization promoting the participation of Latinos in the American political process: www.naleo.org

National Council of La Raza (NCLR): An organization established to reduce poverty and discrimination and improve life opportunities for Hispanic Americans: www.nclr.org

Southwest Voter Registration Education Project (SVREP): An organization founded by William C. Velásquez (see below) and committed to educating Latino communities across the Southwest about the democratic process and the importance of voter registration and voter participation. Its core mission is to empower Latinos politically by increasing their civic engagement in the American electoral system. SVREP believes this can be attained only through the strengthening and exercising of the fundamental right to vote. Thus its motto is "Su Voto Es Su Voz" (Your Vote Is Your Voice): www.svrep.org

Treaty of Guadalupe Hidalgo: A treaty signed on February 2, 1948 to end the U.S.–Mexican War. http:/users.dedot.com/mchs/treaty.html

Tomás Rivera Policy Institute: An organization that conducts and disseminates to decision makers objective, policy-relevant research and its implications on key issues affecting Latino communities: www.trpi.org

William C. Velásquez Institute (WCVI): An organization that conducts research aimed at improving the level of political and economic participation in Latino and other underrepresented communities: www .wcvi.org

■ FIGURE CREDITS

Gus C. García. (Courtesy of the Law Offices of Frank Herrera)

The Honorable Carlos C. Cadena. (Courtesy of Gloria V. Cadena)

1. The thirteen federal judicial circuits. (Reprinted with permission from the West Group)

2. The Sleepy Lagoon defendants. (Courtesy of Alice Greenfield McGrath)

3. A segregated school in Austin, Texas. (Courtesy of Rare Books and Manuscripts, Benson Latin American Collection, University of Texas at Austin)

4. Lemon Grove school children. (Courtesy of Paul Espinosa)

5. Mexican American women railroad workers. (Courtesy of the Arizona Historical Society)

6. Satirical map in response to California voters' passage of the English-Only referendum. (Created by Jose Antonio Burrciaga, courtesy of Cecilia Burrciaga)

7. Cartoon responding to efforts to deny public education benefits to undocumented immigrants. (Cartoon by Jeff MacNelly, *San Antonio Express-News,* October 13, 1996. Copyright © 1996, Tribune Media Services Inc. All rights Reserved. Reprinted with permission.)

8. Protesters marching against California's Proposition 187. (Courtesy of Lisa Valencia Sheratt)

9. Su Voto Es Su Voz (your vote is your voice). (Courtesy of the Southwest Voter Registration Education Project)

10. Society of American Law Teachers marching in Washington, D.C. (Courtesy of Angela J. Davis)

11. Cartoon satirizing the U.S. criminal justice system. (Courtesy of Lalo Lopez Alcaraz)

■ INDEX

abortion, 42–43
Adarand Constructors, Inc., v. Peña,
  140–43, 154
affirmative action, 48, 125, 134–54
African American, 8, 14, 27, 28, 37, 69,
  85, 115–16, 121–25, 127–29, 130,
  134–36, 174
Aguirre-Cervantes v. INS, 55, 60
all-white primaries, 115
Anglo, 8, 13, 23, 30, 49, 67, 68, 83,
  84
Anti-Vietnam War Movement, 28
Arizona, xix, 159; history, 3–4; language, 67–85; *Miranda* Warnings,
  164–68
assistance of counsel, 165, 172
asylum, 55–61

Baker v. Carr, 131
bilingual(ism), 131; ballots, 69–70; education, 29, 81–86; history, 67–68;
  jurors, 162–63
Board of Immigration Appeals (BIA),
  55–60
border, 3, 4, 36, 37, 54, 73, 78, 90–94,
  101–104
border patrol, 54, 90–97, 111
Brown v. Board of Education, 20–21,
  27–32, 159
Bush v. Vera, 122–23

Cadena, Carlos, 13, 19, 159
California, xix, 121, 139; border checkpoints, 94; constitutional convention,
  68; history, 3–9; language, 67–68;
  Los Angeles Board of Supervisors,
  159; Proposition 187, 105–10; Proposition 209, 152–54; Proposition 227,
  81–85; sterilizations, 43; segregation,
  21–26
Campos v. Baytown, 128–29
census (Census Bureau), 65, 89; reapportionment, 117–27; statistical
  sampling, 129–31
checkpoint, 93–98. *See also*
  immigration
Chicana Rights Project, 41
Chicano Movement, 15, 135
circuit, xvii-xix; 5th Circuit, xvii, 78,
  81, 128, 140, 143, 150, 151; 6th Circuit, 141, 151; 9th Circuit, xix, 21, 50,
  55, 60–61, 70, 77, 81, 86, 97, 151–53;
  10th Circuit, xix, 82, 83; 11th Circuit, 151
*Cisneros v. Corpus Christi School Dis-
  trict,* 28
citizen, xv, 3, 9, 20, 23, 49, 65, 70, 89, 93,
  98–99, 101, 103, 109, 134, 137, 158
citizenship, 16, 25, 49, 79, 91–92, 94,
  134
civil rights, 15, 48–49, 69, 134–35, 153;
  organizations, 9, 10, 14, 152
Civil Rights Act of 1964, 13, 47–50,
  78–82
Civil Rights Movement, 28, 69, 135
class action, 14, 30, 100
Coalition for Economic Equity v. Wilson,
  110, 153
Colorado, xix, 3, 28, 67, 85, 142
Comisión Femenil Mexicana Nacional,
  41
common law, xvi–xvii
compelling governmental interest, 108,
  138, 142, 146–54

constitution, xvii, xxi, 3, 11, 12, 20, 23, 25, 29, 31–32, 34, 35, 37, 67–68, 70–71, 76–78, 90, 101, 104, 117, 119, 127, 134, 137, 146–47, 153–54, 160, 169, 172–73
criminal justice, 157–59, 163

democratic theory, 15
Department of Commerce v. United States House of Representatives, 130
deportation, 54, 61, 104, 111
discrimination: against Latinos, 14; against Mexican Americans, 8–10, 13–14, 23–24, 27–29, 31, 128–29; against undocumented immigrants, 49; based on language, 79–85; based on sex, 43, 47–50; benign, 142–46; *de facto* segregation, 20, 27–28; *de jure* segregation, 27–29; invidious, 31–34, 119–21, 142–43; jury selection, 160–63; past effects, 146–50; remedying, 125; reverse, 139–41; Title VII, 13–14, 47–50; voting, 115–17
disenfranchisement, 115
disparate impact, 37, 80
due process, 100, 134
Due Process Clause, 13, 29, 111, 137, 139

Edgewood Independent School District v. Kirby, 36–37
education: bilingual, 81–86; financing, 29–37; fundamental right, 29–35; higher education, 143–52; public benefit, 98–105; segregation, 20–29. *See also* California, Proposition 187; segregation
EEOC v. Hacienda Hotel, 50
EEOC v. Tortilleria La Mejor, 49
employment, 13–14, 78–79, 80–81, 98, 101–102, 129, 135, 152, 153. *See also* language; women

English, 21, 65–68, 71–77, 81–86, 115, 163; English Only, 65–67; English Plus, 86; official language, 69–77; workplace, 77–81
Equal Educational Opportunity Act, 85
Equal Employment Opportunity Commission (EEOC), 14, 49–52, 81
equal pay, 41, 48
Equal Pay Act, 47–48
equal protection, 11, 23, 25–27, 32, 34–35, 76, 84, 100, 134, 137, 146, 153–54, 160
Equal Protection Clause, 20, 21, 29, 31–32, 34, 48, 86, 98–101, 117, 120, 137–40, 146–47, 152–54, 159, 162
Equal Rights Advocates, 41
ethnicity, 41, 43, 48, 134, 138, 147, 153, 161–62
ethnic minority group, 115–16, 120, 128, 130–31, 139, 152

Federal Bureau of Investigation (FBI), 90
foreign-born, 89, 90. *See also* language; immigration
Fuerza Unida in San Antonio, 48
fundamental right, 29–37, 58, 99. *See also* education

García, Gus, 13, 159
Garza v. Smith, 117
gender, 43, 47, 48, 134, 136, 153–54. *See also* women
gerrymandering, 115–16, 126. *See also* voting
Gonzáles v. Stevens, 117
Gratz v. Bollinger, 140–41, 151–52
Graves v. Barnes, 117–19
Grutter v. Bollinger, 140–41, 151

Hernández v. Texas, 11, 13–16, 118, 120, 138, 159–60
Hernández-Montiel v. INS, 60
higher education, 37, 105, 139, 140, 143, 147, 150–52; and affirmative action, 134–43; and criminal justice, 157–58; and discrimination against African Americans and Mexican Americans, 127–29; and language, 67–69; and Mexican Americans, 4–7, 15, 29; and past discrimination, 148–50; in South Texas, 36; and undocumented immigrants, 105–06. *See also* voting
Hopwood v. Texas, 141, 143, 150–51

identity, 4, 10, 14–16, 58, 65, 80. *See also* legal, identity/status
immigration, 65; Antiterrorism and Effective Death Penalty Act, 111; Illegal Immigration Reform and Immigrant Responsibility Act of 1996, 110, 111; Immigration and Nationality Act, 54, 107; Immigration and Naturalization Service (INS), 9, 56, 58, 60; policy, 89–91; Proposition 187, 105–10; public benefits, 98–105; U.S.–Mexico Border, 91–98
indigent, 31, 43; right to counsel, 165–68
intermediate scrutiny, 138–39. *See also* legal standard of review

Johnson v. Board of Regents of University of Georgia, 151
jury, 5, 6, 11, 95, 158, 159, 160, 161, 162, 164, 167, 174; grand jury, 6, 11, 158–60. *See also* jurors
jurors, xx, 161–63, 174; grand jurors, 160. *See also* jury

Keyes v. Denver School District, 28

La Mujer Obrera in El Paso, 48
language, 118; civil rights, 69–77; criminal justice system, 158, 161–63, 171; educational segregation, 21–27; history in United States, 67–68; medical services, 43–47; voting, 128–31; workplace, 70–81. *See also* bilingual(ism); English, English Only; English, English Plus; California, Proposition 227
Latina, 41, 48–50, 70, 121
law enforcement, 4, 7, 8, 41, 59, 62, 95, 107, 158, 167, 173. *See also* police
lawful resident, 101, 103. *See also* citizen; legal, resident; resident alien
League of United Latin American Citizens (LULAC), 10, 21, 49, 86, 107, 108
legal: identity/status, 4, 10–16; profession, 159; protections, 13–14; resident, 49, 54, 98, 111–12; status, 14–15, 49, 61, 105; standard of review, 137–39. *See also* citizen; lawful resident
Local 28, Sheet Metal Workers International Association v. EEOC, 135
Luján v. Colorado School Board of Education, 35

Madrigal v. Quilligan, 41, 43, 44
Méndez v. Westminister School District of Orange County, 20, 21, 23, 27, 29
Meritor Savings Bank v. Vinson, 53
Mexican American Legal Defense and Educational Fund (MALDEF), 10, 41, 49, 86
Mexican American Student Organization (MASO), 28
Mexican American Youth Organization (MAYO), 28

Mexican American: appearance/
ancestry, 91–98; brutality against, 4–
5, 8; early citizens, 3, 14; housing
patterns, 27–28; legal profession,
159; protected class, 11–14, 28, 120–
21; quest for justice, 15–16; use of
legal system, 4, 9–10, 69, 105, 115–
17, 121–23, 127–32

Mexico, 3, 9, 54–55, 67–68, 78, 93; border with Texas, 4–5, 45; border with
United States, 36, 78, 90–91, 94;
immigration from, 86, 89–90, 112;
political asylum and refugees, 55–
60. *See also* border

Miranda v. Arizona, 163–64, 168–69

Movimiento Estudiantil Chicanos de
Aztlán (MEChA), 28

National Association for the Advancement of Colored People (NAACP),
21

National Association of Latino Elected
and Appointed Officials, 10

National Council of La Raza, 10

national origin, 49, 65, 76, 78, 79–82,
85, 132, 135, 153, 160

native born, 93

New Mexico, 3, 69, 82, 83, 159

People v. Zammora, 5–7. *See also* Sleepy
Lagoon

peremptory: challenge, 161–63; strike,
174

Pérez v. Federal Bureau of Investigation,
14, 136

Plessy v. Ferguson, 20

police, 5, 60, 61, 90, 91, 157, 163, 166, 168,
170–73. *See also* law enforcement

poll tax, 115. *See also* voting

precedent, xvii, xix, 122, 141, 143, 147,
151. *See also stare decisis*

race-neutral, 126, 161–63

rational relationship, 139

refugee, 54, 55, 57

*Regents of the University of California v.
Bakke,* 139–41, 143, 146–47, 150–51,
155

reproductive rights, 42–44

resident alien, 95, 101, 103. *See also*
lawful resident; legal, resident

Richards v. LULAC, 37

right to counsel, 158, 166, 168–69

Roe v. Wade, 42

roving patrol, 91, 92, 95, 97, 112. *See
also* immigration

*San Antonio Independent School District
v. Rodríguez,* 29–30, 35–37, 99, 104,
118

search and seizure, 93, 95, 158

segregation: and admissions process,
145–46; educational, 20, 23–29, 37,
138; in the workplace, 48, 61; voter,
124, 145, 146

self-incrimination, 163–64, 166, 169

separate-but-equal, 20, 29

Serrano v. Priest, 35

sexual harassment, 49–54, 61–62; *quid
pro quo,* 49, 50

sexual identity, 60–61

sexual violence, 54, 59

Shaw v. Reno, 122–23, 125, 127

Sleepy Lagoon, 5, 7. *See also People v.
Zammora*

Small Business Administration (SBA),
14

*Smith v. University of Washington Law
School,* 151

Southwest Voter Registration Institute,
10

Spanish: criminal justice, 158, 161–63,
171; educational segregation, 23–27,

37; government functions, 65, 67–77, 131; language discrimination, 9, 29, 82; voting, 117; in the workplace, 77–80. *See also* bilingual(ism), education; language, medical services

stare decisis, xvii. *See also* precedent

statistical sampling, 129–31

sterilization, 43–44, 47

strict scrutiny, 31, 123, 126, 138–39, 142, 146–48

Supremacy Clause, 106

Sweatt v. Painter, 149

Terrell Wells Swimming Pool Company v. Rodríguez, 10

Texas, 3–4, 8, 10, 78; and abortion, 43; and affirmative action, 143–52; and bilingual education, 82; and blowouts/walkouts, 28; and educational funding, 29–37; and educational segregation, 21; and immigrants to, 99–105; and jury exclusion, 11–12, 159–61; and language, 67–68; and lynching, 4; Rangers, 5, 8; and sexual violence, 54; and voter intimidation, 9; and voting, 115, 117–29

Thornburg v. Gingles, 128–29

Tomás Rivera Center, 10

Treaty of Guadalupe Hidalgo, 3, 9, 65

United States Commission on Civil Rights, 83, 157

U.S.–Mexican War, 3, 68, 115

United States v. Paradise, 135

University: of California, Davis, 139–40; of Georgia, 151; of Michigan, 140–41, 151–52, 155; of Southern California, 43; of Texas, 143–51; of Washington, 151

Violence Against Women Act, 54, 112

voting: at-large systems, 116, 128, 129; bilingual ballots, 69, 131; dilution, 116, 120, 128; intimidation, 9; language minorities, 69; majority-minority district, 122–24, 126; multimember district, 118–121; one-man, one-vote, 120; one person, one vote, 131; protections, 14, 116; racial bloc, 125; reapportionment, 117–19, 131–32; redistricting, 117–19, 121–23, 127–29, 131–32; rights, 31–32, 69, 115, 129, 131; single-member district, 118, 121, 128–29. *See also* all-white primaries; gerrymandering; statistical sampling

Voting Rights Act, 14, 69, 116, 122, 126, 128–29

White v. Regester, 117–19, 121–23

William C. Velásquez Institute, 10

women: and affirmative action, 135–36, 141, 153, 155; as criminal defendants, 4–5; and domestic violence, 54, 57, 59, 60, 112; and immigrant status, 47–54; zoot-suiters, 5; and the workplace, 13–14, 49. *See also* asylum; Mexican American; reproductive rights; sexual harassment; sexual violence

Zoot Suit Riots, 5

■ ABOUT THE AUTHORS

HENRY FLORES is a professor of political science at St. Mary's University. He received his B.A. from St. Mary's University, and his M.A. and Ph.D. from the University of California, Santa Barbara. He teaches undergraduate and graduate courses in U.S. Latino politics. He has also served as an expert witness in numerous redistricting cases involving Mexican American plaintiffs and has published in the areas of Latino politics and the voting behavior of U.S. Latinos.

SONIA R. GARCÍA is a professor of political science at St. Mary's University. She received her B.A. from St. Mary's University, her M.A. from the University of Arizona, and her Ph.D. from the University of California, Santa Barbara. She teaches undergraduate and graduate courses in gender politics, judicial process, constitutional law, and constitutional law and theory. She has coauthored a textbook on Texas politics and has published on Latina politics.

JOSÉ ROBERTO JUÁREZ JR. is a law professor at St. Mary's University School of Law. He received his A.B. from Stanford University and his J.D. from the University of Texas School of Law. He teaches courses in civil rights, and has published in the areas of civil rights, language rights, and religion in the Latino community. Prior to joining the faculty of St. Mary's, he served as regional counsel and director of the Employment Program for the Mexican American Legal Defense and Educational Fund.

REYNALDO ANAYA VALENCIA is a law professor at St. Mary's University School of Law. He received his A.B. and A.M. from Stanford University, and his J.D. from Harvard Law School. In addition to teaching courses on gender discrimination and race and racism in American law, he has published on Latinos and the criminal justice system and Latinos and Catholicism. From 1999 to 2000, he served as a White House Fellow in the Office of the Chief of Staff, where he concentrated on race, civil rights, immigration, and Hispanic education issues.